Cottage
for sale*

*must be moved

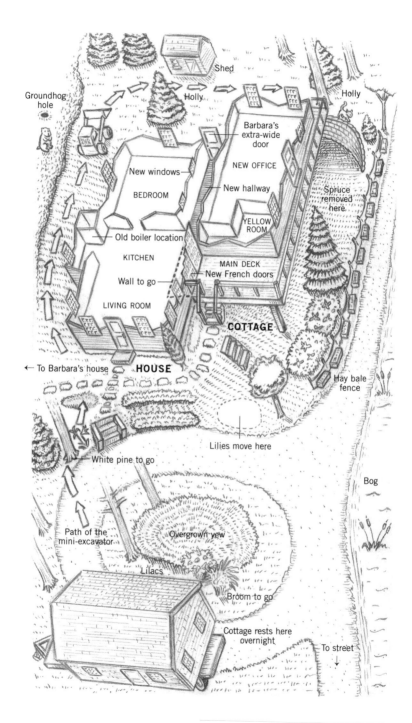

Shed

Holly

Holly

Groundhog hole

Barbara's extra-wide door

NEW OFFICE

New windows

New hallway

Spruce removed here

BEDROOM

YELLOW ROOM

Old boiler location

KITCHEN

MAIN DECK
New French doors

Wall to go

LIVING ROOM

COTTAGE

← To Barbara's house   HOUSE

Hay bale fence

Lilies move here

White pine to go

Bog

Path of the mini-excavator

Overgrown yew

Lilacs

Broom to go

Cottage rests here overnight

To street
↓

Cottage for sale*

*must be moved

a woman moves a house
to make a home

kate whouley

*for Ken —
a veteran
of two moves —
want more? you
a mover AND
a shaker —
Kate Whouley*

COMMONWEALTH EDITIONS
BEVERLY, MASSACHUSETTS

First edition

Library of Congress Cataloging-in-Publication Data
Whouley, Kate.
  Cottage for sale, must be moved : a woman moves a house to make a home / Kate Whouley.
      p. cm.
  ISBN 1-889833-74-6 (hardcover)
  1. Moving of buildings, bridges, etc. 2. Buildings—Repair and reconstruction. 3. Whouley, Kate—Homes, haunts, etc. 4. Cape Cod (Mass.)—Description and travel. I. Title.
TH153.W44 2004
690'.837--dc22   2003023067

Book design by Ann Conneman, Peter King & Company.
Frontispiece drawing by Jeffrey M. Walsh.
Author photo by Anne Williams Sweeney.

Printed in Canada; photos printed in the United States.

Published by Commonwealth Editions
an imprint of Memoirs Unlimited, Inc.
266 Cabot Street, Beverly, Massachusetts 01915
www.commonwealtheditions.com

10 9 8 7 6 5 4 3 2 1

FOR MY MOTHER, MY GRANDMOTHER,
and the long line of bold women who came before them

WHEN LOVE AND SKILL work together, expect a masterpiece.

—ATTRIBUTED TO JOHN RUSKIN

contents

1   FIRST SIGHT

22   RESOLUTION

43   FOOTWORK

66   TOWN HALL

84   MAKING WAY

107 KEYLINES AND BUTTERFLIES

120 PARADE ROUTE

137 LIFTING OFF AND LANDING

156 THE HISTORY OF CONCRETE

177 PROGRESS

194 THE DAY OF DOORS

204 BIRTHDAY DECK

223 OPENING UP

242 FINISH WORK

258 MOVING IN

273 THE TWELVE DAYS OF CHRISTMAS

291 MARRIAGE

note from the author

A MEMOIR is a series of memories with a point of view.
In this case, the view is mine. My guess is that if you asked
any of the people in this book to tell you their version of
events, you wouldn't hear exactly the same story. I take
full responsibility for my own subjective observations, and
any mistaken impressions or information I might inadvertently pass along in the telling. And while I make no claims
of objective fact, I do promise I've told the tale—and the
truth—exactly as I experienced it.

KATE WHOULEY
CAPE COD, MASSACHUSETTS
FEBRUARY 2004

cast and crew

IT TAKES A VILLAGE to move a cottage—namely, house-movers and house-makers, planners and officials, family and friends. Everyone on this list has a real-life counterpart, though a few names have been changed for reasons of privacy.

MOVERS AND MAKERS

Mr. Hayden	Owner of Hayden Building Movers; he speaks in shorthand and knows how to move a house. Sidekick: Glen.
John Baxter	Owner of Baxter Crane and Rigging; his company owns and operates the biggest crane on Cape Cod.
Rick	Knight in shining armor at the controls of above-mentioned crane.
Ed & John	My builders, father and son; they have home construction and firefighting in common. John's daughters—and Ed's granddaughters—are Katelin and Nicole.
Peter	John's right-hand man, also a firefighter.
Brian	Bobcat-driver and firefighter.
Howard	Retired financial advisor who once owned a general store in Vermont; now works with Ed and John.
Eric & Paulie	The building crew on the six-guy days; both are active firefighters.

Scotty	Tree-man, landscaper, and neighbor who speaks passionately about the oak take-over of Cape Cod's piney landscape.
Ronny	Concrete forms man and mastermind of the cottage foundation.
Jeff	Concrete-pumping man who comes to our rescue more than once.
Vito	Mason, concrete historian, and creator of the smooth foundation wall that links house and cottage; another firefighter.
Stan	Electrician and surfer dude, relocated from California to Cape Cod.
Kevin	The plumber, who eventually shows up; Lyle is his principal assistant.

PLANNERS AND TOWN OFFICIALS

Tom Howes	Keeper of the cottages; he is charged by Eastward Companies with selling the colony to make way for new homes.
Dave	Soft-spoken civil engineer and my friend Erika's dad. His associate is Nick, the Bog Scientist.
Mr. Van Buren	Chief Conservation Officer; Darcy is his associate.
Ralph Crossen	Chief Building Inspector; Mr. Martin is his associate.
Tom McKean	Tuba player and head of the Health Department; Ed Barry is his associate.

FRIENDS AND NEIGHBORS

Barbara	My original next-door neighbor, whose father and brother built my house by hand.
Harry	Musician, computer programmer, woodworker, carpenter—and one of the Bog Boys.
Tony	Social scientist, cat-sitter-in-chief, careful house painter—and the other half of the Bog Boys.
Bruce	Bookseller and poet living on Martha's Vineyard; Egypt's biggest fan and occasionally his cat sitter.
Erika	Elementary school teacher, oboe player, and doctoral candidate; Sara is her sister.
Tina	Flight attendant and independent scholar.
Katrina	Hypnotherapist, counselor, and Egyptian dancer. Her fiancé, Ruben, is an architect-in-training.
Sandy	Jungian psychologist and cat sitter who reinforces my house-marrying fantasies.
Cindy	My best friend since high school; mother of Brooke and Drew.

first sight

I AM A COMPULSIVE READER of the classifieds. For this reason, I do not get the daily paper. But each week, the *Pennysaver* arrives in my mailbox, and I cannot resist the urge to read: *Wedding Gown: Priscilla of Boston, Ivory Lace. Size 8, Never Worn; Paid $2,500. Sacrifice $1,200.*

Imagine selling your unused wedding gown. Soon-to-be-wed women calling you, the disappointed bride-not-to-be. Worse, they come to your house, full of undimmed hope and in search of a bargain; they look critically at the gown of your dreams, decide not to buy.

The classified ads, for me, are like reading stories, or maybe like reading the skeletons of stories, waiting for me to invent their skin. But my compulsion is not merely recreational. I am a dedicated finder of desired objects. Seven years ago, I bought an all-in-one washer-dryer from a woman who told me she needed a large-capacity machine to handle her husband's heavy work clothes. My stackable is still running, and I bought it for a quarter of the price I'd have paid had it been new, pristine—and without a story. Through the classifieds, I found the slate to build my patio and a full-size gas stove to replace the two-burner model with the oven door that had to be tied shut. I've located daylilies to plant on my hillside, an Adirondack-style love seat, handmade. But I don't shop only for myself. I take assignments. My mother's first computer came from the classifieds, as did her most recent fridge. Not to mention the deep blue canoe I once found for an important man in my life. A beautiful canoe, with a maple leaf embossed on the side, and shiny padded seats. Orange life vests came with it, along with varnished hardwood oars.

I mention all this by way of explaining why I am reading the *Pennysaver* on my lunch break today, a Wednesday in early December 1999. As I scan the aptly named "Things and Stuff" listings, I am looking for nothing in particular. At least nothing to purchase. The stories today suggest simple lifestyle upgrades: a few pieces of living room furniture, a couple of TVs, a computer and a printer. "Wanted to Buy" is just as mundane. Dealers of antiques wondering if I have any to sell; a man willing to come to my home to buy my books. He's always in there.

I move on to a new heading, "Buildings," with a single listing:

Cottages for Sale. $3,000 each. Must be moved.

I imagine these cottages, all in a row. Waiting to be adopted. I wonder where they are. I don't recognize the exchange.

$3,000 each. That doesn't seem like very much money for a completely assembled cottage, even a very small, completely assembled cottage. Even a very small, completely assembled summer cottage with no insulation.

Must be moved. I wonder how much it costs to move a building.   *

* I LIVE ON CAPE COD in a three-room house that was built in 1950. It is a quintessential seacoast home: weathering

cedar shakes, yellow shutters, summertime window boxes filled with lavender impatiens, a white picket fence out front. To reach the house, you travel a long dirt driveway and climb six brick steps, walk through the arbor and along the slate path that separates the shade and sun section of my perennial garden. Knock on the front door—there is no doorbell—or come around and rap on the glass panes of the kitchen door. I am more likely to hear you there.

The house sits on a flat bit of land in a hilly landscape; the downslope from the south-facing patio leads to an ancient way, now a gravel drive for my neighbors to the rear. From the kitchen you can see past the drive to the overgrown cranberry bog, home to cardinals and catbirds, doves and quail, robins, purple finches, crows, jays, red-winged blackbirds, the itinerant warbler. Turtles occasionally climb up the hill from the wetland; I find them nosing around in the myrtle or behind the house under the holly tree. A woodchuck makes his way, regularly, slowly, low to the ground, in the opposite direction. I know where his hole is: just outside my bedroom window, on a rising hillside, overgrown with white pines, chokecherries, and wild raspberry vines.

Though people are not far away, I am shielded by hills and trees from all my human neighbors. It is the birds and animals I see and hear more often. Raccoons arguing late at night; skunks small and beautiful, more white than black, moving silently on their nocturnal errands; a red fox that circles the house just before dawn. At the feeders, I host chickadees and goldfinches, titmice and nuthatches, downy woodpeckers, white-throated sparrows, pine siskins, and winter juncos. Gray squirrels make acrobatic attempts to rob the birds, but the fortress-like feeder forces them to the base for scraps, which they share with their furtive red-squirrel cousins and small striped chipmunks. The bunnies live closer to the road, preferring grasses and the apples that fall from the ancient tree. Egypt, my large gray cat, is sometimes less than hospitable to the smaller ground-dwelling animals, but all in all we live peaceably on this tiny patch of Cape Cod.

As long as I have lived in my small home, I have contemplated enlarging my space. I work from home, too. File cabinets and clothing fight for space in my bedroom closet; my printer sits atop my dresser and my fax machine is on the kitchen counter. The space—any space—would be welcome. Yet when I think of adding on, I think of the disruption it would cause us all: Kate, cat, home, business, and animal bystanders. Because my house is built on a four-foot concrete block foundation, adding a second story would mean first lifting up the house to make new foundation walls. I imagine disconnected plumbing, a house on stilts, and the rumble of bulldozers terrorizing Egypt's dreams. When I think of expanding into the hillside instead, I realize I cannot bear to displace the ruddy old groundhog, who sometimes suns himself in early spring at exactly eye level from my desk.

Rather than adding on, I have managed, these many years, to squeeze home and business into just three rooms, to limit my possessions (or to build more bookshelves), to create space in odd places, to blur the boundaries between home and office, to keep the kitchen counters clear—to be content, if slightly crowded, in my lovely little house. *

✳   THERE WERE SHARDS of window glass in the backyard and spider castles in the living room when I first laid eyes on my little house, though it wasn't advertised—or priced—as a fixer-upper.

Hollies abound on the wooded setting of this unique one-bedroom cottage.

After months of low-budget house hunting, all the houses I hunted were looking pretty much the same. They were little ranches, situated on postage-stamp lots, treeless, and much too close to my least-favorite road on Cape Cod: Route 28. An abundance of hollies was exactly what I wanted, even if the wooded setting was starting to claim the little cottage situated between the cedar trees, even if the kitchen was last painted in 1952, even if the old wooden gutters were probably last cleaned that same year. Much to the dismay of my realtor, I made a lowball offer. After an evening of phone calls, we settled on a price that I could afford and that the owners could accept.

We passed papers on a clear day in May in 1987. I spent a month of nights and weekends scrubbing walls and windows, waxing floors, and removing the cheap white paneling in the bedroom. It was slow going, and the bedroom wasn't yet ready for occupancy when the lease on my apartment ran out. I piled all my possessions in the living room and slept in front of the fireplace, my mattress the only object in the room that was allowed to lie flat.

After the bedroom, I worked on the kitchen. Almost every surface—walls, cabinets, ceiling, even the refrigerator—had been painted a jaundiced beige. I began by stripping the two knotty pine walls. The unfortunate yellow was not easy to remove. On the advice of the True Value hardware man, I purchased a stripping tool, a heat gun with a blade, which came in handy when I moved on to the kitchen cabinets. The cabinets I stained cherry; the wood walls, when they were finally revealed, I left in their natural state. The rest of the kitchen I painted white, as white as possible; same in the bedroom, same on the ceilings. Nonyellowing white I bought, as white as white gets. The kitchen counter I replaced with a speckled blue laminate, saving a piece of the original: it resembled a composite of hazardous waste sealed in gleaming plastic. I replaced the peeling beige-pink linoleum with blue-gray and white vinyl after I had the fridge refinished into shiny white. Then I moved on to the sickly green bathroom. ＊

＊ NOWADAYS, the nonyellowing whiteness is gone, replaced with saturated colors, colors that take risks. The still-bare wood in the kitchen meets warm red walls, walls the color of mulled wine. My bedroom is deep peach. The bathroom is painted an unapologetic pink. The wood floors still need refinishing, but Indian Sand Treewax—another recommendation from the True Value man—does a great job covering up the scratches and imperfections.

I have lost the eagerness to do it myself, and I rely instead on Harry and Tony, two old friends who happen to be handy around the house. Our friendship predates my Cape Cod life. We met in Boston back in 1983, when we all worked at the Boston University Bookstore. Harry's a musician and Tony is working on his doctorate now; both have the flexibility for and interest in the occasional odd job that entails a Cape escape, and I am happy to have them here. I've known these guys for seventeen years; they've known each other for seven years beyond that. As a result, the three of us spend a great deal of time debating the merits of any project before we actually begin, and we tend to take long lunch breaks to discuss the politics of the day. It's close to impossible to win an argument with the well-informed and tenacious Tony, but Harry and I do our best to help him perfect his scholarly form. In the summertime, we often end the workday with a swim at Long Beach, followed by Indian food for supper.

One Saturday, a few years back, when Harry and Tony were making me bookshelves in the kitchen, we decided they needed a corporate umbrella, a name. In minutes, they became the Bog Boys, named of course for the bog at the bottom of the hill. Two superintelligent men who are wonderful to have around the house. Two middle-aged guys who like to eat donuts and read the *Boston Globe* before they begin their workday. The Bog Boys? Oddly, the name is a perfect fit.

It is the Bog Boys who created the bookshelf that encircles the living room just above doorway height, who made the doors that enclose that washer-dryer I found in the *Pennysaver*. The Bog Boys made me a spice rack that spans the refinished cabinets on either side of my kitchen sink, and it was the Bog Boys who made my kitchen red, my bedroom peach, my bathroom first blue then briefly red, blue again, and finally spunky pink. The Bog Boys built me a pine vanity for my bathroom sink, and many years ago now, they made a cat shelf, a place for Egypt to land when he jumps up to bang on the bedroom window, demanding to be let in. As the kitty has aged, his cat shelf has become two shelves, stairway-style, to make his leap a little easier, and for this comfort, he can thank—who else— the Bog Boys. *

* I MET MY CLOSEST NEIGHBOR about a year after I moved in. She knocked loudly and with the certainty of someone who had watched this house being built almost forty years earlier. I opened the door to find a white-haired woman standing on my step. "I don't want to come in," she said, her voice at least as loud as her knock, "I just want to say thank you for fixing this place up. It had gotten to be a terrible mess."

Of course I invited her in, but she would have none of it. "I'm Barbara Dowe," she said as I stepped outside to continue the conversation. "My father built this place, you know, and my mother designed it. I live up the hill." She pointed at the white bungalow with the colonial blue shutters. "My father built that house, too," she added. "We used to have a cranberry bog right down there." She lifted her head in the opposite direction, as though she were pointing with her nose. "Now it's all grown up. A shame. I have a picture around somewhere that shows this cottage when it was first built, you know. You can see down to the bog. You might be interested in it."

"Oh yes, I'd love to see it." I introduced myself.

She nodded, then looked down past her bright red coat to her shoes, old-lady shoes, tan-colored, a little scuffed, but proper enough. A beat and a half passed before she looked up at me again. "Well, I won't take any more of your time. I know you're busy. I just wanted to say that it does my heart good to see you fixing this place up. Those last people that lived here, they didn't care about anything. There was trash in the yard, a real mess, and I hate to think how the inside must have looked."

I invited her in again, to have a look, but again she refused. "No, no. I know you're busy."

"Some other time?" I offered, and she looked right at me. In that moment, she was almost scary looking: her eyes froglike behind thick glasses, her mouth open, revealing her teeth — large, perfect, and I am pretty sure, all her own.

"Very nice to meet you, Katie," she said, immediately lengthening my name into its diminutive form. "I'll bring down that picture some time." The interview was over. She turned to walk up the overgrown path between the two houses. "Damn vines." The thorns were catching on her dull beige stockings. "I just can't keep up with them anymore." *

* IN THE YEARS since that first meeting, Barbara has become a friend and teacher. She gave me my first bird feeder, the first flowers for my garden, and a sense of my home's history. Recently, she moved into a nursing home, and I have yet to grow used to the sight of her house, dark and empty on the hill. She is rarely lucid now, but she has left me with a deep appreciation of my hand-built home. It is a simple floor plan. You enter through the front door straight into the living room; to your left is a brick fireplace; to your right, a triple window takes up the entire wall. From the living room you

move into the kitchen, with the bathroom tucked off to the side. The bedroom is behind the kitchen. It's a pretty big room, with windows on the three exterior walls. If you move back into the kitchen, and take a left, you can step through an extra-wide door onto the slate patio. Tucked in against the house, the herb garden thrives in afternoon sun, and the beach roses planted on the hillside scent the air with the fragrance of vanilla and cloves.

What is wonderful about my house is the way the light moves through the many windows I imagine Barbara's mother instructing her husband to install. In three rooms and a bathroom, she planned thirteen windows, and she planned them in just the right places. The sun rises in the eastern corner of the bedroom, and the light moves around the house as the day progresses. The long southern exposure means that there is daylight in all the rooms all afternoon, until the sun sets in the western corner of the living room. The moon, too, shines into the house. In the wintertime, when the trees are bare and the moon is full, I sometimes have to pull my bedroom blinds, blocking out the silvery light bright enough to make a shadow of the windowpanes on the floorboards. Or there will be no hope of sleep.

It is because the elder Mrs. Dowe lived next door that she could plan this perfect play of light and day and night. She and her builder-husband knew how to situate the cottage on the land because they knew the land. I never met her; she died a longtime widow, somewhere in her nineties, the first year I was here, the spring before her daughter came down the path to introduce herself. ✻

✳ I AM LISTENING for the squeak of the hinge on the black metal mailbox that is mounted to the right of my front door. It's Wednesday again, and I await the arrival of the *Pennysaver*. I find I have been thinking about those cottages for sale. Thinking: Maybe I'll call that number. Maybe I'll do a little bit of investigation. For while it is true that I was not seeking a cottage when I saw that listing last week, I am always seeking more space. A place to put my office that is not my bedroom. A place to put the fax machine that is not my kitchen counter. But when I comb the *Pennysaver* today, I find no listing. No cottages for sale. No cottages to be moved.

Is it the story I am already inventing of the sad little cottages, abandoned in the name of progress, waiting patiently to be adopted, that drives me to scour the *Pennysaver* again the following week? Or is it the sense I may have missed an opportunity? I'm not sure, but I realize that the cottages have come to live in my mind, that I find myself wondering if they are still for sale, if I could find them, and if one would fit my circumstances and my site plan. And I find myself sharing my classified curiosity with Ed, a retired firefighter who is a working builder. Ed and I are almost-relatives of the blended family variety. He's someone you trust the moment you meet him, the moment you feel the warmth in his eyes and the good humor in his soul. "Am I crazy to think of moving a cottage and attaching it to my house?" I ask when I see him on Christmas Day.

"Not at all," he says, and I think he is being generous in the face of a theoretical possibility. But he continues. "I think I know where those cottages are—or some cottages for sale, anyway. They're just down the street. You ought to go have a look." I am tempted to depart the gathering at once, to follow Ed's directions to my classified destiny. But dinner is served, and the sun sets on those cottages just down the street.

"You don't think I'm crazy?" I confirm with Ed before we say good-bye. He smiles and his blue eyes twinkle in response. "I'm going to go see those cottages tomorrow," I tell him.

"You do that," he says, "and let me know."

"What cottages?" my mother asks, as soon as we are in the car. I tell her about the ad in the *Pennysaver,* about my conversation with Ed. "And what would you do with a cottage?"

"Attach it to my house—as an addition. Put my office in it."

"Now that's a good idea. Maybe I could get one too." My mom's house is even smaller than my place, another Cape Cod cottage turned year-round residence. She downsized a few years back, and her furniture and possessions are still in the process of adapting. Case in point: the one hundred-plus versions of Santa Claus who surround us now as we open gifts in her tiny living room.

"You could use an addition just for all these Santas," I say.

"You don't like them?"

That's a tough one. I like my surfaces clear, perhaps a generational response to my mother's tendencies in the opposite direction. It isn't that I don't like the Santa display, but I am less than comfortable sitting amidst all these white-haired men—thin Father Christmas Santas and round jelly-belly

Santas; Santas dressed in red, blue, green, and even in black leather; the Harley Santa my mother bought last year and gave to me, without realizing he was dressed like a biker. I found him exceedingly creepy. My mother agreed that on his own, he was a little much. She happily adopted him into her fold, where his bad-boy vibe helps balance out all the good-natured Santas in the room.

"Well, it isn't that I don't like the Santas, per se. But there are an awful lot of them. They make me feel like I'm in a gift shop. Like I could turn one upside down and find a price."

She laughs. "You probably would. You know I never remember to take the price tags off." Which brings us back to our gifts, price tags intact, and not a Santa among them.   ✳

✳   AS SOON AS I GET HOME, I call Harry. He has a gig the next evening on the Cape. Can he come down early and look at some cottages with me? Harry is willing, even intrigued, but not as enthusiastic as I hoped he'd be. I want at those cottages, as soon as possible, but I also want Harry, Bog-Boy-in-Chief, to give me his professional opinion. Doesn't he want to come first thing in the morning? No. Okay, early afternoon. Settled. Our friend Bruce will come too—another friend from BU Bookstore days who is visiting from Martha's Vineyard.

Sunday dawns bright blue and bitterly cold, the kind of day when it is better not to know the "windchill factor." When Harry arrives, I give him barely a moment to say hello to Bruce before I bundle the three of us into Harry's car. "I really need to find you a car," I say, as we pull out of the driveway.

"I've been looking, you know." Another classified assignment.

"I know," he says, without enthusiasm. He is not convinced his 1986 Toyota Nova is on death's door, and he feels a certain loyalty to the aging vehicle. I, on the other hand, believe it is time to move on. I worry about his late-night gigs and his unreliable vehicle. I don't feel safe in the car, which rattles and shakes and farts without apology. But we are three, and his back seat accommodates full-sized passengers. Mine requires the folding of body parts and elicits complaints from any adult who is forced to ride in the rear.

We follow Ed's directions to a small cottage colony in Harwich Port. Once the vacation retreat of choice on Cape Cod, only a few cottage colonies are still in business these days. They once offered families a homey alternative to motels, more comfortable than a campground but with some of the same benefits: room for the kids to roam, other families nearby, and the sense of being part of a vacation village. In recent years, cottage colonies have hit upon hard times. The cottages are too tiny and too primitive for today's vacationers, and the colonies are often located too close to what are now too busy roads. Most cottage colonies have been redeveloped, many demolished. In this case, they are making way for new homes. The sign by the road confirms the price and availability of the buildings and reminds us they must be moved.

We discover the cottages are open to visitors, front doors unlocked. Each has a living room, a tiny galley kitchen, a minuscule bathroom, and a very, very small bedroom. They all have little screened-in porches. I imagine the vacationing families who came home to them all those years ago. Sitting on their porches late at night, content in their week on Cape Cod, they would play cards and music and sip vacation drinks. They were happy families, and these are happy cottages, though empty now and a bit worn out.

We walk through each little house, noting the slightly varying layouts, the positioning of windows and doors. I am Goldilocks, visiting the Bear family compound in their absence, searching for the cottage that is just right. And I find it. It is at the very back of the cottage colony, the cottage farthest from the street. Though it is not discernibly different from its neighbors on the outside, the inside of "my cottage" is warm and appealing, with Mexican tiles hand-laid on the tiny kitchen wall, a deep green living room with real knotty pine paneling, a bold purple bedroom, scuffed but promising wood floors, and bright white ceilings. There are odd built-in features that speak of a weekend carpenter, and a yellow bar of soap still resting on the white porcelain sink. While the other cottages feel as though they have been abandoned for some time, this last little cottage has been loved, and recently. We tour all the cottages one more time, comparing details, measuring rooms with Harry's footsteps, making notes, but we know we'll return to the last little cottage in the row. Inside, I jump up and down, up and down, making my way across the floorboards. I detect no soft spots. "It seems sturdy," I say, and Harry agrees. Bruce is slightly dubious about my research methods.

I open up the little notebook I have brought, the gridded paper perfect for sketching a floor plan. I outline the cottage, rough the locations of the doors and windows, and Harry provides the measurements.

"I could live here," Bruce says, "just as it is." Bruce has had an ongoing fantasy for as long as I've known him. A small-house fantasy. I first learned of it when we worked at the BU Bookstore and he was visiting me in Marblehead, a town full of charming old homes. We were walking around the Old Town section when we came upon a little house, snuggled into a hillside, a tiny porch only a few feet from the sidewalk. "Now that could be my house," Bruce said. I agreed it was a sweet little house.

"Whenever I see a little house like that, I think: The owners could give that house to me. They would see me looking with admiration on their home, and decide to give it to me. They'd walk outside, and say to me, 'This little house is just the right size for you. We have decided to give it to you.'"

I wanted to ask, What will happen to the couple; where will they live? But I understood I was being picky in the face of his fantasy. In the years since, Bruce has refined the scenario, and I have dared to ask a few questions. No strings attached, I have learned, in this house-gifting, and no worries about the couple (I think it is always a couple) who give him the house. They will not be homeless, but instead will move into a bigger house when he moves into the smaller one.

Bruce is an economical man; he is a poet for whom every word counts, and he lives sparingly in a two-room apartment in Vineyard Haven. As long as I have known him, Bruce has been a bookseller. He's a voracious reader, but due to space constraints, he limits the number of books that he owns. He invests only in art books, and takes most of what he reads home on loan.

I too can imagine Bruce living in this tiny cottage, seventeen by twenty-five, according to Harry's feet. I wonder if the cottage could take the ferry over to the Vineyard. House-moving is an old and honored tradition on Cape Cod, dating back to times when wood was scarce and transport to this spit of sand was expensive, even dangerous. I have heard stories of houses crossing the channel from the Cape to the islands. But I have already taken possession of this cottage in my mind. And I am not gracious like his fantasy couple. I want to keep this small house. I want to take it home.

"This is the best of the bunch," I say, not yet willing to admit I have fallen deeply, irretrievably in love.   *

*   IN THE CAR Harry blasts the heat at my request, pointing out that his radiator is in excellent repair. We talk about the little cottage as we ride around seeking a quick bite before we pick up champagne for a New Year's party. In Massachusetts, what we call the blue laws keep the liquor merchants shuttered on most Sundays. Only during the holiday season could we hope to purchase spirits on the day of rest. The original blue laws shut down all retail on Sunday, and frankly, I preferred it that way. My reasons were more pragmatic than spiritual. I was a bookstore manager in those days, and I found peace of mind knowing the shop was closed up tight one day a week. But it was more than that. There was a quiet in the streets around the shuttered shops, a quiet interrupted only by meandering Sunday afternoon drives, a quiet that made napping on a Sunday afternoon easy—and entirely guiltless. But slowly the laws eased, and less slowly the stores

opened, one after another. Soon enough, everybody was open, pretty much all of the time. Convenient, sure, but I have this unkickable sense that something valuable was lost.

On this day, though, I am happy to find a package store open where we can buy our holiday spirits. (A famous Massachusetts expression, "package store"; in the "package" are always alcoholic beverages.) Happy too for our midafternoon meal of pizza, salad, and root beer all around. Between bites, Harry and I take turns with the notebook. We draw an outline of my house, an outline of the cottage, and the three of us discuss the possible placement of the addition. "Leave it detached? Maybe with an interesting walkway to it?" This is Harry's suggestion. He's carried an image of a glass walkway connecting to an outbuilding on my property for many years.

"But where?" I ask him.

"Out on the corner by the shed."

"Won't meet setback requirements. That's right on the property line."

"Take the shed out and put it there."

"Too close to the septic. We need at least ten feet."

"You know all this stuff," he says.

"I do." I have looked into adding on so many times in the past eight, ten, twelve years that I know every pro and con of every option.   *

* WE MAKE OUR WAY HOME, only to pack up Harry's gear and head out again, this time to Hyannis—the downtown of all Cape Cod. We find parking across the street from tonight's venue, The Prodigal Son, a coffeehouse with an eclectic entertainment calendar. In any given month, you can hear rock bands, attend poetry slams and unpredictable open-mike nights, listen to folk music, and see Middle Eastern dance performances. Tonight, Harry backs up Tiffany Park, a young singer-songwriter who has a loyal following in the area. Bruce is eager to hear them; he hasn't heard Harry play since the days of the BU Bookstore, more than fifteen years earlier.

Bruce wears a neat brown beard streaked with gray and slightly outdated aviator glasses. He could easily be mistaken for a literature professor, especially when he opens his mouth. Bruce is highly intelligent, and highly verbal in the right setting. I think because he lives on an island, he saves up all his deep thinking. That might explain why he speaks in paragraphs rather than sentences, and why almost every observation he makes is thoughtful and well considered.

Self-schooled in music appreciation, Bruce has a CD collection that must rival the Smithsonian's, at least in the contemporary and minimalist departments. But he doesn't hear too much live music outside a concert hall. He is immediately disconcerted by the sound level at the coffeehouse, and upset that he is without earplugs. He folds his arms across his chest and refuses a drink. I find myself annoyed with his behavior, or maybe it is my defensiveness at work. Would a more thoughtful hostess have suggested ear protection?

I make my way to the bar for a glass of white wine. I bump into my friend Katrina, who has come to hear Harry, too. Katrina is tiny, beautiful, and blonde, and she is known to the bartender-owner because she hosts the Middle Eastern dance events here at The Prodigal. I introduce her to Bruce, who remains disgruntled. Usually the sight of Katrina improves the day of any person of the male gender. I allow myself one more moment of guilt for Bruce's bad feelings, and then I sit back to enjoy the show.

Tiffany is young, in her mid-twenties maybe, and obviously talented. She wears 1950s-style plastic eyeglasses, a red plaid woodsman jacket, and army boots. Her voice is resonant and evocative, and so are her own songs, of which, Harry tells her, she does not write enough. Harry, close to twenty years older, is just as gifted. He is as much Tiffany's cheerleader and coach as he is backup to her lead. He prefers the backup role, he says. He plays a mean guitar, a double-mean bass; the depth of his voice complements his own complex and lovely songs. What Harry lacks are the psychological components to solo success in the musical world: abiding confidence and unstinting ambition. He is happier helping someone else along.

Tonight Harry wears his usual uniform: black jeans and a black T-shirt. He is a big guy, tall, strong, and rounding slightly as he hits the middle of his life. He's been bald as long as I've known him, since he was not yet twenty-five. Harry has what another friend calls "a well-shaped head," and he looks great without hair. Perhaps it is his clean-shaven head that makes his eyebrows appear so unruly. I have known him for so many years, I sometimes fail to notice his distinctive looks.

On the tiny stage, Harry and Tiffany create an unlikely aesthetic, an odd yet perfect combination of sight and sound that is precisely wacky now: In their own version of "I'm Gonna Love You Just a Little More, Baby," Tiffany is Barry White, while Harry, in falsetto, joins her for the chorus.

I steal a glance at Bruce. He has unfolded his arms, opening himself to the music. I see his fingers tapping out a rhythm on the table, and a smile playing on the edge of his lips. I shift my attention back to the stage, where Harry has become Barry, leaning into the mike and making every attempt to maintain a serious demeanor as he lowers his voice to a deep-throated rumble. As they finish the tune, Tiffany and Harry are grinning, and we are clapping, laughing, clapping.

resolution

THE NEXT DAY, a Monday, I call the number on the sign.

"Eastward Companies."

I notice speaking voices more than most people do. Perhaps it is my musician's ear, or maybe all these years of listening to the radio instead of watching TV. I appreciate any lovely voice, whether it is male or female, and I am apt to idealize the person behind the voice. Many years ago, I met the late Robert J. Lurtsema, legendary host of *Morning Pro Musica*. The gray-white beard I expected, and I was unsurprised that voice, more bass than baritone, would reside in a barrel chest, supported by a big belly. What stunned me was Lurtsema's height, not to mention his apparel. That voice belonged in a tall man's body; that voice belonged in a tuxedo jacket. But the voice lived in a short, round man; the voice wore a red chamois shirt from L. L. Bean.

Voices, I have learned, are not always to be trusted. Broad voices live in thin bodies, young voices in old bodies, and voices, it turns out, dress however they like. Still, I persist in reading voices, and I am not always wrong. I met a significant man in my life over the telephone. His voice was warm, unconstrained, and so appealing that I wanted to curl up inside it and live there. When we met in person, I was not disappointed. Now we communicate only occasionally—usually through e-mail—and for this I am grateful. To hear him speak requires a deafness my heart can barely achieve. It is one thing to lose a lover; another thing entirely to give up such a voice.

"Eastward Companies."

This voice is female, and she breathes the greeting into the phone. If Marlene Dietrich had answered telephones for a living, this would have been her voice. Deep, sexy, yet remarkably professional. This voice makes me want to pack my bags and head for the Eastward Companies, wherever they are. Just to satisfy my curiosity. I wonder what effect this modern-day Marlene would have on male callers. I know my ears are more sensitive than most, and I've learned to tone down my aural fantasies. Even as I try to dress her voice in lumpy pink sweatpants, I am willing to bet contractors hear fishnet stockings when they call Eastward Companies.

 "I'm calling about the cottages—" I begin.

"Yes, you'll need to speak to Tom Howes." Tom wasn't in at the moment; could he call me back? She is efficient, too, handles me so smoothly that I am barely aware she has taken my number and gone on to the next call. I am still holding the receiver to my ear, but the voice has disappeared. ✳

✳   WHEN TOM HOWES returns my call, his voice is businesslike, agreeable, an easy tenor. I realize as we speak that I am already invested in that little cottage; I want it, and he has it. Tom is polite and helpful, able to put me in touch with a house-mover, willing to estimate for me what I might pay to have the house moved. "Around $2,500," he says, "depending on your location."

My location, I think, my lovely location may cause a string of problems. I push those thoughts aside and continue with my information gathering. The owner would like the houses moved as soon as possible, Tom Howes informs me. Within a couple of weeks, by the end of January at the latest.

I explain I want to attach the cottage to my existing house, that I will have to figure it out, get permits, clear the land before I can move the cottage. I cannot get everything done within that time frame.

"Do you have any place on your property you can put the cottage for the time being?" he asks me.

He is obviously assuming that my "property" is more sub-stantial—and flatter—than it actually is. I wonder if I will have to give up the cottage, simply because of bad timing and the fact that I am surrounded by hills and trees. I change the subject. "Have you had many calls?"

"Yes and no. Lots of people dreaming, nobody who is really serious yet."

"Well, I am really serious."

"I can tell," he says, and he promises not to give away the last little cottage until I report back to him with the results of my investigation.

I hang up from Tom Howes and make the call to Bob Hayden, owner of Hayden Building Movers. A deep voice rattles out of an old answering machine. "You have reached Hayden Building Movers." The voice does not apologize for missing my call, but tells me instead that I can reach a live person between 7:30

and 8 in the morning or 5:30 and 6 in the evening. This is the voice of a man who does not believe in receptionists — or office hours, for that matter. Can he possibly spend all his time between 8 A.M. and 5:30 P.M. moving houses? Are there that many houses to move on Cape Cod? The ragged voice of Hayden Building Movers, whom I suspect is Bob Hayden himself, offers a return call if I leave a message. An innocent, I leave one.   ✳

✳   NEXT, I CALL ED'S HOUSE, where his wife, Susan, answers. "You saw them?" she says. "Let me get Eddy. He's dying to know." I hear her hollering for Ed before she asks me to hang on. "I think he's running the saw. I have to go get him."

"They look good," I say, after Ed says hello.

I tell him about the cottage I like best and what I have learned from Tom Howes. We talk about ways we can attach the cottage to the house. Harry and I have been conferring, and we are thinking that the cottage needs to nestle in next to the house, where the patio is now. It's the only place where I can imagine a crane could deposit a cottage safely. As I speak, I can almost hear Ed trying to recall the lay of the land. He hasn't been here in a few years. "Just outside the kitchen, there's a patio, remember? It runs the length of the house, and it's about twelve feet wide. Then the land slopes down to the bog. I'm thinking the crane could lift it in from my neighbor's driveway."

"That does sound like the easiest place to put it," Ed agrees.

But not easy with the Conservation Commission, I know. A few years ago, I hired an architect to help me come up with a plan for an addition. She urged me to expand into the far hillside, on the side of the house that was farthest from the bog. But I had two problems with those far-side plans. One: We were adding a room with a full concrete wall that backed into the damp earth only to get the second-floor room with the light I wanted. Two: The woodchuck would be displaced. As would the wrens and the quail who nest in the thick undergrowth. She assured me the animals would find new homes, but I was unconvinced. We are eating up so much of the Cape Cod landscape. How many creatures can we relocate before there are no homes for them at all?

I suggested we look at the other side of the house, where the southern exposure meant the rooms would get more light. It would be more accessible, and only the ants that build their hills between the stones on my patio would have to move out. "On that side," she said, "we'd have to deal with conservation permits." No one wants to deal with conservation permits on Cape Cod, I learned. It takes longer, it costs more, and there is no guarantee you'll get your way. She continued: "It isn't even worth your paying me to draw a plan until you hire an engineer and find out exactly how far you are from that bog."

I didn't hire the engineer. By that point, I was too discouraged and too broke to consider pursuing this fantasy any further.

"The bog could be a problem," I say to Ed. I fill him in on what I know already. "I guess I need an engineer." *

* JUST BEFORE CHRISTMAS, I sent out invitations for a millennium bash. The invitations have a color picture of a funky Y2K wand-wielding fairy, and guests are instructed to come prepared to be a Wish Angel. My concept is this: Upon

arrival, each guest will select another's name from a basket. During the course of the evening, the wishers must divine their wishees' deepest desires, and they must do this without arousing suspicion. At midnight, we will exchange wishes.

I have invented the Wish Angels as party glue. It will be an excuse for a conversation with someone you don't know, or don't know well. I figure that in order to keep your angel identity hidden, you will want to circulate. But the idea has met with some resistance among my invitees. My friend Erika feels too shy to be a Wish Angel, she tells me on Tuesday, on our way over to see the cottage. "I'm not sure I could just strike up a conversation with someone I don't know," she says. And then, after a moment, "Would we have to wish our wishes out loud?"

I decide immediately that we do not. As we drive along Route 28, we devise the plan for the evening. All wishes will be anonymous. The slips of paper with the names on them will also serve as the slips of paper for the wishing. For selection purposes, the names will be folded inward, blank sides showing. After the Wish Angel writes the wish, he or she will return it, folded name outward, to the basket. I am pleased with Erika's attention to the folding details. Until she went to Columbia to get her doctorate in education, Erika taught first grade. I am pretty sure she would approve of Wish Angels if she were asking her six-year-olds to make wishes for each other.

Erika is just the person you'd want to teach your first-grader. She is young and lovely, energetic, sweet, and calm, and she loves kids. When she first thought of applying to the doctoral program at Teacher's College, Erika considered instead making a request to follow her kids for their first three years in school, teaching them first, second, and third grades. She wanted to stay with them, provide continuity, and make sure the slower learners got the attention they needed, especially the kids who were having trouble reading. Blonde, soft-spoken Erika is passionate about teaching children to read. She loves to lead them to words, to open up their worlds. She thrills at the steady progress of her classroom, and approaches her role with a certain reverence. "In one school year," she told me once, "most kids learn to read. When you think about it, that is an amazing amount of learning in ten months' time." I didn't point out that it is an amazing amount of teaching, too.

When we finally get to the cottage colony, I take her right to the last one. "It's perfect," she says. "And you're right, it does match your house!" The knotty pine paneling, the deep colors on the walls, the many windows. And they are both about the same age. It is my thought that house and cottage were separated at birth. It is my fantasy that both were built by Barbara Dowe's father. But I doubt this is true. In a Cape Codder's mind, any one town is very far away from the next. There is a joke that in summertime, Falmouth and Hyannis are twenty-four miles and twenty-four hours apart. We've traveled almost twenty-nine miles to reach the cottage colony. Light years, in the geographical lexicon of Cape Cod.

"I called your dad," I mention as we visit another cottage. Erika's father is a surveyor and civil engineer.

"He's off this week."

I have met Erika's father only in passing. I know he is the tall, blond, and silent type. Erika thinks the world of him, and I know I can trust him completely. I got his machine when I called. His disembodied voice was assured, quietly authoritative. I hope he can take me on. In my message, I tried to strike a balance between urgent need and downright desperation for his services.

"He's swamped. I'm amazed he took this week off, but I'm glad he did. He works too hard."

"He may be too busy, then?"

"He's always too busy. But I mentioned your cottage idea to him at supper last night. I'm sure he'll call you back." *

* IT ISN'T AS COLD TODAY, but still we crank the heat when we get back into the car. In another fifteen minutes, we pull into Eastward Companies. I enter the office with a sense of anticipation. Sure enough, the voice is at the front desk: I recognize her as she speaks into her headset. She is an attractive blonde, fiftyish, and dressed at the exact midpoint between pink bunny sweatsuit and black-with-gold-buttons Coco Chanel original. She smiles an acknowledgment while she finishes up with her caller.

My $300 check is already written. She has papers for me, and a map that shows all the little cottages and their square footage. They are labeled. Mine is H1. She asks me if I have decided which one I want and I point to that one just as Tom Howes comes through the door. When she introduces us, he asks me if I looked at H5. Tom is pushing this other cottage because someone else wants mine.

"I called first," I told him this morning, when he informed me of this development. He conceded that this was true.

"But he wants two of them," he explained. In other words, I am being run over by a cottage-moving high roller.

"What does he want to do with them?" I asked. "Are you sure it matters which ones he takes? The one I want matches my house. Can't you ask him to take another?" Tom agreed to ask, but urged me to look at the other cottage on my way over today.

"I looked at it," I tell him now, "But I still like the one in the back better."

"H5 is bigger," he reminds me, "and there is already a gas heater in the living room."

"Have you asked that guy if he cares which one he takes?" Not yet, but he promises that he will. *Do you have a deposit from him?* I want to ask. But I don't. Instead, I say it was nice to meet him, and I promise to take one more look at H5 on our way home.

Erika and I make our way back. Route 28 in late December is another landscape entirely. I love this stretch of road in the wintertime almost as much as I hate it in the summer. The traffic is light; most locals use the back roads year-round out of habit. The T-shirt shacks are all sealed up, and you can't get any saltwater taffy till next spring. The miniature-golf courses look like small abandoned kingdoms, their moats drained and their most dazzling structures shrink-wrapped in brown Hefty bags. The motels claim "No Vacancy," and by this the owners mean to say, "No Heat, No Business, and We're in Florida, Anyway." Fried clam joints and ice cream parlors and seafood restaurants have signs out front. "See you next season!" If it weren't for these upbeat declarations of future possibility, you would think the place abandoned, left behind. In the clear winter light, the tackiness and 1950s style of these roadside attractions is evident. It seems entirely possible that you have entered a time warp.

Across from the Dairy Queen, we take a right into the cottage colony and get out of the car. H5 is at the very front of the colony, facing the street. It is larger, and it is in fine shape. It has a closet in the living room, which is a bonus feature, and there is an extra window. The layout is slightly different. This cottage has a back door off the kitchen, instead of a side door out the living room, and the orientation of the rooms is the reverse of H1. There is no reason not to like it, but there is also, for me, no reason to love it.

We head back to my cottage for one last look, and I hear their voices before I see them—a man and a woman, the kids circling around. He has a clipboard. They are standing in the screened porch of my cottage. I can barely hear their conversation, even as I intentionally, guiltlessly eavesdrop, but I make out enough to realize he is a realtor! Showing her my cottage! *Don't bother writing a check!* I want to tell her. *I just put a deposit on this one. Have a look at H5, why don't you? It's bigger, too!*

On the way home, Erika and I speculate about the woman and the children, about the man who wants to buy two cottages. We consider how much it matters what cottage I move. Do I want to move a cottage, any cottage, or do I want to move the last little cottage in the row, that cottage only? The answer is not clear to me. I suppose I am willing to move any cottage that fits, but I want the cottage with the crooked Mexican tiles in the kitchen, the funny purple bedroom with the tiny round hole in the wall where someone connected a hose to the water heater—to provide water for the aquarium that must have rested on the rough built-in table. I know I'll take down the tiles, pull out the table, and patch the hole in the wall. But the sense of life and caring in that cottage still appeals. If I'm going to move a cottage, I want to move a cottage with personality, with history, a cottage that has been loved.

With no traffic, it takes less than light years to get home from Harwich, and in that time I resolve to hold fast to my quirky cottage. To guard it jealously, to defend it, to tell Tom Howes to find another cottage for that greedy man who wants two. ✳

✳   IT'S A TWO-PARTY WEEKEND. On Saturday, my mother and I drive to Worcester for the Big Family Christmas. The family, in this case, is my mother's family, and the Big Christmas is just two days before the New Year. Sometimes we're late and sometimes we're early, but we never aim for the actual day. The location changes annually as well; this year, we gather at Jack's house. My uncle Jack is the elder of his generation, the keeper of the family history, and the force behind most family reunions. He is also the reigning patriarch. It is a role he seems to enjoy. He likes to gather us together, to stand in the center of our family circle, to tell stories and give small speeches. If my uncle Bob were still alive, he would challenge Jack's authority, but now it falls to his younger sisters—my mother and my aunt—to tease Jack when he takes the patri-archal thing too seriously.

On this day, Jack pulls me aside early in the gathering. "There are so many of us," he says to me. "We only get together once a year now, and when we do, it's hard to talk to everybody here. I think it would be nice if we got everyone in one room and each said a few words about our lives—you know, what we've been doing, what's new. What do you think?"

I am the oldest of my generation, and though it doesn't look like I'll ever qualify for matriarch, I am honored that Jack has turned to me for my opinion before he makes the announcement to the larger group. But I am horrified by his idea, and I tell him so. He laughs. There is no dissuading him, and there is no Bob on hand to tell Jack he's been working in human services too long. Jack has thought about this for some time. No, he doesn't think his exercise sounds like a workshop-opener. He thinks it is a good way for all of us to get to know each other better. Yes, he'd like me on board, but he'll go it alone if required. He is determined to host this show-and-tell session.

It's after dinner when Jack gathers the family for his talking experiment. We are all squeezed into his family room, an addition with lots of windows and a view of the Worcester High School playing field in the distance. It's time for the grab, the yearly and often controversial entertainment at our family gatherings. We select gifts from a stash in the center of the room, and then we do our best to trade our selections for something we'd like better. According to the rules of the grab, you are allowed to exchange the gift you choose for any gift you prefer, so long as that gift has been unwrapped before you take your turn. Number Nine can trade with Numbers One through Eight, for example, but Number Twenty-one has a larger selection of gifts to steal. Number One makes out best of all. After everything is open and displayed (you aren't allowed to hide your gift if you like it, hoping no one will remember you have it), Number One gets to re-select from the full array of opened gifts.

There are at least two camps of grab participants: those who would never take a gift away from someone else just to get what they want, and those who are merciless, even going so far as to rob the children in the room. Then there are those who just hate the grab, period, and don't want to play, and those who would rather give gifts as they wish and forget the grab trinkets, which nobody wants or needs. Finally, there are those among us—interestingly, this contingent consists mainly of cousins—who would prefer to skip the gift giving altogether and just visit. Perhaps because there is no clear majority opinion, the tradition of the grab continues. Year after year, we gather to be entertained by the surprises in the middle of the room and the horse trading that follows. Like many others in my family, I rarely take advantage of the rule that says I can exchange my gift with anyone who has gone before me. But I am always ready to participate in the consensual, often multiple, trades that occur after all the gifts have been selected.

"Before the grab," Jack begins. He is standing in the center of the sunroom, a politician ready with his speech. "I thought it might be nice if we went around the room and said a few words about what we're doing these days." He pauses. "Now, I already know Kate's opinion." He nods in my direction and I make a face at him. "But I've been thinking how we don't get to hear from everybody at these parties. And we miss what is happening in each other's lives. My son-in-law, for example, just got promoted, and I bet he hasn't mentioned that to anybody here. But we'd all like to congratulate him, and this would be a chance to do that."

My aunt Rosemary jumps in. Though she works as a buyer for a defense contractor, she is trained as a psychotherapist. This is right up her alley. "Jack, you are so right." She turns to my cousin's husband. "Congratulations! That's great!"

"It isn't that I hate the idea, it's only that I feel awkward," I say.

I'm relieved when Jack does not suggest I go first as a way to alleviate my awkward feelings. Instead, he lets his son-in-law lead. Someone asks him what he does for a living, and we go from there. Even the little kids say something, with a little coaxing from their parents. Jack, who stays in touch with most of the people in the room, asks encouraging questions to nudge people along. To my mother, he says, "And you are active in the town now, too, right?" This leads her to speak about her work with the Cultural Council of which she is the chair, and which she neglected to mention when she mumbled something about being retired and "hanging in there on Cape Cod."

When it is my turn, I feel nervous. Even as I listened to everyone speak, I thought about what I would say. I always feel a little bit the oddball at these gatherings. Forty-something and unmarried, no grandchildren to contribute, and a job that nobody really understands. Jack's right in the sense that we know only pieces of each other, small items that are true, but in no way add up to the whole picture of our individual lives. I know my cousin's husband as a great cook, a pie- and cookie-maker for family gatherings, an ex-Marine, but until a few minutes ago, I had no idea what he did in his civilian life. It is also clear from this exercise that we are a family of second-hand braggarts. None of us are inclined to announce our achievements; instead we let news travel through the family grapevine, mother to sister to son to wife. Today, Jack asks everyone to speak for himself, herself. It isn't easy for any of us.

But the questions people ask, the coaxing and talking, help every reluctant speaker along, and also provide evidence that everyone in this room genuinely cares about every other person here.

"I'm thinking of moving a cottage," I begin when my turn comes. "I found it in the newspaper, and it is part of a cottage colony they are clearing out to make new homes. I want to attach it to my house and make it into my office. I've been looking into it all this week. There are a lot of issues with the town, and I don't know yet how I'll finance it." No one speaks, and so I continue. "I've been running my business out of my bedroom for twelve years now." There is laughter, and I realize that does sound funny. I go with it. "Even if this doesn't work out," I say, pausing for dramatic effect, ready to overstate my goal, "I am determined to get my business out of my bedroom this year." Everyone is laughing again. I smile, and I sense the power of stating my intentions to the twenty-something assembled relatives in the room. Hearing myself speak the words, I realize I am determined, and that I am going to do my best to make this cottage thing happen.

Questions follow, which I do my best to answer, and then we move on to the next family member, and the next and the next. When we finally begin the grab, it is with a new spirit of knowing and curiosity about each other. Jack's genius is apparent as we help ourselves to dessert and coffee. In smaller groups now, we are quizzing each other, asking more questions, telling stories and laughing, pleased to learn more about the strangers we call family.

"Great idea you had," I say to Jack, as I give him a good-bye hug.

"Keep me posted about that cottage." *

✳   ON NEW YEAR'S DAY, Bruce arrives on a midmorning ferry to help with the preparations. I love to cook when I have the time, and Bruce has the patience to act as sous-chef on the long days of cooking madness that precede any event I host. But he is not always comfortable in the chaos I create in the kitchen. Today, Bruce is horrified when I drop dried cranberries next to the pecans on top of the goat cheese rounds. It looks so pretty and festive, and I am pretty sure the tastes and textures will work well—sharp with tangy, rice cracker–crunchy with white-cheese smooth. We'll heat them later, so they can be served warm.

Tony arrives next, with his significant, Anna. We chat for a few minutes before I ferry Bruce, Tony, and Anna to the bed-and-breakfast around the corner. I am putting up my off-Cape guests overnight. You don't need to do that, they told me, but I feel rich at the moment. Though I mostly work for independent bookstore owners, I've been working almost full-time on a high-tech project for the last three months. My big-business client owes me a bundle of money. In three more months, I'll be back to making my project-to-project, hand-to-mouth living, but for the moment, I feel the security of a soon-to-be-paid contractor. I want to share the wealth with friends. And I don't want them driving back to Boston in the wee hours of the next century. Call it a bout of Y2K paranoia.

In the wider world, there are warnings about terrorist plots; the survivalists are in full gear; and emergency workers will be on alert overnight, just in case something horrible happens. There are some who believe the world is going to end tonight, but most people are just worried their computers won't work tomorrow. I'm pretty sure there will be a world in the morning, but I think I'll stay off the Internet after midnight. I've brought in extra firewood to keep us warm if the power grid fails, I am well stocked with candles, and I've made sure we'll have plenty of leftovers. I'm thinking God doesn't work on Earth-time, but if lightning or terrorists or electronic madness strikes at 12:01, I'm glad I'll be surrounded by friends.

Tina calls from the bus stop, and I make a run to pick her up while Bruce keeps his eye on the kitchen. She is a flight attendant for American Airlines. She flew in from London this afternoon, and she is "on reserve" for New Year's Day. That means Tina could be called for a trip in the dead of the night and be forced to leave the Cape by 4:00 for a 6:00 A.M. sign-in. We've worked this out already. Harry has offered to take her to the airport, whenever she needs to go. "I hardly sleep anyway," he says. "It isn't a problem. I'll just take you on up, and then maybe I'll go to an early mass." I am pretty sure that Harry has a crush on Tina, but it is also true that Harry has offered just because he's a genuinely good guy. An early-morning ride to Boston, I think, will be the perfect way for Tina to find that out. I am hoping for romance.

I am not normally a matchmaker, but Tina is a special case. I want to encourage her to begin dating. She is twenty-eight, and her sweetheart died about a year and a half ago—unexpectedly, prematurely, far away from home. He was my friend and colleague and we were working together on a project in Hong Kong. I met Tina when I picked her up at the Hong Kong airport, delivering her to his side. The sad circumstances of our meeting explain why our friendship, though not old in years, is deep in meaning.

Now Tina sits on the stool by the counter and writes out the Wish Angel names in big block letters. She and Bruce share a passion for the movies, and they are speaking in a language I barely understand, filled with names of directors and actors I do not recognize. I am cin-illiterate. Bruce, I register, as I listen to them, also has a small crush on Tina. Anyone would have a crush on Tina. She is beautiful, with big brown eyes that give a clue to her deeply sweet nature. I know Bruce well enough to believe he probably won't act on his infatuation. I know Harry well enough to hope that he will.

The 9:30 start of this party means that I have time to change out of my cooking clothes before the other guests arrive. Often when I cook, I end up wearing my garlic-infused clothes to the table. Tony and Anna return, feeling pleased with the progress of their Cape Cod mini-vacation.

We are moving from the kitchen to the living room when Harry pounds his big Harry fists on the front door, not a request to be answered, but only a signal he is about to open the door. He's just played a First Night gig in Providence. When he sees the spread, he curses himself for eating Burger King on the drive up. I reassure him he can just nibble tonight and eat leftovers tomorrow. Because he calls me the Leftover Queen, Harry finds this an acceptable, even welcome, fate.

We eat and we drink and we talk, talk, talk. We are few enough to talk as a group, but there are enough of us to break into smaller conversations. Bruce and Tony catch up with each other. They know each other from the BU Bookstore days, but aren't in regular touch. Tina chats quietly with Anna, Tony's young love. Anna is from Italy and her gentle beauty matches her lilting accent exactly. Tony seems happy around Anna, and we are all happy for that. I watch Harry watch Tina, and I am pretty sure my hunch is right. And I feel good about the Wish Angel thing, too. Everybody is circulating, I notice, and everybody is talking to everybody else. It is a slightly mixed group of old and new friends, and they are all getting along. It is possible to throw a lot of wonderful people (who don't know each other) into the same room with not-so-great results. So far, so good, I think.

Around quarter to twelve, pens in hand, I remind everyone to write their wishes. People scatter to odd corners of the house, needing privacy for their compositions. "Is this all right for Bruce?" his angel asks me, because she has met him for the first time this evening. With her intuition as a guide, she has wished him well. Tina, too, shows me her wish for Harry, which is more than perfect, and filled with details she has learned from me. Another guest shares her wish for Bruce's angel with me, and I nod a secret approval just as her wishee walks by. Anna does not check with me, perhaps because we have met only a few times, or perhaps she is my Angel. None of the men ask for advice, either. They write in silence.

At midnight, or possibly a minute late, we stand in a circle and lift our glasses. I bought twenty crystal flutes for this party. A dollar a stem at Ocean State Job Lot, and well worth the price to hear the clink of our glasses as we toast. We drink. We make our private wishes. (Three wishes for the new century, I'd said on the invitation—one for yourself, one for the world, and one for the person whose name you select.) For the world, I wish for more peace, less hunger, more love, less anger. It's an easy, predictable wish, if compound. For myself,

I am torn. I've been working on a novel for at least five years, and I'd love to finish it this year. I wouldn't mind a change in my relationship status either—from unequivocally single to say, single, but happily involved. I also want to move a house. In some way, the other wishes come with the cottage: a place to write, the space for a man to share. As I wish for a successful cottage-moving, I am aware I am wishing for much more.

There is Middle Eastern music on the stereo now. I study Egyptian dance with my friend Katrina, and I'd organized the CDs to segue from quiet jazz to music that makes you want to move. I was hoping that Katrina and her sweetheart, Ruben, might arrive late, but she has two dance engagements this evening; their appearance is unlikely now.

"This is dancing music," Tony says, and I nod. "Show us some moves." As we stand in the circle, I do. Some basic hips, some shoulder shimmies for the men, and we move together, smiling, holding our glasses, a circle of friends. I cannot imagine being luckier than this.

We pull our wish-slips from the basket. And as if it is choreographed, everyone returns to their seats to read their wishes. "Let's read them out loud," someone suggests.

"If you want to, but you can keep your wish to yourself, too, if you like." I am thinking of the conversation with Erika. She and Bill didn't make it after all, but I know there is more than one shy person in this crowd. Bruce takes the silent wishing option, but everyone else chooses to read their wish aloud. I am impressed by the wishes, by the details that each person has found for their wish-ward. Someone has wished Tony a 1990 Volvo station wagon, in excellent condition, low mileage and cheap. Tina is wished that she will be able to sleep late in the morning, that she will not be called by American Airlines at 4 A.M. Harry? I wonder. Anna gets good wishes in her new job, and Harry's wish from Tina is the best of all. It is long and complicated, but at the center is the wish for "the creativity to keep writing great songs like 'When We All Get Finished, We Can All Get Happy.'" Harry is convinced the wish is from me. I deny it, emphatically, laughing. "But who else would know about that song?" He wrote it when we were opening the BU Bookstore, claiming it was a song about my management style, assuring me it was a compliment. I've never been 100 percent sure. He turns to Tony, who shakes his head; then to Bruce, who echoes Tony's denial.

"It's a secret!" I say. "Your Wish Angel is a secret!"

Of course the figuring out of Wish Angels is the perfect complement to the figuring out of wishes by those very angels. This is not unpredictable. What is funny, though, is the fact that almost everybody is convinced I am their Wish Angel. And when I say, truthfully, that I am not, each guest is entirely baffled. "Who else would know to wish me this?" A shrug, a smile from me. "Wish Angels," I say in my best guru voice, "have special Ways of Knowing."

footwork

ON THE FIRST WEDNESDAY of the new millennium, I have an 8 A.M. appointment with the chief building inspector. "Get him involved from the start," Ed told me. "You'll have a better chance with the town if you do."

"Ralph Crossen," he says, standing to greet me. I climb the single stair that separates his office from the rest of the Building Department, and shake his hand. I introduce myself and take the seat he indicates. Then I tell Mr. Crossen what I want to do, and lay my plans on his desk.

While he examines my plans, I contemplate the last week and a half. In the days since that first look at the cottage, I have been attached to the telephone, with an occasional break for some computer-aided design. I've managed to defend my cottage from the cottage-grabbing man, and I have hired an engineer—Erika's dad—and secured the services of Ed and his son John as my builders. I have not yet met with the house-mover, but on Monday, he finally returned my many calls. It appears that what I want to do is possible—not without complications—but possible.

Ralph Crossen, conspicuously more awake than I am, fires questions at me. Why do I want to go to the trouble of moving a house? Am I certain the cottage is structurally sound? Am I sure moving a building would be less expensive than adding on?

Because I make a chunk of my living designing bookstores, I know enough construction jargon to answer Ralph Crossen with confidence. I speak of cost per square foot, comparing the cost of building from scratch to the cost of moving a ready-made structure, requiring only minor cosmetic work.

The cottage itself looks to be in good shape, Ed has told me. He has visited it twice, taken some measurements, given my choice his seal of approval. "We might have to blow in some insulation to meet code. It probably isn't insulated. And you'll need storm windows." I made careful notes on the back of an envelope. We estimated costs for the foundation, the move, building the connecting passage, and the required electrical and plumbing work. When we added everything up, it came to $15,000, plus the cost of the cottage move. "Say $18,000 when you're done," Ed said.

"Say $20,000," I replied, thinking of my hillside. I suspect I'll spend more. Even so, I know it will be cheaper than starting from scratch. Except for the house-moving, all the other costs would come with any addition. And we'd have to build it besides.

Ralph Crossen takes to his calculator, jots down some numbers, and eventually declares I may be right about the savings. At this point, he becomes more interested in the story. How did I find it? Where is it now? Who will move it for me?

"Hayden?" he asks, and I nod.

Finally, I get to ask some questions. I'm concerned about some new regulations that specify how many bedrooms can exist on how much acreage. Will my office be considered a bedroom? I don't want to use up my bedroom allotment in case I want to add one later. But if I call my working space an "office," the town could assume that I have a parade of clients, that I need zoning approval, parking permits, handicapped access, who knows what else.

I juggle bookstore projects with writing work; clients rarely come to me, and I hope to do more writing than consulting in the coming years. In the spirit of hopefulness and with some guile, I have called my office "a writing studio" on the floor plan in front of Mr. Crossen. He approves of the terminology, and tells me to leave at least a five-foot opening into the space, no door. A door that closes makes a bedroom.

"I don't see any issues from a Building perspective," he says at last. "We're not your problem. And I think you'll probably be okay with Health. It's Conservation you need to worry about. This wetland," he says, pointing to my site map. "That's your problem. You'll need special permits, maybe even a variance. If I were you, I'd go right next door and talk to them while you're here. Find out where you stand."

He gathers the plans into a stack and hands them back to me. The interview is over. He stands, shakes my hand, looks me in the eye. "You are an enterprising young lady." He says it approvingly; he smiles for the first time since we have met. I decide to let the young lady part go by. "It's an original idea, sounds like it will work. But," he says, pausing, holding onto the hard *t*, "first you'll have to get it past Conservation." He breathes extra emphasis into the last word in the sentence, slowing on the third syllable. *Con-sahh-vayy-shun*. I notice his smile has vanished and that when he wishes me good luck, he says it in a way that suggests I will need it. ✳

*   DARCY IN CONSERVATION is pleasant and helpful. She looks at my site map, takes out her ruler, and measures the distance from my house to the bog. "All depends on where the edge of the wetlands actually is," she says as she lays her ruler on the counter between us. "It could go either way. If you go sixteen feet out from your existing dwelling—"

"Twenty with the hallway. I need a hallway to connect the two buildings."

"Twenty," she repeats. "At twenty, you'll probably land in the buffer zone." She explains to me that building in the first fifty feet from any certified wetland is prohibited by town ordinance. "You'll have to make a full filing and go before the Commission to request a variance for the part of the structure that will be in the no-disturb zone."

This is not surprising news. Erika's engineering father, Dave, has already told me that locating the exact edge of the wetland is essential. That how much or how little of the buffer zone we would disturb could make or break the project.

"I can't shrink the building," I say. "It already exists. And there isn't another spot to put it on the property. It's all hills and trees. Doing it this way makes much less disturbance than building from scratch. Will they take that into consideration?"

"Possibly. But that's up to our commissioners. I can't speak for them. Do you have an engineer?" I mention Dave's name, and she nods in what seems like pleasant recognition. "Good. He'll represent you at the hearing."

Represent me? At a hearing? "Can't I represent myself?" I ask Darcy, trying to keep the panic out of my voice.

"Well, generally, the engineer represents the homeowner." She says this kindly but firmly. I sense I have made a faux pas, a municipal mistake that she is willing, because I am a beginner, to overlook. Darcy continues. "You'll need a survey and a plan drawn up. Dave will locate the edge of the wetland and make the filing." She hands me a thick packet of forms. "Then, we'll schedule a hearing. You're in luck now. At this time of year, it only takes four or five weeks to get on the calendar."

Four or five weeks! "Can I put my name in now?"

"Not unless you can complete your paperwork within the next five days. We won't schedule a hearing until your application is ready to be submitted. As part of your filing, you'll have to notify abutters within three hundred feet. They need a minimum of ten days' notice before the hearing date, and a notice has to go into the paper. And before you submit your application, you have to post and stake the property, so the commissioners can visit the site. The Commission meets every other Thursday." She pauses; perhaps she notices I am having some trouble taking all this in.

I begin to understand the sense of foreboding I'd heard in Ralph Crossen's elongation of *Conservation.* It isn't that I don't appreciate the need for conservation, even with a capital C, Conservation. I do care about the environment. I don't drive an SUV. I reuse tin foil, and I don't buy zip-lock bags. I recycle, even though that means I have to pay Macomber's Sanitary Refuse an extra four dollars every time they pick up my carefully rinsed and sorted glass, tin, plastic, and paper. I belong to Co-op America. I truly consider the impact of my actions, my purchases, my footsteps on the earth. I try to tread lightly.

Moving a cottage appeals to me in part because it is a form of recycling, a way to conserve resources.

As I stand on the other side of the counter, I feel caught in a web of bureaucratic requirements, even while I appreciate the value of having rules to preserve our diminishing wetland resources. According to Darcy's rough measurements on my imperfect and outdated site map, my cottage will stretch four or five feet into that fifty-foot buffer zone. *This isn't a shopping center.* I think of the hay bales protecting the pond behind the Cape Cod Mall when they expanded the parking lot to its very edge. I am not a developer with deep pockets and money to hire a sly attorney to get around the rules. I am someone who will struggle to pay the engineer, someone who isn't even certain yet she'll qualify for the home equity loan she'll need, assuming the project is approved. I am someone who thinks about quail and groundhogs and turtles and foxes. I have no intention of disturbing any of them. I know my property; I know the bog. I know I can do this without hurting the land or its inhabitants. But the fact of my knowledge, my well-meaning, good-hearted awareness of my small ecosystem means nothing in the face of regulations. Regulations I recognize as critical, regulations I support, regulations I would happily enforce—on someone else.

"I guess I was hoping to get some indication from you," I begin. "I mean—if there's no chance the town will allow this, I don't necessarily want to hire an engineer and begin this whole expensive process."

"It all rests with the commissioners," she says. "And a lot will depend on exactly where the wetland ends. Maybe there is a way you can attach the addition without infringing on the no-disturbance zone?"

"Maybe," I say. I thank her for her time, take my wad of papers with instructions, and make my way downstairs to the Health Department.

Now that I understand the timing with Conservation, I realize I will probably have to purchase the cottage before I know for sure that I can move it—or use it. It looks like another one of those situations where bold action and deep faith will be required. The boldness that I mustered to buy my house almost thirteen years ago, even knowing that my job might disappear. The faith that I summoned to start my own business a year later, with a week's vacation pay and just one client lined up. I remember the books I read about going freelance, advising me to save six or twelve months' worth of salary before going out on my own. It is what I would have done, if I'd had the luxury of time and a habitable interim workplace. In an unlikely twist that signaled his imminent departure from the book business, the entrepreneur-owner of the company where I worked had moved the bookstore offices to his concrete plant. My asthma was kicking up every day on the job. I couldn't afford to breathe in any more of that white dust that covered my desk or the diesel fumes that wafted into our space from the adjacent truck garage.

To begin a new venture from a position of financial strength makes sound business sense. If you are going to take the plunge, dive at high tide. It is counsel I have given others. The tide was low when I ventured out. You could smell it, even. There was the risk of plunging headfirst into mud. There was the chance that high tide would arrive in time to carry me in. You can dive, I realized then, when you know the water is high, or you can dive believing that the water will rise. If someone asked me now, I'd say wait for high tide if you can, but if you can't, just make sure you have the deepest sort of faith in what you are about to do. The tide looks to be on the low side now. I don't have three thousand dollars to spend on a cottage I may not be able to use. Or another thousand dollars for engineering plans for an addition that might never be built. On the other hand, the question of how far I am from the bog will have impact on any project I can contemplate, now or in the future. Clearly there is a corresponding benefit for that financial risk. And the cottage—well, if I don't have faith in the project, who will have it for me? Besides, I think to myself, as I push open the blue door of the Health Department, if I can't use my cottage, I can always run another ad in the *Pennysaver.* *

* AT THE HEALTH DEPARTMENT COUNTER, a white-haired man helps me. He locates the plan of my septic system. If I didn't already have a copy of the card in my packet of plans, I'd be surprised to learn this official document is a three-by-five index card, with the location of my septic system sketched in soft dark pencil on the back. On the front, the number of bathrooms and bedrooms is indicated, along with some basic information about the system itself. On my card, it says I have three bedrooms. In fact, I have just one, but when we updated the septic, it was certified for three bedrooms. As always, I was thinking of adding on. I explain this to the man, who has introduced himself as Ed Barry. I show him the plans; he sees the single bedroom. "Well, if these plans are

correct, and you are telling me the truth—" He pauses to get a good look at me, and I feel as though I have become Ralph Crossen's "young lady."

"And I am telling you the truth."

"Well, then I don't see a problem. You have a Title V system for three bedrooms. So you can add two."

I restrain myself so he does not realize how thrilled I am at this news. I am Title V–compliant!

Ever since the Massachusetts legislature passed what is known as the Title V Septic Systems Regulations, the average Health Department official has had tremendous power in the life of the average citizen. Or more specifically, the average citizen who is not connected to a municipal sewer system. That includes almost every homeowner on Cape Cod. If you want to sell your house, it has to be Title V–compliant before the sale will go through. If you want to add on, Title V compliance kicks in before any building plans will be approved. If you are doing nothing except filling up your old septic system (or worse, old cesspool) with waste, you are okay—unless you have it pumped more than four times in a year. Time to upgrade, says the town, which tracks the destination of every pumping truck.

Title V is a good thing for the environment, another regulation I wholeheartedly support in theory. Especially on the Cape, where the water table is high and the land is low, we need to be mindful of where we plant our waste. The problem with Title V is that it costs a lot of money to comply. It isn't uncommon to spend five or ten thousand dollars for a simple system. Some people can't afford compliance. I had a neighbor several years ago who lost her home over a costly septic problem. She couldn't afford the very expensive system required by her low-lying property, and she couldn't sell her house without it. In a situation like that, the regulation seems intrusive, blatantly unfair. Yet without some regulation, we place our environment, and even our own health, at risk. For the second time today, I find myself contemplating the intersection of what we want and what is good for the land we borrow.

Mr. Barry warms to the idea that I hope to move a cottage, now that I am established as a truth-teller with two bedrooms on the way. He asks me where the cottage is now, how we'll move it. While we speak, Tom McKean steps out of a back office. Tom and I play in the same community band, a wind and percussion ensemble of fifty pieces, give or take, in any given year. We sit at opposite ends of the group: He plays tuba and I play flute, and we don't have much more than a nod-ding acquaintance. But we do nod and smile across the horns and clarinets that sit between us. From his baby face and clear blue eyes—and the two young children I know he has at home—I'd say that Tom is in his mid- to late thirties. That makes him one of the younger members of our musical ensemble, where I would place the average age somewhere around sixty-two.

Behind the counter, Tom hangs back, almost loitering; his curiosity transparent. He nods my way, but doesn't interrupt. I notice his blue suit, his serious demeanor, the way he is lis-tening in without joining the conversation, the way he doesn't even act surprised to see me. I decide Tom is probably the boss of the Health Department. And I didn't even know I had friends in high places. *

✳ JANUARY FLIES BY. I'm finishing up my big contract, writing reports and editing PowerPoint presentations. I haven't worked for big business—ever—and the volume of their documentary requirements overwhelms me. But their timing has been perfect. I've been chained to my computer through November and December—months when my bookstore clients want me to leave them alone to sell books. Now this project is drawing to a close, and I'll need to line up some other work—especially if I want to move this house.

I visit a longtime client in the middle of the month; we plan a series of management training classes. Back at my hotel, I hear from another client who is concluding a lease agreement on a new space in San Francisco. Can I fly there—in three days? Before I leave, I hear from another client, a bookseller in Maine, with whom I've worked for many years. He's opening a second store in the fall. We've already worked through sales projections, budgets, lease negotiations; now he is ready to think about the space. I'm delighted to help, looking forward to the freedom to work in three dimensions instead of two. With three projects in the offing, it looks like I'll have plenty of work for the spring.

While I am in California, Tony is on Cape Cod. He likes the small escapes from the city; he loves Egypt. Sometimes Anna joins Tony on a Cape weekend, but mostly he comes alone. He believes that Egypt needs some "guy quality time," and it is his mission to provide it. I'm not sure what happens when I am away, but I know that movies are watched and lots of chips and salsa are consumed. And when I come home, Egypt is nonchalant about my arrival, the best sign of all that he is well cared for and happy in my absence. It is a perfect arrangement. Tony juggles a number of jobs while he is working on his dissertation. He teaches part-time, is coauthoring a book with one of his professors, works as a statistician at a sociology think tank, and also works for me. Sometimes his tasks are mundane—keeping my accounting records up-to-date—and sometimes they are more in keeping with his expertise—decoding the results of an employee survey for a client of mine.

This week when he visits, I have asked him to take some photographs for me. He is an excellent photographer, and I can't think of anyone better to take some photos of the cottages being moved—since I can't be there myself. While I am in San Francisco, the cottages will be lifted off their foundations and moved to another section of the property. Eastward wants to get moving on their project, and they have come to realize that they will not be able to sell and relocate those little cottages by the end of this month. They have found a place to put them. The colony will stay together, each cottage set on concrete blocks until an owner claims it, takes it to a new and permanent home.

Tony enjoys this assignment, though he tells me when we speak that evening that it was a cold, cold day. You can almost see that in the photographs; the blue in the sky is pale and blunt, clear in a way that speaks of temperatures in the single digits.

"It was pretty cool," Tony says, now speaking of the cottages rather than the weather. "I saw them move two of the cottages, but they didn't get to yours. Yours will probably get moved tomorrow."

Tony can't make it tomorrow. He needs to be in Boston for work, so we won't have pictures of this first relocation of my cottage. I'm a little disappointed, but Tony assures me I will get the general idea. He watched the process twice and it was pretty much the same. He's right that the general idea is really what we need. I sent him to take the photographs because I am thinking of writing a children's book based on the cottage story. I've talked to my local postmistress, Nancy, who is also an artist, about the possibility of illustrating it. "Take lots of pictures," she said, and so we will. For Nancy's purposes, the photographs of any cottage being lifted off its foundation will do. But for sheer documentary purposes, for the thrill of seeing what I missed while I was in California, I wish we had a shot of my very cottage in midair.

"Hayden's guys sawed through the screen porches first thing. So they just fell to the ground as the cottages went up in the air. It was something," Tony says. The cottages were already loosened from their foundations when Tony arrived, so he didn't witness that part of the process. But he saw the liftoffs and he saw the crashing porches, and he saw the cottages being carried on a flatbed truck to their new location. "And those guys—they really get right under the house. Man. There were two or three guys working underneath one cottage while they were moving it from the flatbed to the concrete blocks, and something slipped. They got out from under there so fast! One of them barely made it. And I was shooting the whole time. I was afraid what I might get on film. But those guys know how to move!"

Of course I am concerned for the house-movers, but this story of a house almost missing its landing worries me for the cottage as well. "Oh, they righted it just in time," Tony says. "And after that, they decided to use the crane to lift the cottages off the truck. Mr. Hayden said they had the crane; they might as well use it. Even though it was really big for the job. I guess it was the only crane they could get today."

"You talked to Mr. Hayden?" Somehow this surprises me, even though I'd told Tony he should get permission from him to take pictures. It wasn't until Tom Howes made a call on my behalf that the house-mover returned any of my five—count 'em—phone calls. On that return call, he identified himself as Mr. Hayden, and so our uneven relationship of names and titles began. He was Mr. Hayden to me. I was Kate. Once, I think, he even called me Katie.

Mr. Hayden didn't exactly apologize for taking so long to return my call. "I get calls from a lot of kooks who aren't serious about moving houses. They just want to waste my time." His voice matched exactly the gravelly message I'd heard so many times. I recognized it immediately, even at 7:30 in the morn- ing, a time when I usually refuse to answer the phone. But I'd been rising early, waiting for his callback for many days in a row. I was as ready for him as I could be.

I assured him, as I had Tom Howes, that I was serious, but that I needed him to see my location, to make sure it was possible to move the house. I told him about the driveway access, the big spruce trees, the steep hill, the bog. Could he come take a look?

A weather-beaten man of few words, Mr. Hayden could just as easily be spearing whales as moving houses. He has a rough, reddish-blonde beard on its way to gray, and his matching hair has been styled by the time he spends outdoors. He talks in spurts and you have to listen fast to hear what he says. He is not fond of repeating himself. We walk the property; I show him where I want the cottage. I fill the space with details he may or may not want to hear. But I don't know how to talk to him, or what he needs to know. He wrinkles his brow, he squints, he nods occasionally, but he says next to nothing.

"Need a crane," he finally says. "Can't do this mechanically, too steep. Have to get Baxter over here."

"Baxter?"

"He owns the crane. Get him to figure out how to do this. If he says it can be done, it can be done." Mr. Hayden almost smiles as he makes this pronouncement. Meanwhile, I am wondering, who is the missing subject of his sentences? Me? I need a crane? I need to get Baxter over here? Is he telling me to have Baxter figure it out, or is he telling me he'll have Baxter figure it out?

"But what do you think?" I ask him.

"Need a big crane. I'll call Baxter. You around?"

"Early next week?" I suggest. I am trying to get the hang of speaking to him in his own language.

"Be in touch," he says, as he heads for his car.

"Thanks for coming out," I say to the distance between us, wondering whether it is he or I who will be in touch. ✳

✳　"THAT'S THE CRANE that will lift my cottage," I say, when Tony shows me the pictures. It is huge and red, and it says BAXTER in big block letters on the boom. Mr. Hayden brought Mr. Baxter over to see my site just before I left for my most recent San Francisco trip. John Baxter, who introduced himself with his first name, was friendly and chatty. In his presence, Mr. Hayden seemed a little more approachable. We paced out the landing site and John made calculations. He had a blue binder with him, full of charts and numbers. Distances, heights, ratios. Picking up a house with a crane—and landing it successfully on a new foundation—requires a lot of math.

I showed them where the cottage would sit and asked about the two big spruce trees between my house and my neighbor's driveway. Erika's father had managed to get Darcy from Conservation to make a site visit the week before. "What a nice spot," she'd said when she got out of her truck. "Not too many places like this left on Cape Cod." Her next remark was the one that worried me: "Those are gorgeous spruce. You won't have to lose those, will you?"

They are beautiful trees, as old as the house, maybe older, at least fifty years. They are planted below the house, near the base of the hillside that leads down to the bog. At their widest point, the trees are about eighteen feet apart (we measured this). From the house, you see into the treetops, or tree-middles to be more precise, and often you can spot a cardinal, poised on the edge of a branch as if he were posing for a Christmas card, red against evergreen. When it snows, I feel like calling Hallmark.

"Is there any way to do it without taking down these spruce?" I ask the men now. "Conservation may want them to stay."

"Excuse me?" Mr. Hayden says, loudly, indignantly. "Aren't

these trees on your property?"

"Yes, but they're in that buffer zone. I need their permission to take them down."

Mr. Hayden, disbelieving, shakes his head, grumbles something unintelligible and nasty about town government. John Baxter makes some fresh calculations, takes some more measurements. "If we had to," John says, "I think we could do it. We can swing the cottage up this way—he gestures to indicate the long side of the cottage would move through the trees—and then swing it around ninety degrees to make the landing. But it wouldn't be easy." The cottage is sixteen feet wide. It would be a very tight fit.

We walk back up the hill and designate the trees that will have to come down, no matter what—a few small oaks, a larger one by the corner of the house. "I can't make any guarantees," John says, looking back at the spruce closest to us. "It would be better to take one tree down, probably this one."

"You can cut it down ahead of time, or we can knock it over with the cottage." Mr. Hayden clarifies. I let that image lie.

"If they both stay, I could end up hurting both of them during the move."

"Killing 'em is another way they could come down," Mr. Hayden says. It's clear he is still mad at the unavoidable regulators of my backyard.

"It would be a lot better to take this one down." John Baxter repeats his message. "Besides, you'll have to cut it way back, won't you? It will be too tight to the house."

"You're right. It might be better if we take it away, rather than hack at it." I pause for a moment, staring at the space where I imagine the cottage will land. "Okay, assuming we can solve the spruce issue," I say to Mr. Hayden now, "you're saying you can do this job?"

He shrugs, nods in the direction of John Baxter.

"We'll need to use the biggest crane I have," John says, "because the hill is so steep. But the driveway is just wide enough, and as long as we can dig into the hill a little for the pads, there's enough room. Damn, it's tight! But I think we can do it."

"If he says he can do it, we can do it," Mr. Hayden says cheerfully.

John Baxter shakes my hand as I thank him. He gives me some advice on the Conservation hearing. "Go yourself," he says. "Don't hire some attorney to go for you. I watch those hearings on TV. They hate the big shots."

"What about an engineer?"

"Oh yeah, you need an engineer, but do all the talking yourself. You'll have a much better chance."

We walk toward the circle. Mr. Hayden is getting in his car. "Get back with a price," he calls—I think—to me. *

*   I MAKE FIVE TRIPS to California in six weeks. Leave on Wednesday, return on Saturday, three days at home, leave again. It is grueling, and the travel is that much worse because the project is not going smoothly. There are too many people involved in the design decisions; every meeting is a clash of sensibilities. I feel annoyed most of the time—and jet-lagged.

On the other hand—and on the other coast—the bookstore in Maine is a breath of fresh air. The architect and I are in tune, talking and sketching and faxing back and forth. Already, I can see the space. It will be beautiful.

I'm grateful for Tony's willingness to kitty-sit and back me up at the office. He is eager for hours as he saves up for that new, old Volvo wagon he was wished for the New Year. The one he's been driving is about twenty years old. He's looking for something about half that age, and he's looking hard. Online, in the papers, in person, his search is earnest and thorough. Just like Tony.

I am thrilled he wants more work. I am also thrilled by the news he brought a few weeks back. He and Anna were married the first week of the New Year. A city hall marriage—no fluff, and not a ring bearer in sight. "We'll probably do it again later, for Anna's parents," he said. They live in Italy and don't yet know their daughter is a married woman. "I wanted to tell you, because that New Year's party of yours was kind of a catalyst." They had applied for a license back in October, he told me, but they hadn't made up their minds how or when to get married. The license would expire in early January, and they figured they would just let it go. Apply again when they knew what they wanted to do. "But our time on the Cape, and your party, and then driving back—we said, 'Oh, let's do it.'"

There is nothing like a car ride early in a millennium to spark a romance. Harry and Tina are dating now, and I am pleased to see my friends discover the wonder of each other. My own love life has been actively—and classically—disappointing: lunch without lust, and one former girlfriend stealing back the only promising man I'd met in some time. Tony, my unofficial romantic advisor, is also my personal advocate. He is hopeful when I am hopeful and always on my side when things don't work out. "No great loss," he says about the latest disappointment. He tells me I deserve better. "You're such a great catch. If you lived in the city, you'd be turning down the offers. You just have to get out more."

Get out more? I'm barely home at all. I thank Tony for his moral support as I recall the desires tucked inside that master wish I made for the New Year. First comes the cottage, I remind myself—the place to write, the space to share. I have no doubt that opening up my workspace will also open up my work. And taking the work out of the bedroom? Surely, that can only help in the romance department. Create the space, I tell myself. The man will arrive when I have room for him. In the meantime, I have this cottage to move. ✳

✳   THE HEARING IS ONLY a few days away. Everything is ready. I've spoken to Scotty, an arborist and neighbor, who assures me that taking down one spruce is the thing to do. "There's a beech tree here that needs room to grow. Clear out that spruce and a couple of these oaks, and you'll have a beautiful European beech." Scotty is a fan of beech trees, of which I have a few on my property, all young, all self-seeded—from where, we aren't sure. The closest beech is in front of the library, a couple of blocks away. Those trees are seventy-five years old, huge and graceful and unmistakable. Scott considers my baby beeches a mystery to be solved; he is on the lookout for a closer parent that he may have missed in his travels through my neighbors' backyards.

Mr. Hayden has been back, in person, with an estimate. "Around $3,000, maybe $3,500 depending on the crane. Challenging site," he says. "Have to rent the crane for the whole day. $800 right there, unless I use it on another job."

"No problem," I say. "Sounds good."

When I ask him, Dave says we are ready, and he feels optimistic. The plans have been submitted, and the bog scientist has located the border of the bog. It's true I'll be edging into the buffer zone with the cottage, but the zone includes my neighbor's driveway, which is disturbed every day, many times a day. My neighbor, too, has pointed this out. He's on my side, happy to lend me his driveway for the cottage delivery. I know I'll pay later; when he applies to pave the gravel drive, he will expect my support. For now, I am grateful he is so gracious and agreeable.

Ed has visited twice, once alone and once with his son John, who will oversee the project until Ed is back from Florida. We walked the property together, tracing the invisible outline of the cottage. It was a warmish day, so we stood outside to talk. The project was new to John, and he was listening carefully to his father as he spoke.

"We have to get the equipment in over on this side on account of Conservation, and we have to use small equipment—maybe a couple of Bobcats."

"My mini-excavator?" John asked. Ed laughed and turned to me.

"John needs to do something to justify that mini-excavator he bought last year," he says to me. "He promised Margaret he'd use it to make her a garden, but that hasn't happened yet."

"Are you guys going to do the clearing?"

"Looking that way." His excavator friend is out of business, Ed told me. But they know someone else who will work with them.

"Brian's done a lot of this," John said, reassuring me.

"Anyway," Ed continued, "we have to be very careful with the digging, and we can't get too close to this house. Foundation's only four-foot block."

John nodded.

"We'll get Ronny in here to pour the new foundation. Hayden will deliver the cottage."

John listened some more to his father, got his questions answered before he said, "I just can't see the roofline." We were standing by the kitchen window, just in front of where the cottage will land.

"Well, you know, we won't be sure of it till we see the cottage sitting right here. But that's the beauty of this job," Ed said to John. "We have to get the excavation done as soon as Conservation says it's a go, because we have to get the foundation in so the cottage can get over here before the summer traffic. But once that cottage is here, we can just relax a little, and figure things out. We'll pour another little foundation wall here, to support the hallway, and we'll connect them with the deck—that will be the floor in the hallway," he clarified for me. "When the rooftops are side by side, we'll know what to do. And Kate has an idea what she wants." John looked at me. "The main thing is to get it over here onto the foundation.

Then, we build the connecting passageway, and finally we marry the houses together."

Marry the houses together. I love the language. I love the image. I love the metaphor. And I love Ed's kind and easy manner. It turns out that Egypt does, too. In an unprecedented act of affection, he came racing down the hill straight to Ed, giving him a head butt and a sideways rub just below his knees. A certain seal of approval for our builder, and all the more amazing, given that Ed was wearing steel-toed work boots. Egypt is uniformly frightened by men in big boots. Even the Bog Boys, whom he adores, make him nervous when they wear boots.

I take Egypt's affection as a good sign. I am looking for good signs wherever I can find them. When I find a lucky penny, I pick it up, and so far, I have found heads-up pennies at the entrance to the cottage, in the parking lot at Eastward Companies, on the threshold of the Building Department office. It was a little tricky to pick that one up, as I trailed Mr. Crossen's secretary on the way to his office, but I just bent down and scooped it up like a lost button. I am certain these pennies mean something. Find a penny, pick it up, and all the day you'll have good luck. I haven't found a penny yet at Conservation, but I plan to keep my eyes on the carpet.

town hall

I'VE LIVED IN THIS TOWN for thirteen years now, and if on average I pass by twice a week, I've driven by Town Hall more than thirteen hundred times. More than once I have wondered about the people who turn into that parking lot. Most, I have assumed, work there. When I was growing up, my grandmother worked at City Hall in Somerville, Massachusetts. It was a beautiful building, clean red brick with white-trimmed windows—right next to the high school, and just past the billboard that said, "You May Be Dead Right and Still Be Dead. Drive Defensively." I remember puzzling over those words for years, my reading skills far ahead of my comprehension. Each new administration repainted that billboard to accommodate the new mayor's signature. Sometimes the grim graphics would change slightly, but never the message. As I grew older I wondered if this were the city's slogan, and if so, thought they could do better.

When I was small, and still confused by the words, I thought of them only as the curtain rising on my view of City Hall. We'd turn soon, and I'd run through the maze of corridors to the Planning Department, where my grandmother worked as executive secretary. "Well look who's here!" she'd say, acting as though I were the biggest surprise of her day. In fact, every trip to my grandmother's was planned well in advance. She'd wrap me up in a hug and show me off to her coworkers. I remember Fred best of all, a draftsman for the city who would draw me pictures to color, running copies on the mimeograph machine so I could color, recolor, and recolor. Even when I wasn't visiting my grandmother, Fred would send me pictures in the mail, stacks of purple outlines, all the same design, usually with a seasonal flavor—a stained-glass window with the Virgin Mother at Christmas, a leprechaun smiling with a pot of gold for St. Patrick's Day. I used to smell each sheet before I began to color it. I can still recall that sharp scent, lost now, of mimeo ink.

I loved my grandmother's domain of maps and plans, and I loved especially the stamp she had with her signature. *Mary A. Ford*, it read, in her distinctive, beautiful script. She'd let me dip it and stamp it all over the scrap paper she saved for me. She had stationery of her own, too: *Mary A. Ford, Planning Board.* I could not help but notice that it rhymed.

As much as I loved visiting the Planning Department, the maps and the mimeos, my favorite part of City Hall was down the hall from where Nana worked—the home of the switch-board and another Mary, who wore a headphone and spoke into a tiny mike, and who knew the giant maze in front of her by heart. "City Hall," she would say, and after the caller announced his desired destination, she would plug one of the rubber-coated wires into the numbered extension that repre-sented the department he sought. It was fun to watch Mary and her huge board, but it was even more fun to be Mary, or Mary's little helper. She'd let me sit on her lap and wear her heavy headset. When the phone rang, I'd put the right wire into place, and in my most grown-up voice, I'd answer, "City

Hall." Then I'd repeat the caller's request, so that Mary could show me where to plug the caller in, and I would stretch to make the connection. Sometimes, when I was feeling extra bold, I'd imitate Mary's efficient reassurance to my caller. "I'll connect you," I'd say, as I plugged the wire in tight to the extension Mary had indicated.

To this day, I wonder whether the callers at the other end of the phone thought it odd to hear a child's voice when they called City Hall. Or whether they noticed at all. Certainly we had no complaints. It was usually late enough in the day that the call volume was light, but every call was a thrill, a delight. For many years, I believed that Mary's was the perfect job. ✱

✱ XEROX MACHINES and laser printers have replaced Fred's mimeograph machine, and voicemail would make Mary redundant at the Barnstable Town Hall. Here, the Town Hall is a three-story dark brick building designed by H. H. Richardson, that great architect of public buildings. It was once the Normal School, a training ground for young women who wished to teach. Through the years, this handsome building has morphed from college to elementary school to maritime academy before lending its space to county business. It is only since 1979 that Town Hall has been Town Hall, probably around the same time the county offices moved over to the new addition on the courthouse in Barnstable Village. Maybe it is because the building has served a succession of public masters that some of the town offices have a haphazard feel to them. The Building Department comes to mind: housed in the attic, with angled ceilings and exposed beams, floors covered with indoor-outdoor carpeting. Chief Ralph Crossen's office looks like an indoor shed, complete with roof and window. I have wondered if they got all the inspectors together one Saturday and said, "Go build your offices."

After so many years of passing right by, I am beginning to feel like a resident here. I know building inspectors and health officials and conservation agents, and I no longer need to check the directory to find them. Tonight, I am turning into the parking lot for the Thursday night meeting of the Conservation Commission.

Three months have passed since I first played Goldilocks in the cottage colony, three months of running around and making calls and deciding to go forward even knowing I may be stopped in my tracks this very night. Tonight, at the end of a heavy agenda, the commissioners will decide whether my cottage will be allowed to live four feet into that buffer zone. Erika's dad, Dave, is here with Nick, the bog scientist he hired, and Scotty is here, too. Tina is visiting from Boston, her timing coincidental but perfect.

As I walk into the hearing room, a large space equipped with microphones and video equipment, I think of my grandmother. So many years at City Hall. She'd know just how to handle this situation. I invoke her spirit and ask for her blessing on the project. And when I sit down next to Tina, just in front of Dave and Nick, with Scotty over to the left and ahead of us, I sense Nana is near, maybe even in the empty chair next to me. "Why look who's here!" In my head I use the same tone of mock surprise my grandmother used all those years ago. Beside me, Tina grins.

Tonight's agenda is ordered by the perceived complication of the requests before the commissioners. It crosses my mind that they might do better to get the hard stuff out of the way first, but perhaps taking care of a number of smaller items in quick succession gives them a feeling of accomplishment, warms them up for the tougher stuff. Last in line, I don't personally believe my situation is so complicated, especially as I listen to an engineer defend a project his company wishes to undertake. In Barnstable Harbor is a tank they want to remove. He displays studies and evidence that there will be no hazards involved in the removal, but the commissioners are skeptical. He cites water quality studies taken near the tank, at the top of the tank, at the bottom of the tank. There is no evidence it is leaking. It will come up easily. He shows them how. "But, why, if it is doing no harm to the harbor, do we want to haul it up?" inquires a commissioner. The engineer, a large man, clasps his hands tight behind his back as he speaks into the mike. This is the audience view: back of head, neck, shoulders, back, hands. His hands are clearly ill at ease.

He tries another tack with the commissioners, raising the possibility that there could be a problem with the tank and its contents (which are unknown). Wouldn't it be better to get it out now rather than later? This does not go over well with the Commission.

"You just told us the test results indicate no toxicity. Now you are telling us we may have toxic waste in the harbor?"

An excellent point, I think, and I begin to wonder what exactly is the truth of the matter. Meanwhile, the man's hands are moving from discomfort to frustration to anger. The commissioners are not pleased. It is evident to me that there is a history between this board and this engineer, his company, perhaps his mysterious client. Mr. Van Buren, the head of the Conservation Department, weighs in. He sits at one end of the dais, and although he is not a member of the Commission, it is obvious that the department recommendation he delivers before each vote weighs heavily on any Commission decision. Now he makes it clear to the engineer (and the room, and the TV viewers) that the Commission was very unhappy with the applicant and his company on their last project. These remarks lead to a heated exchange between Mr. Van Buren and the man I am now beginning to think of as the defendant. I hear the man's voice tighten, even as it increases in volume. Mr. Van Buren remains calm. His sitting position, his height on the dais, his normal tone of voice make it clear who is in charge here, at least tonight.

Finally the engineer loses it. "You're calling me a liar," he says. Behind his back, his hands are clenched together, tight and bright red. *Red-handed*, I think, and I decide that I am with the commissioners. Perhaps the tank should be taken out of the harbor, but I'm not sure I want this man or his client in charge of the operation. In the end, the project is "continued" to a meeting almost two months away. The commissioners want more information. Is it dangerous or is it not? If it is hazardous, how will the removal be handled to ensure the harbor is protected? It is up to the engineer to return with the answers. *

* DURING ONE OF THE EARLIER, less complicated cases, Dave and Nick and Scotty and Tina and I met on the bench in

the hallway outside the meeting room. Nick, the bog scientist, took over as our strategist. "You go up there with Dave, and field their questions," Nick said to me.

Dave nodded his agreement, and I remembered what John Baxter said about the Commission hating big shots. "I'll review the plans with the commissioners, walk them through the photographs we submitted with our application. I won't say any more than what is necessary," Dave said. Erika's dad is a gentle, slow-spoken man of few words. It struck me as funny that he could even imagine a situation where he might say too much.

"You sit at that table, where the other mikes are," Nick instructed me. "Just tell them why you want to do this—if they even ask. They may not ask anything. Emphasize how small your house is now. Do you know the exact square footage of the cottage?"

"Yes," I said, "just 386, and the original house is 750."

"We are not talking trophy home. How much of this will sit in the no-disturb zone?" Dave gave him the number, 4 feet into the buffer times 24 feet across, 96 square feet.

"I'd have avoided the buffer altogether," I said, "but this is the only way we can attach the cottage given the contours of the land. And the cottage is the size it is. It isn't as though I'm building from scratch."

"Excellent!" Nick said, pleased with me. "Remember to say that if you have a chance. Very good point."

As a bog scientist, Nick has an interest in preserving wetlands, rather than destroying them. He's willing to coach me and support our application because he doesn't believe my project will harm the bog—or the plant or animal life it supports. He gives me some more pointers. "You're using small equipment, and you're going out of your way to minimize disturbance in the buffer. That's key. And don't forget to mention the driveway," Nick continued. "If they start talking about non-disturbance, your neighbor's driveway is already in that zone." I never thought I'd be grateful for my neighbor's driveway, but it's now true that I am. "We're here if they get technical," Nick assured me, nodding to Scotty, who was pacing the hallway, "but let's not even mention us unless we have to. They have more sympathy for homeowners than they do for experts."

I see that Nick is probably right as I watch the red-handed engineer stalk out of the room, angry to be "continued." Had his client been in evidence, perhaps the engineer's case would have been bolstered. Now he has another nine weeks of waiting before he has a shot at convincing the Commission again. Many of the more complicated cases, I notice, are continued for dates in May, June, even July. I think of my little cottage waiting in Harwich Port, already up on blocks. The developers have been kind to store it, but they will not wait forever. If the Commission doesn't give me an answer tonight, I'll have to give up the whole idea. I wonder if the stalling tactics cause a certain number of applicants to give up the fight.

"I just had no idea how much drama occurs at Town Hall," Tina says to me during the break between the tank removal case and the next case on the docket. "Do you think this happens in Boston, too?" she asks. But before I can answer she adds, "Even if they have hearings I could go to in Boston, I bet there wouldn't be any clam people."

She's referring to an earlier case, when one of the commissioners, after listening to the town's own request to rebuild a crumbling boat ramp in Cotuit, looked out into the hall and said, "Are the clam people here?" Sure enough, they were, though they were on hand to testify against another project. Still, they were happy to step up to the table and express their opinions and concerns about the impact on shell fishing if the ramp were constructed as outlined. The issue once again was dredging, disturbing the beds where the clams lie sleeping. How much would be required? Too much, thought the commissioners, as deeper questioning revealed that the town had money left over in the dredging budget. It appeared they were intending to enlarge the ramp simply because they could afford to do so.

The clam people said the area was in enough trouble already; a boater in favor of a new ramp asked who goes clamming under an active boat ramp anyway? A neighboring resident said a bigger boat ramp would only mean more traffic, more disturbance to the people as well as to the clams that lived nearby.

"You're right. If you want clam people, you'll have to come down here. Every other Thursday night. I'd love to have you."

"I just might come," she says. ✳

✳   FINALLY, IT IS OUR TURN. Dave walks up to the lectern; I move to the table nearby. I am aware of the video camera, staring down from its perch in the corner of the room. The hearings rate local TV coverage, but evidently not a cameraman. I sit silently as Dave begins to explain what we wish to do. He refers the commissioners to the plan, to the photographs, walks them through the process of moving the cottage, lifting it, attaching it to the house. In our discussions, we have anticipated many of the issues Conservation might raise. The narrative indicates that we will use only small equipment, John's mini-excavator and a Bobcat, to do the digging, and the plans show the equipment will enter the property outside the buffer zone, on the other side of the front yard, and travel around and through the backyard to reach the side where we will be working. "We'll be able to reuse the fill," Dave continues, anticipating their next question. "There is a dug-out area, indicated on the plan, which we will refill." This too is outside the buffer, so the Commission will be less concerned about it. I am pretty certain that the dug-out spot is a result of an illegal attempt to fill the cranberry bog many years ago, an attempt that was halted by the state, according to the records I've seen. It seems to me appropriate that we will replace the soil stolen those many years ago.

When he is finished, Dave asks for questions, and there are plenty. Surprisingly, they are all directed to me. Why can't the cottage be placed outside the buffer zone? Because it must be lifted with a crane, and given the contours of the property, there is no other place to put the cottage. Why move a cottage in, why not add on—outside the buffer zone? I explain that I have wanted to add on for many years, have looked at many plans, that I am a writer and work from home. I tell them that I would like a room where I can work, just work quietly, and remind them that because I do work from home, any addition would disturb not only my home but my workplace. This would result in the least amount of disturbance, I say, both to me and to the property. I point out that the hill slopes almost straight up on the other side of the house, that although it is outside the buffer, building there would require much more disturbance of the land, and create a larger possibility of erosion on the bog side of the house. When they seem to accept that I am intent on moving the cottage, they get more detailed in their questions.

"What about this hallway?" An older man on the Commission asks me. "If you eliminate this hallway, you'd be within the fifty-feet rule, or pretty close. Am I correct?"

I was expecting this question, though hoping it would not be asked. I can't bear the idea of giving up my hallway. The hallway is what makes the plan work; it is the elegant connection between the houses, the neutral space that makes the union possible. "I did consider that," I say to the commissioners. "But without the hallway, we'd have to eliminate walls and do some major demolition in both buildings. We'd be compromising the structural integrity of the main house, which is on a concrete block foundation. It would be very expensive work. At that point, I'd lose the savings I anticipate by moving a fully built structure. The cottage is in good shape. It is structurally sound and doesn't require much cosmetic work either. The beauty of the hallway is that both buildings remain intact—and I get the full use of the new space, rather than cutting into it to create a passageway."

They take this in silently. I look at the Commission, waiting for their next question. It comes from a small white-haired woman, seventy-five if a day, sprightly and intelligent and ready with the pointed questions. I'd been watching her all evening. I had to laugh when she quizzed the engineer representing the town about the Highway Department's application to repave a road. "This application says repave," she said, "You aren't planning to widen it, are you?"

"No ma'am," the man replied. "There may be some minor topographical changes when we repave—"

She interrupted him. "Are you saying you will widen it?"

"No, no," he assured her, "we just want to make sure the drainage will be right."

"Well," she said, "all I know is that every time a road gets repaved in this town, it seems to turn into a superhighway!" He conceded that the department does often take the opportunity to widen a road when they repave, but reminded her they would have to indicate their intention on the application. "My point exactly," she said. "So the road will stay the same width?" She asked one more time, and she looked at this man as if she were his mother—or his grandmother—as if he would go to bed without dinner if he hedged his reply.

"Yes, ma'am," he said, "This road will stay exactly the same width."

Now this same woman is ready with a question for me. "The foundation," she says, "why do you need a full foundation for the cottage?"

Ed had warned me on this one. "They may not want the full basement. They may even require pilings instead of a foundation."

"Pilings?"

"Sunken concrete and wood, the way we'll do the deck. You've seen it on beach houses." Yes, I have, and I do not want pilings. I want a basement. I will gain no storage space in the little cottage, and I have only my bedroom closet in my house. My backyard shed is so packed that I have to rearrange it every season, moving the more-required items from back to front. Even when I keep up with this plan, I inevitably need an old client file, a paintbrush, or a piece of leftover lumber for some small project in the middle of gardening season. This means relocating all shed contents onto the backyard until I reach the item I need. Yes, I want a basement, and I have plans for it.

And there is another reason I want a full basement. I want the cottage to support a full second floor. Not that I am planning one in the immediate future, but I want the option. It is the four-foot cinderblock foundation on my original house that makes going up, my first preference in expansion options, impossible to contemplate.

I decide to lean on my contractors as a first line of defense. "My builder recommended a full basement," I begin.

She interrupts me. "I did a similar-size addition on my house. A four-foot basement was fine structurally, no problem at all."

I take this in. "Yes," I say, "I'm sure a crawl-space basement would work, but it's the crawl space on my main house that has caused me trouble. You see, there isn't room for my furnace or hot water heater under the house, so they are in a closet off my kitchen. My space, even with the addition, will be small. I'd love to move that furnace to the basement, and for health reasons, too. I'm asthmatic. It isn't really a great thing to have a gas boiler in my living space. Anyway, the contractors I've talked with have told me it would be a much easier and cheaper proposition to move the furnace, the water heater, and all the plumbing that will go along with that if I put a full foundation under the cottage."

There is silence from the board when I finish that little speech. Everyone sitting on that dais—indeed everyone on Cape Cod—knows that plumbers charge a disproportionately larger sum of money if they have to crawl on their bellies to do their work. It strikes me, too, that my addition, my whole house, could probably fit inside the living rooms of some of these esteemed ladies and gentlemen of the Commission. I bet not a one of them has a furnace in their kitchen closet. I'm a good person. I mean well. I don't intend to build a strip mall. Can't they just say yes?

Mr. Van Buren takes note of the silence and asks if there are any further questions from the commissioners. There are none. They ask him for the department recommendation, which he has provided on every case this evening that was not continued or otherwise delayed. "I'll be glad to give the department's recommendation on this," he says, glancing down at the paperwork he has prepared. He settles back into his chair, puts down his pen, and looks right at me, smiling oddly.

"Of course, this case cannot fail to remind the commissioners of another, similar case that came before the Commission a little more than a year ago. It was an old house in Osterville," he says, "and they also had to file with us and we gave them an approval. In that case, the house was lifted up by the crane, too." He pauses for a breath, looks right at me again. "And it fell completely apart in midair."

He smiles a devilish grin, and before I can wonder why he is recounting this tale to me at this moment, in front of the Commission and on local-access television, the members of the Commission jump in. The older gentleman who'd asked about the hallway: "Mr. Van Buren, please don't frighten the applicant!"

And in the same moment, the spry woman who had objected earlier to my foundation: "That was a case of poor engineering—and a very old house! That certainly won't happen to this young lady!" They peer down at me from their positions on the dais to see if I have been adversely affected by Mr. Van Buren's indiscretion.

I move closer to the mike. "Well," and here I pause a little dramatically, myself, "I dearly hope that will not be the fate of my cottage."

I don't think he meant to do so, but I believe Mr. Van Buren, in raising the specter of the lost house in Osterville, has brought the full force of his volunteer commissioners onto the side of this beleaguered, earnest homeowner. He felt it too, along with the satisfaction of telling his tale.

"It seems clear that the Commission will favor this proposal," he says, moving back to his paperwork, picking up his pen. "The department recommendation on this case considers the drive already in the nondisturbance zone, which changes the complexion of this request. Also, I would like to mention that the proposal is very thorough, and the applicant has made every attempt to minimize disturbance to the Bordering Vegetative Wetland. Therefore we recommend approval with no special conditions." He looks at me. "In terms of revegetation," and at this point, he makes direct eye contact with me, "we feel you have done an excellent job in maintaining the natural surroundings for many years. We won't place any special conditions on you, but trust that you will replant accordingly."

This is a big deal. I was so afraid they'd question the removal of one of the spruce, ask me to squeeze the cottage between the trees. That's why Scotty is here, to wax rhapsodic about the baby beech tree that will thrive when the spruce and those few small oaks are out of its way. But they didn't ask. They trusted me. Though I think Mr. Van Buren is one odd duck with a pretty sick sense of humor, I feel thrilled that he trusts me to revegetate responsibly! I assure him that the natural setting is as much a benefit to me, to my peace of mind, as it is to the wetland and the wildlife.

He nodded, a benediction.

The commissioners agree with his recommendation, motions are made and seconded, and it is over. The hearing, the night. Dave thanks them as do I, and I walk back to collect Tina, trying to maintain an air of detached pleasure. I do not yell Yippee.

"What you said about wanting to move the furnace from the kitchen into the cellar was a stroke of genius," Nick marvels when we get outside of the room. There is real admiration in his voice.

"It's only the truth."

"Impressive," he says.

We walk to the parking lot together, the winning team. "They didn't ask a single question about the trees," I say.

"I was just as happy not to have to speak," Scotty chimes in.

"But I appreciate your coming all the same," I say to him, "and you too, Nick. It really helped to know I had expert allies in the room." They shrug this off. I thank Dave for all his hard work, and compliment him for saying only what was required, just as he'd promised he would. "There is no way I could have made it through these three months without all your help and guidance," I say. I can't tell if he takes in how much I appreciate his hard work, his insight into the most important issues, his planning and support. I suppose this is just another Conservation evening for Erika's dad.

"No problem," he says. "I'm glad it worked out."

Tina and I go out for Indian food to celebrate. We order wine.

"To the cottage!" Tina toasts.

"To the house and cottage together!" I reply.

"To the Conservation Commission."

"To the lady commissioner who wants the roads to stay the same width!"

"Yes, yes, to her, definitely."

We drink.

"She was great," Tina says. "Don't you just want to be her?" she asks me as the appetizers are delivered.

"Yes—maybe—but not just yet," I say as I scoop a pakora onto my friend's plate.

making way

"IT'S A GO," I tell John the morning after the hearing. I explain there is a ten-day appeal period, but we aren't expecting any opposition. We can proceed at our own risk, and I'm in favor of moving forward as soon as we can. The closer we get to the tourist season, the harder it will be to maneuver a cottage on the back roads of Cape Cod. This fact is not lost on the public servants who will approve the required moving permits. The longer we wait, the more difficult it will be to obtain permission to tie up traffic in the four towns that separate the cottage from my house.

"You'll need your building permits before we can excavate," John reminds me.

I have the drawings ready, but I need some help with the forms. I don't know how to fill in the blanks on the cutaway drawing provided by the Building Department. Size of wall studs, size of floor and ceiling joists? How do I know these answers without x-raying the cottage? John says he'll come over on Saturday to help me out. If Conservation gives me my Order of Conditions on Monday, I can march right over to the Building Department. I need the order before I can get the permit.

I call Tom Howes with the good news, which he promises to pass along to Mr. Hayden. Mid-April, we think, we'll have a cottage on the way. I ask about the other cottages, all lined up on their blocks. None of them has moved yet, and this comforts me. I am not the only cottage-mover who is keeping him waiting. After I hang up with Tom, I try Ed in Florida. I share my good news with his answering machine, encouraging him to come home soon so he won't miss the excitement.

Tina is still talking about the clam people when I drop her at the bus in Hyannis. She has an eager, playful intellect, and when she is introduced to a new idea, Tina runs with it. The machinations of Town Hall are on her radar now, and the clam people have come to live in her mind. Or rather the concept of the clam people, the fact that clam people exist; defenders of shellfish have enlarged Tina's perception of the world. "Come back soon, and I'll take you to another hearing." We laugh as we hug good-bye.

Ten minutes later, I am pulling into my driveway. Scotty's red pickup truck is parked low on the circle. He probably wants to talk about the trees we'll be taking down. Scotty never calls ahead; he just shows up. Maybe this is because we are almost neighbors, or more likely because we know each other through Barbara, who has always referred to him by his little-boy name. The Barbara connection bolsters what might otherwise be a strictly business acquaintance. We feel at ease with each other. In the same way I call him Scotty because that's how Barbara introduced him to me, he knocks on my door at odd hours without a warning call. Though prepared to find him on my doorstep when I come around the circle, I am not prepared for the sound of chainsaws, the four men scattered around my side yard, and the golden retriever circling them as they work. I have not been gone more than an hour, but already the old spruce is down; I can smell its sap when I get out of the car. I wanted to see that one go, to say good-bye in some appropriate way, to thank the tree for its long and faithful service, and I feel sorry it has been taken without ceremony.

Egypt greets me at the door and does not hesitate to let me know he is unhappy. His territory is changing before his eyes, and worse, there is a dog loose in the yard. We watch through the big windows in the living room, Egypt hunkered down into a four-legged squat and disbelieving when I try to convince him this is change for the better. I've been worried all along how my aging kitty will take to this project. He came to me because he wasn't happy in a series of earlier homes, and it took him about ten months to settle in full time. Even though he's stuck around for almost eleven years now, Egypt holds the potential to pack his bags and go should he be displeased. Or so I imagine. He's strong-willed and supersensitive, a hyperthyroid cat who requires medication twice a day. Any decision I make involves consideration of Egypt's response, and he has a way of making his opinions clear. He's not happy today, this surprise inaugural day of the house-moving. "A cottage is coming," I tell him. "You'll like it." He gives me a look that conveys his disbelief before he jumps down from the windowsill and leads me into the kitchen where he sits facing his empty food dish, suggesting with his back to me that it would be a good idea to feed him. Now. *

*   CRUEL APRIL IS KIND on Saturday, sunny and warm enough to sit outside at the picnic table to review the requirements for the building permit. John, the star student in a class where he knows all the answers, fills in the blanks. Rafters 2 x 8; ceiling supports 2 x 6; wall studs 2 x 4; floor joists 2 x 8. All 16 on center. He's not positive about the thickness of the

foundation walls and the size of the footings required. "We usually come in after the foundation," he explains.

"I can find that out," I assure him, and he fills out the rest of the forms, including an estimate of costs.

They want building costs, and all we're building is that connecting hallway. We puzzle over the formulas, which allocate a certain amount for windows, doors, and walls, interior versus exterior, house construction versus deck. John comes up with a number: $15,000. Close to the numbers on the back of my envelope. I do some more addition in my head: The hallway plus the cottage plus the cottage-moving will come in around $22,000. Add a couple of thousand for engineering, another $1,500 for tree removal, and that's $25,500. I've applied for a home equity line of credit for $20,000. And I've got just about $6,000 in the bank. As long as I stay busy with work, I'll be all right.

The next day I visit Katrina and Ruben, and we haul out Ruben's fat book on home construction. He's trained as an architect, and has recently reentered his field after a stint of odd jobs: bartender, tour leader, trolley driver. Ruben is movie-star handsome. He'd play the Latin lover, irresistible, passionate. But he'd have to work to fit the dark, stormy stereotype. Ruben is as warmhearted and kind as they come, and when he smiles, you'd swear someone turned on a light in the room. Together, he and Katrina are a knockout couple.

"Ten-inch walls, ten-by-twenty footings," Ruben announces. "You might want to read this section about foundations," he suggests, and hands me the book—dense, but interesting all the same. I love learning this stuff. Take footings. I never thought about the idea that something needs to hold the foundation walls in place. I guess I thought the floor did that, through some bizarre principle of expansion. But then that wouldn't explain dirt cellars. Footings. I taste the word, think of the expressions I have heard, the metaphors of certainty and security that I have understood without any knowledge of this construction term. Footings. I study the illustrations in Ruben's book and sense, almost as much as I see, the thick perimeter of concrete that will be the solid resting place for the foundation, the very base of what will one day be my office.   *

* THE WEEK TAKES ME BACK to Town Hall. I want to make sure my building paperwork is good to go as soon as I get the official document from Conservation. On this my second visit to the Building Department, I am introduced to Mr. Martin, the building inspector who is in charge of my section of town. He is kind and patient with me, and intrigued with the cottage-moving plan. I show him some photos of the cottage we will move, and when he hears of my time constraints, he advises me to show him everything I have before I actually apply for the permit. He'll look it over and make sure nothing is missing. "You don't want to get hung up on some technicality," he says with a grin.

"I have my stuff with me now," I offer. "Do you have a minute?"

He leads me into his office and offers me the plastic seat next to his desk. His workspace consists of a small metal desk in a windowless room he shares with at least two colleagues. The room could use a paint job, but at least he doesn't suffer with that strange shingled façade that delineates the boss's office at the rear of the space.

As soon as we are seated, I show him my foundation plan. The existing house sits on a concrete block foundation that is only four feet high. To avoid disturbing that foundation wall, we have designed something Ed calls a "shelf." The back section of the cottage foundation (which will be poured a distance of four feet from the original house) will match the existing foundation, with a four-foot depth. The front section, starting about ten feet away from the existing house, will be a full eight feet deep. To create this split-level basement, we will actually construct two separate foundations. Looked at from the side, the base of the shorter foundation is like a long shelf four feet above the base of the taller foundation. Thus, the terminology.

I've drawn the plan on the computer, with phone support from Harry. Mr. Martin looks it over, listens to my explanation, and asks about the extra wall that will support the section of hallway that leads to the kitchen. Concrete block, I tell him, and he tells me I need to specify that on the plan. "Show me where it's poured and where it is block. Do you have elevations?"

"I'm working on those." Elevations—face-on drawings that in this case will show the walls, the locations of windows, and the cellar door—are my least-favorite thing to draw. I can see in space better than I can represent what I see in two dimensions, especially with a computer program. I knew I'd need the elevations for the foundation guys, but I didn't realize that the Building Department would want them, too. Mr. Martin also needs a basement plan, he tells me, and all the smoke detectors must be indicated on the plan. The code on "smokes," as he calls them, is based on square footage of living space and requires one in every bedroom, but the enforcement in my case is complicated because the bulk of my project is not new construction.

"Is the one you have already hard-wired?" I confirm that it is. That smoke alarm was added about ten years ago—when the new furnace was installed. "Well, that might do it for the old house. But you'll need at least one up and one down in the new section. And one in the hallway." ✳

✳ THREE DAYS LATER, Conservation order and building application in hand, I begin my long march through the offices in Town Hall. The assessor's office is a breeze. I'm all paid up on my property taxes; the signature is easy. Planning, no problem; another few minutes, another signature. But Health. Despite my earlier conversation with Mr. Barry of the Health Department, I am now informed my application is questionable.

"You're adding bedrooms," she says.

I explain that I have only one bedroom now, but that I have a three-bedroom septic system. "Yes, but you're adding bedrooms," she says.

"I am adding one room that qualifies as a bedroom. That will make it a two-bedroom on a certified three-bedroom system."

"Yes, but you're adding bedrooms," she repeats, and this becomes her mantra, a response to every argument I muster. I tell her that I have already discussed this with her colleague. I try to explain my hurry, that the cottage is coming, that I don't have the luxury of building an addition at my leisure, that the addition will simply arrive—and it needs to do that before Memorial Day weekend. She has no sympathy. Mr. Barry is not here, and I am adding bedrooms.

As we grow more frustrated with each other, I begin to suspect that she is giving me a harder time because I am a woman. I have watched three male contractors come and go, joking, flirting, asking her about her vacation. She helps them with a smile, signs on their dotted lines, chats about Disney World before she returns to me with a frown, withholds her signature.

I am not feeling very warm toward the fact of her femaleness, either. I find myself wishing I were dealing with a man. I hate my gender-biased, antifeminist thinking, but I do suspect I could charm my way out of this questionable application were I facing one of her male colleagues across the counter. When at last she decides to get a second opinion, I am hoping it will come from her boss, Tom, my bandmate, but he is nowhere in sight.

"It's a gray area," her colleague agrees, as he looks at the plan, and the little 3-by-5 card with my septic system on it. "Did you check the codebook?" Together, they consult the Title V Septic Code, an 8 1/2-by-11 sheaf, which is easily one inch thick.

"I am only a one-person household," I say, while they search for the answer in the fine print. "Well, one person and a cat, and he uses the litter box." No laughter. They confer some more and decide my septic system may be adequate, but must be inspected. I'll need to produce a completed report from a certified septic inspector before the Health Department will sign off on my building application.

I thank Ms. Adding Bedrooms for the list of town-approved and certified septic inspectors and consider I should have never come to Town Hall before lunch. If I weren't hungry, I could put this setback into perspective. As it is, I am close to tears when I run into Tom in the hallway outside the Health office. In the few rehearsals since the last time I saw Tom at Town Hall, he's learned about my project. I am always slow to pack up after playing—we flute players have a lot of swabbing to do after a two-hour session, and Tom tends to linger a bit, reviewing the tough passages on his horn. With two small kids at home, it's hard for him to practice uninterrupted. Lately, we have been leaving the auditorium together, walking to our cars while he quizzes me about my project. Until recently, our small relationship was largely based on the fact that we respect each other's playing. We hear each other across the band; I play soprano to his bass. It's funny getting to know someone in such a setting: You know the sound and skill before you know the person. The cottage has provided us with a reason to know each other just a little better.

"Kate," he says, because he sees me first.

I pull myself together in the manner befitting the principal flute player he knows. "Your colleagues sent me packing," I say, holding up my building application and the list of inspectors.

"You need an inspection?" he asks. I realize I could put him in a very awkward position if I tell the whole story, so I just nod. "Let me see the list." He runs through it. "Some of these guys charge way too much for the same job. But we can't control the pricing." He tells me whom he would call if he were in my shoes. "They all fill out the same form, do exactly the same thing. This guy only charges $125 or $150. Some of these guys try to get $300—even $325—for the same job." I can tell this really bothers him.

I thank Tom for his insider information, but I have already decided to call Mr. Macomber. In the town of Barnstable, his family controls all the elements of our lives that we would prefer not to mess with ourselves; septic systems, trash collection, and bookkeeping services represent the three branches of the family. I tell Mr. Macomber, when he answers the phone himself, that I've been getting my trash taken away for the last fourteen years by his brother's company, and that before I had my new septic installed, I'd been a customer of his. I explain my situation, the cottage, the hurry, and then I beg him to write me in for an inspection this week.

"Tomorrow or the next day. How about that?"

"That would be great."

"Now, it will take me two more days to fill out all the paperwork. Sounds like you don't want me to mail it—that will take another day. You're close by. I can probably just drop it in your mailbox when I'm done. Or send somebody by your house on their way to a job."

My thanks are profuse, excessive, and completely sincere.

Thirty minutes later, a big red Macomber's truck backs into my driveway, and I can tell the driver is amused by my enthusiastic welcome. "This is great! Are you really going to do the inspection right now, today?"

"Had some time between jobs, so he sent me over," he says.

"Where is it?" I lead him to the approximate location of my septic system, where he sticks a metal stake in the ground, brings it up, moves a few inches, taps down, hauls up. This process continues for several minutes until he strikes concrete. Then he begins to dig. Egypt, fascinated by this process, stays behind with the inspector when I decide to move inside, out of the rain, away from the contents of my septic system, which I fear may be on display at any moment.

"Let me know if you need anything else."

"I'll knock on your door when I'm done," he says, and gets back to his digging. "Hey, what's with this cat?" he yells after me. Egypt is poised several feet from the inspector, watching his every move.

"He thinks he's in charge of you," I call back to him. "He thinks he's a dog." I know Egypt would be insulted by this remark, but the man hears it as a recommendation on my cat's behalf. I walk back towards him. "Do you want me to bring him inside?"

"No, that's okay." He leans on his shovel, takes another look at Egypt, shrugs. I hear the sound of metal scraping concrete as I walk away. ✳

✳ FRIDAY AFTERNOON, I emerge triumphant from Town Hall. I feel like skipping down the steps, shouting my good news to the world. *I have a building permit!* It is a small, everyday thing that builders do. But I feel like I have accomplished a great and enormous feat. I am exhilarated. I want to call friends, celebrate, have a party. I settle for paging John. He calls me back immediately.

"I have the permit!"

"Seriously?"

"Seriously. It's right here in front of me." I am pleased that he is surprised.

"When you told me you had to get a septic inspection, I figured we'd just lost two weeks, easy," he tells me.

"I'm glad you didn't say that then."

"How'd you do everything so fast?"

I tell John about Mr. Macomber and the red truck that came so quickly. I tell him how I called each morning for two days to check on the report, and how, once the passing grade was hand-delivered to my mailbox, I gathered everything up and raced to Town Hall, arriving within the confines of that critical one-hour window, and how when I got there, my friend Tom was at the counter, how he smiled and signed off, accepting as evidence, but never opening the report to verify I had passed. I tell John how I made my way up to Conservation to find no one available for the sign-off, but how when I explained my situation to the secretary, she told me to pay the fees over at Building, and leave the package for her to pass back with the signatures. I tell him about the holdup in Building over the estimates, and how I had to show Mr. Ralph Crossen himself some photos of the cottage to prove it was in fine shape.

"I didn't realize that the fee for the permit is based on the size and cost of the project. He thought we bid low. But he approved it in the end."

"Yeah," John says after he listens to my excited monologue. "That's great." He's low-key, but I can tell he does think it is great, and he is happy we won't be delayed. It isn't a champagne toast, but I'm glad I called John with the good news. "We can start Monday like we planned. I'll call Brian and get the Bobcat lined up. I still can't believe you got the septic that fast."

"Perseverance," I say. "Oh, and also having my system pumped the next day. A thank-you for the quick service that I was asking Mr. Macomber to provide."

"Did it need to be pumped?"

"Probably. It hasn't been in years."

He laughs. "See you Monday morning." *

* I WAS HOPING for another warmish day, the kind of day that makes you want to be outside, to be in the dirt, to welcome spring, but this Saturday morning is chilly, gray, and threatening. Tony and Harry are here already, and Katrina is on her way. The plan is to move as many plants as we can in a day's time. We need to dig up more than half the perennial garden in the front yard to make way for the equipment and rescue as much as we can from the patio area where the cottage will land. The Bog Boys will take care of the heaviest work—pulling up the slate patio, moving some of the larger shrubs—and they will also construct the silt fence with the hay bales and fencing material that Scott dropped off yesterday. Katrina and I, meanwhile, will dig and dig, moving the tender shoots that we can see and the invisible roots that I know are there.

Katrina is an unlikely helper for this garden-moving project. Aside from the glamour-girl image that she projects on a daily basis, she has a deathly fear of earthworms. It is not so surprising that a certified hypnotherapist has never been able to conquer a small but deep phobia, but what astonishes me is that Katrina is absolutely fearless in the face of giant snakes. She has danced in Egypt with two live cobras wrapped around her torso, but she is afraid to encounter the tiny worms in the damp April earth. I too embrace the symbol of feminine power that the snake represents. I wear a ring with two little serpents intertwined, but I could never dance with even a single cobra. As for earthworms, I try not to disturb them, but I welcome their presence in my garden, a sign of healthy dirt.

When she arrives, Katrina is dressed for a farm-girl photo shoot. She's wearing blue denim overalls with a cinched waistline and a lace-up bodice. "I got them from the Victoria's Secret catalogue years ago, but I've hardly ever worn them."

"You look the part," I tell her, laughing. "Though I'm not sure that farmers wear eyeliner." I show her the equipment we will use, and I give her a pair of little flowered garden gloves. "These are yours to keep, to promote your gardening inclinations in the future, and they will also protect you so you can't touch an earthworm by accident." Involuntarily she shivers at the thought. "Don't worry, I'll be right next to you all day long. And Harry and Tony will be nearby." I mean this as additional reassurance, though I am not sure exactly what the Bog Boys would do in the event of a worm-related incident.

We talk about men to keep Katrina's mind off the creatures in the dirt.

"He was too self-absorbed anyway," she says of my most recent prospect. "All he thought about was his work."

"You're right."

"You weren't interested anyway, were you? I mean you weren't attracted to him physically—were you?" Katrina believes in love at first sight. I believe love comes on tiptoes, often in the dark. How can you see to know?

"Well, we met under awkward circumstances. It's so hard to know when it's a fix-up. I was willing to give it a few more dates."

"Forget him," she says, and I assure her that it will not be difficult.

The subject changes to dancing, to the next Evening in Egypt, a monthly event of Middle Eastern dance and music. It's Katrina's invention, and a showcase for student performers. My solo debut was a year ago August, and I am a regular now. I love the dance, the control and concentration that it requires, the freedom of expression that it allows, and I love the costumes, all sequins and beads and glitter and gloves. I remember once, when Katrina was asking my opinion on a costume, saying to her, "It looks great, but what will you wear for jewelry?"

She looked in the mirror at her black-and-gold costume with gold beaded fringe, the gold sequined finger-sandals, the veil that she had in one hand. "Does this woman need jewelry?" she asked, striking a pose.

"Of course!" I said. "You look practically naked."

In the garden now, she asks me about my costume for our next event. "Are you going to wear your turquoise?"

It's raining now, a steady drizzle. The men are pounding the stakes into the hay bales with the new fifty-pound sledge-hammer I bought this morning. We are kneeling in the wet earth, the hoods up on our slickers. We speak of silk veils and finger cymbals and I describe my pale turquoise handless gloves with little swirls of seed pearls that move when I do. We relocate plants and more plants, and we set aside a small lilac, a forsythia, and some purple coneflowers, primroses, lilies, and daffodils for Katrina to take home: the beginning of her garden.

The beginning of my garden can be credited to Barbara. "I need to thin these daffodils in the back. Why don't you come up and dig some out?" I learned that day—on my knees in Barbara's backyard—that there was a link between the flowers and my home builder. "My father planted the daffodils on the side over there," she said, gesturing to a mass planting on the hillside facing my front yard. "He was the gardener." Barbara paused. I kept digging. The daffodil bulbs were entangled with the irises, and little roses were trailing all through the garden. It was tough going, and I was a novice.

"He planted them one fall, and we didn't even know he'd done it—until the next spring when they bloomed." She paused again. "He died that winter, so it was like the daffodils had come from God."

Daffodils from God, a reminder of a gardening-father. I stopped my digging, stared hard at what must have been hundreds of thriving daffodils on that hillside, blooming years and years later, the man who buried the bulbs long deceased. I contemplated the weigela, planted by Barbara's back door, and the azalea between the side windows, the white lilac blooming by the cellar door, and the tough-to-dig irises interlaced with what Barbara told me was a rose that came to Cape Cod on a ship with her first American ancestor.

As I give the offspring of Barbara's bulbs to Katrina, I want to share some bit of gardening wisdom. Maybe tell her that one day the earthworms in the ground will seem a happy reassurance of the richness of her soil, a sign that all is well, an omen of buds and blooms to come. But then I think of Barbara. Her gardening tips were always of the moment. "A little lime will help those lilacs to bloom," she told me when I moved some of her father's plantings from the shade to the sun. "Miracid is what you want to feed those rhododendrons. Azaleas like it too. Acid. The lilac needs alkaline. Don't plant them near each other, or they'll be fighting over the soil." I consider that a changed relationship with worms is far, far into Katrina's gardening future. I focus on the present with my advice.

"You might want to add a little bulb booster when you plant those daffodils," I tell Katrina now. "Remind me to give you some before you go." ✴

✴   A MINI-EXCAVATOR is parked outside my bedroom window; there are three men conferring on what used to be my patio; and my cat is scratching madly at the window because he thinks the safest place to be is outside, far away from this heavy loud yellow machine that could eat him at any moment.

We are under way.

I have a feeling that these days of digging and heavy equipment will be the worst, especially for Egypt, who has moved, tail down, out to the kitchen for a better view of the yellow threat. I reassure him, remind him that I have permitted this, that I am calm in the face of the men and monsters outside our window; and while I am hoping my calm will be contagious, he seems certain it is only another symptom of my declining sanity. Why else would I invite this disruption into our perfect space? The windows rattle and the floor shakes beneath his sure cat feet. Giant roaring beasts could invade our home at any moment. *Listen to me,* he is saying as he pounds, paw over paw, on the kitchen door. *We need to get out of here.*

I join him at the door and regard the scene. Brian is operating the orange-and-white Bobcat, John the yellow mini-excavator. Ed, just back from Florida, is manning the Dunkin' Donuts station he has improvised on top of my barrel of good dirt out back by the shed. It's raining, still, and the colors of the men and the machines stand out all the more. Ed in bright blue slicker and hat, John in a tan coverall and an orange watch cap that matches the Bobcat, Brian more subdued in a navy blue windbreaker with the white seal of the Hyannis Fire Department over his heart. His baseball cap also advertises his affiliation, and when I mention that he is almost in uniform, he laughs. "Always wear this cap on a job in case I need to ask a favor. Like your neighbors and their driveway. They aren't likely to say no when a firefighter asks for a favor."

"They think it's an emergency?"

"That too," he says, grinning. "But mostly, they want me to remember where their house is."

Finally I get it. It's firefighter humor, an imitation of intimidation. Brian, like John, works for the Fire Department in Hyannis. It is the same department that came to my rescue ten years ago when I had a very serious, very sudden, very scary asthma attack. I'd dropped my car off that morning for repairs and had walked over to the mall where a bus would take me home. It was bitter-cold, in the single digits, with a hard wind that whipped across the empty parking lot. The cold took my breath and I could not regain it. The only open entrance was at the far end of the mall. I struggled to get to it, stopping and starting, turning my face from the wind, sitting on a bench, rising. My inhalers weren't working. The coughing was uncontrollable; my lungs felt squeezed shut. I finally scaled the door, flagged down an incoming mall walker. "Asthma," I rasped, for to speak in sentences was more than I could do. "Bad. Hospital." She understood.

"Don't try to talk," she advised. "I'll be right back." I watched her, my mouth open, sucking in the air my body refused to process, as she headed for the bank of black pay phones, and then returned to sit with me, murmuring reassurances. She was wearing a pale green warm-up suit and sneakers. "They're here," she told me, as the siren screamed toward us, only moments after her call. "They'll take care of you."

And they did. They gave me oxygen and medicine to breathe and one of them held my hand. They asked no questions because they knew I could not speak, and they moved quietly, efficiently in their tiny mobile hospital. I fought for consciousness, even as I felt a part of me preparing for departure. *Look at everything in this truck. Memorize every shiny surface, every bottle and syringe. Pay attention. Pay attention.* I listened as one of them called the hospital, speaking of me, and I felt only a mild interest in learning that I was turning blue. *Bottles, syringes, shiny metal boxes, the sting of an IV needle.* A comforting voice without, a stern voice within. *Pay attention, pay attention.*

Years later, I remember only the feeling of surrender to capable hands; hours later I could not even place the faces of the men who owned those hands. There were two in the back of the truck with me. One tall, older, and one very young—shorter, wiry, like John—with a tenor voice like John's. I wonder. I wonder as I deliver hot coffee to the backyard and coax John and Brian off their tractors, as we laugh at Brian's impersonation of a firefighting Mafioso, as Ed tells a story and John empties his mug, refuses my offer of a second cup. I wonder, but I don't say a word. I wonder if I ever will. *

* LAST NIGHT MR. HAYDEN CALLED and told me he probably won't be able to move the cottage and put it into place on the same day. That means it needs a resting place, a place where it can spend the night. He suggested the parking lot at 4 Seas Ice Cream. "Call Dick Warren," he told me. Four Seas has world-renowned homemade ice cream, and Mr. Warren staffs the place with smiling high school kids. He has an advantage in hiring; until he retired a few years ago, he worked as a guidance counselor. Once the shop opens, there will be no room in his parking lot, which is actually two parking lots because they need at least that many to accommodate the endless stream of customers between mid-May and early September.

As long as the cottage moves before Mr. Warren opens up, he might be willing to lend us his lot, but I couldn't get to sleep last night thinking of all the possible things that could happen to my cottage, sitting on a trailer in full view for an afternoon and an overnight. I call Mr. Hayden back this morning and find him in at 7:35. He cuts me off mid-sentence. "Just call Dick Warren." Instead, I call Harry, who offers to sleep in the cottage, to protect it from the cottage raiders of my imagination. By the time we say good-bye, he is planning his camping trip.

"Thanks for calling Bog Boys Security," he says as we hang up, and he promises Tony will sleep there, too.

But the more I think of the cottage in that parking lot, even if it were protected by Bog Boys, the less I like the idea. It occurs to me that a business owner, even a kindly, community-minded business owner, wouldn't let me just leave a cottage on his property without worrying about his own liability. I don't want to ask Mr. Warren. I want the cottage to come here. No stop-overs, no sleepovers. I leave a message on Scott's machine and he stops by on his way home with an extra long tape measure. If he prunes back the oak branches and pulls out the midnight broom, we decide, the cottage will fit at the bottom of the circle, without interfering with my neighbors' right of way. It gives me great satisfaction to call Mr. Hayden with this bit of news.

"The cottage can stay here," I tell him when he answers the next morning at 7:25.

"Where?" he asks me.

"The bottom of my driveway. We figured out a way to make room." I spare him the details.

"You measured it?" His only question.

"Uh-huh."

"Fine." ✱

✱ FOR SEVERAL DAYS, the men and the machines decon-
struct my yard. The cold never lets up, nor does the rain.
When Brian has to work a shift at the firehouse, John takes over
the Bobcat and cedes the yellow mini-excavator to his father. I
snap pictures when the rain slows to drizzle, and I watch the
hole that used to be my hillside grow deeper and deeper.

When I look out my bedroom window, I have the feeling I am
living on the second floor. There is no going out the kitchen
door anymore, and no going out at all for Egypt, who is displeased but now more curious than worried. He seems to be
adapting. Every night when the machines are quiet, we go out
together and explore the yard. We have to take the long way
around the excavation site, across mud mountains in the
backyard, to reach the sand pit where the patio used to be.
One late afternoon, the sun breaks through, the sand sparkles,
and Egypt rolls, belly up, scratching his back with the crys-
talline earth. *Maybe tearing up the grass wasn't such a bad idea.
You can have a much more satisfying roll in the dirt.*

I haven't climbed into the hole myself, not wanting to give my
cat any ideas, but John is scampering up and down the sand
walls routinely as the week wears on. He holds a giant measuring stick that rises well above his head. Ed sights him through
the surveyor's box that sits on a tripod in the midst of the
relocated daffodils, and thus determines the depth of the hole.

More of the digging is by hand now, and another man, whose name I have not learned, has joined the crew. "I'm the oldest guy here," he notes on a day when Ed is absent. "How come I'm the only one with a shovel?"

"You got to learn how to drive these machines," John replies.

He nods, and I can see he is a little envious of the men who get to be boys for a few days. This is what I have come to realize. John, Brian, Ed—they are having fun driving these vehicles around my yard, making sand piles and digging holes, yanking out tree stumps and every once in a while banging into the side of my house. The longer I watch them, the more I understand the look in the eyes of the hand-digger. I'm beginning to wish I could take the Bobcat for a spin myself. Egypt, on the other hand, prefers the yellow mini-excavator. He's claimed it as his own, sitting on the black vinyl seat, grooming, mugging for the camera. "All you need is a little yellow hard hat," I tell him as I snap his picture.

Fat chance, he tells me, as he stares straight ahead, but he does allow me to join him. I take the seat and he sits on the flat yellow metal plate just in front of the steering wheel. I hear his purr, *Vrroom, vrooom.*

"Vrroom, vrooom, vroooooommmmh," I answer, but quietly, so my neighbors won't notice that I am playing trucks with my cat.

keylines and butterflies

THEY POURED THE FOUNDATION TODAY. For the uninitiated, this would seem a beginning. But this newborn construction maven knows better. This is easily the middle. We have run the gauntlet of local regulation, cleared the land of trees. We have disturbed the earth, uncovered the sand base of Cape Cod, and just last week poured the footings. The footings are the very bottom of what will become the walls of my basement. Thanks to Ruben, I know they are ten inches deep, twenty inches wide. Along the center line of each, the concrete workers placed a two-by-four right on top of the concrete, while it was still wet. "Why?" I asked the concrete man today, as he removed the board to reveal a long thin line in the center of the now-solid rectangle of cement.

"To lock the walls in. It is called a keyline." I like this new word and add it to my growing vocabulary of building terms. *Keyline.* I want to write it down right away, before I forget it, but I am too busy with the camera, taking endless shots of concrete being pumped and poured and moved around with shovels.

The walls of the foundation will be ten inches thick and eight feet tall when they are dry and free of the concrete forms. The forms are interlocking rectangles with faded printing that once advertised their manufacturer. They resemble a strange fortress built into the hillside, wooden frames around panels whose color can only be described as pale corrugated, the color of boxes left in the shed for a few years. Setting the forms is a process that looks like something you could do on a smaller scale with Legos. But before the forms are set, Ronny, the head honcho of On-Cape Concrete Forms, comes and measures and levels and sets up strings and makes sure that the foundation will land exactly where it belongs. This is especially important in this case, as we are planning a foundation that will hold a house already built. What's more, this already-built house will be deposited by a crane. There is no room for error.

That is probably why I've been seeing so much of Mr. Hayden recently. He visits at the end of the workday, on his way home. I am learning to expect him—or, more accurately, to expect anyone at any time. My house, my schedule are no longer mine alone. Men and trucks and tractors come and go. They knock on my door before 8 A.M. They surprise me in the garden in the late afternoon. "Make sure Ronny calls me," Mr. Hayden said to me early last week, while I was patting some dirt around yet another transplant. "Have to give him some very specific measurements. Need some bolts in the founda-tion. Maybe some butterflies. Not sure yet which, maybe both." With each visit, my Haydenese has been improving. I've hardly begun to notice the missing subjects in his sentences; I've just been filling in the blanks in my head. *Butterflies?* I didn't ask. For a moment, I held the image of thousands of small beating wings—orange and black; blue and yellow—circling the foundation, holding my little cottage in place. But I didn't share this thought with Mr. Hayden. I was pretty sure his butterflies were of the hardware-store variety, something like those hooks that expand on one side to hold hanging pots.

Ronny visited the site a few days later, and I passed Mr. Hayden's message along. He nodded, pocketed the card for Hayden Building Movers with Mr. Hayden's numbers. Ronny was not worried yet about the bolts, or even the measurements for the walls. He was worried about my hillside. "We'll pour the footings if we can, but we'll probably have to pump the walls." It seems the contours of my land present a challenge. We can't get a concrete mixer up high enough to pour the concrete between the forms to make the walls. The pump truck, Ed told me yesterday, costs $700 every time it visits. The price does not seem so outrageous when I realize the pump truck is essentially a pale yellow crane. I struggle to fit it all into one picture, holding the camera vertically and getting myself onto the top of the woodchuck hill.

When the concrete mixer arrives, they hook his chute to the pump truck, and soon the concrete is coming out of a big rubber tube that hangs off the crane. The guys, stationed atop the forms, hug the big tube, get a good grip on it, and move it into position. They signal to the driver. *More water, pour harder, lighten up.* The man on the crane adjusts his controls, repositions according to their signals.

As they pump the first section of the foundation, I am adding up how much it will cost just to create a resting place for the cottage waiting in Harwich. Two more trips of the pump truck, $2,100 total. Then there is concrete, labor. And I found out only a few days ago that a concrete floor is an accessory item. You want the radio in the car? You have to pay for it. Ditto with the basement floor. We make the walls. You pay extra for the floor. I fought hard for a full basement with the Conservation

Commission. Damned if I'll settle for anything less than smooth concrete at the base of my eight-foot walls. ✳

✳ I WAS IN BOSTON this morning while they were setting the forms for the walls. Just before I went into a meeting, my cell phone rang. A question about the elevations. The man at the other end of the phone asked to speak to the person who had done the drawings. "That would be me," I answered. I sensed the confusion at the other end of the phone. "You have some questions?" I asked, urging him along. He wanted to confirm the location of the door and the windows. The south-facing wall will boast two windows, side by side, and a door, which I also imagine with windows. I want to draw in as much light as possible to the basement, not because I plan to spend so much time there, but as an antidote to the mold and mildew that come gratis with any Cape Cod cellar. There will also be small casement-style windows on the sides of the foundation, for ventilation more than light. I had a copy of the plans with me. In the front seat of my car, I felt like a real construction super. He promised to call again with questions.

On the second call, he asked about the four small openings I'd specified in the front and rear of the cottage. "Those are for the straps," I explained. "When the house is lifted up, it will be held with two big straps. When it lands on the foundation, there has to be somewhere for those straps to go."

"You on your way home?" he asked. He wants me to see the forms, make sure everything is in place correctly before they pour. The concrete truck is scheduled for noon.

"I should be there unless there is big traffic." ✳

＊ IT IS JUST A FEW MINUTES before twelve and I am driving down the steep little road that leads to my street. I see the top of a crane through the trees. For a split second, I am worried there has been a horrible mistake, that the cottage and the giant crane have arrived before the foundation. Then I pull into the driveway, spot the cement mixer, and see the guys hooking up the mixer to what I now realize must be the pump truck.

I feel a surge of pure pleasure at the sight of the concrete mixer. Despite my unpleasant experience working in the white dust of the concrete plant, I love to watch these mixer trucks, their huge drums set to spinning, graphics going round and round. Mixing sand and water and stones, adjusting the recipe for the job. I have had a few different mixers on this project already, but my clear favorites have drums painted to look like the Cape Cod license plate: red-and-white striped lighthouse, a bit of blue sea, a sailboat. I love to watch the scene on the truck spinning faster, faster into abstraction, then slowing down, moving back, resolving finally into what is recognizable, bright, simple.

Indeed, we have a Cape Cod drum today, and I view this as a good omen. I jump out of my car and run over to the men, conscious of my heels, my dress. We triple-check the drawings, walk to the front to make sure the forms look right, that the openings are okay. "Looks good," I say. "I'm going to quick-change. I'll be right back. Do you mind if I take some pictures?"

I climb atop the sand mountain in my backyard to get a shot, but I am not happy with the angle. At the highest point on the far hillside, I can get almost all of the crane into the picture.

Better. Watching the men, the movement, listening to the sounds of the pump and the mixer, I think about how long it has taken to reach this point: four and a half months. From the first reading of the classified ad to the Conservation hearing, that fateful night at the end of last month, Mr. Van Buren's odd sense of humor.

I do hope my cottage doesn't fall apart. Ed says it is good and sturdy. When I visited for more measurements a couple of weeks back, I got down on my knees to have a look underneath. The wood was clean and dry, reddish, maybe spruce; it looked brand new. It's been sitting in a sunny spot on sand for the last fifty years. A few more pine trees in that cottage colony and there would be wood rot, maybe even termite damage. I stood up to resume my measurements: base of cottage to base of kitchen window. The underbelly of my cottage is beautiful and strong, I thought. I drew an arrow to the spot on my drawing, made a note of the span, and felt something like pride in my sturdy, well-built cottage-to-be.

My thoughts turn back to money. I have never had much of it in my life, and I tend to trade in risk rather than in security. In the early days of my business, I barely eked by. I accumulated a good deal of debt, and not just the good kind my old boss had recommended to me. Over the years, my income has become a little more predictable, but still there are times when the IRS gets paid with a Visa card, or the mortgage payment requires a cash advance. I've learned to live with the uncertainty of cash flow, and most of the time, it all works out in the end. Right now I have a lot of work, but tax time is coming, and I know I'll need more than the equity loan to complete the cottage. But I am committed now, and I have no intention of turning back. I may have to adjust my expectations, perhaps take more time to finish the inside work. Chances are, I think, as I watch the concrete spill over the forms and onto the ground, as the concrete worker wrestles the tube into another section, chances are I will not be able to afford the furnace move. Chances are the furnace will stay exactly where it is. But I am getting a cellar floor, for sure.

Now the men are smoothing out their work with shovels, making sure that all is even. The tube is being pulled up into the air; it is still spitting concrete. "It's very rocky," I remark to one of the men.

"That's what makes it strong," he replies.

"Makes sense," I concede, but still I am struck by the sound, the chortling sound as the rocks hit the form, and I wonder: Is there enough water? Will they take away the forms tomorrow, and find tumbling piles of rocks? It is an image I suspect Conservation Chief Van Buren would enjoy. ✶

✶ THE NEXT DAY they remove the forms, and I have walls. The concrete looks almost wet, it is so dark, but it is smooth and sturdy. No tumbling rocks in sight. The foundation sits in the rain for a couple of days before the strongman of the concrete crew—the one who was hugging the big rubber chute, moving it around to make the walls—comes back to tar the foundation. He asks me roughly where the soil line will be, and I give my best guess. He paints the black tar onto the outside of the foundation, from the bottom up, following the contours I've indicated. When he is done, the tar gleams and the foundation looks all dressed up. I shoot a photograph, pleased with the aesthetic of shiny black against dull gray. The tar will be covered by earth when we backfill around the foundation, but I like the security of knowing it is there, protecting my basement from the elements, keeping it dry against the damp.

John and Ed and Brian return with a black-topped Bobcat and their giant ruler. They do a little filling around the completed portion of the foundation and make way for the smaller section that will sit four feet away from the house. They calculate depth using a nail hammered just under the kitchen door as their reference point, and they dig carefully, working very close to the house. More than once the house is hit with the scoop of the Bobcat, and every time this happens, Egypt gives me another dirty look. But he has gained some ease with this process, with the machinery, the noise. He likes our walks at dusk, when all is silent except the birds, calling and chattering like crazy in the trees around us. He enjoys surveying the progress of each day at least as much as I do.

My kitchen plumbing has been disconnected now, so that any water I use at the sink runs out the open end of the waste pipe and into the ditch outside the kitchen window. I take to using a dishpan and dump the wastewater in the tub. It's a relatively minor inconvenience; at least I have running water. After the inspector comes to give his seal of approval for Part One of the foundation, I let a little more water run out the pipe, but I still send the big loads down the drain in the bathroom. I don't want to create any more erosion of the earth close to the house. The four-foot margin between the unpoured foundation wall and the house has been cut in half by excavation, and we want the house to stay standing on its four-foot block foundation. This is where the issues of "structural integrity" come into play.

Part Two of the two-part foundation will require another set of footings, four more walls, two more visits from the concrete truck. The weather is not cooperating; we need a clear day to pour the concrete. Otherwise, the mix could be diluted by rainwater. On the first sunny day we have, I expect to see Ronny and his crew. But I am not at the front of the line, and another three days pass before they arrive. The strongman is with him, but the boss is a man I don't recognize. He hasn't been on this job before, but he tells me he's sure he can pour (rather than pump) the upper footings. I have my doubts about this, as he attempts to angle the chute through the window openings in the basement. Sure enough, it goes badly. Very badly. There is concrete all over the side yard. There is concrete atop the hay bale fence, which is halfway destroyed by the attempt to get the truck into a better position. There is concrete on my neighbor's driveway. And all this concrete dumping has occurred while I stepped inside to take a business call. When I come outside again, the guys are long gone. I waver between outrage and fear. The already-hardening puddles of cement, I am sure, violate every conservation regulation in the book. Not to mention the fact that I wasn't planning on concrete as a prominent landscape element. (Involuntarily, the bookseller in me performs free association: *The Cement Garden,* Ian McEwan; grim book, great writer.)

"Ed," I say, when he answers my page. "The yard's a mess. There's concrete everywhere."

"Oh, they always spill a little," he starts to reassure me.

"No, this is not a little. This is a lot. And if Ronny thinks I am paying for this trip, he's crazy. And they wrecked the fence, didn't even put it back. And there's concrete in my neighbor's driveway. It's all getting hard. It's a mess. I'm sorry—but can you come over?" I wonder if he can tell I am on the verge of tears.

"Don't worry," he tells me. "It's okay if it hardens. We can hack it up and take it away easier. And we'll just use some of it as fill. Remember we have to backfill all around the foundation. I'll come over just as soon as I can finish up here—say, around four o'clock—is that okay?"

"Yes." I'm afraid to say anything else, because I know I will start crying.

"I'll take care of it with Ronny," he says. "Just don't worry."

But I am worried. I shoot an entire roll of the spills, a photojournalist documenting an unnatural disaster, and I go to work on sweeping up my neighbor's driveway. When Ed arrives, he takes over the driveway cleanup, and he reassembles the fence. He assures me the pools of concrete on the hillside will not be that hard to break up, that concrete spills are common, that all will be well. I don't know whether to believe him, but I bask in Ed's soft-spoken reassurances, in his blue eyes, silver white hair, the redness in his face that tells you he needs to watch his cholesterol. His upward inflections and his south-of-Boston accent. His competent, easygoing presence. Maybe Ed is right. Maybe everything will be okay. ∗

∗ RAIN AND MORE RAIN slows down the foundation work, but the following week, the pump truck arrives again. At the end of the job, the driver comes up the hill to see me. "Who did this?" asks a man who introduces himself as Jeff. He is surveying the concrete on the hillside. "Wasn't my guys."

"It's a mess, isn't it?"

"It is a mess. What happened?"

"They tried to pour instead of using a pump truck."

"Stupid," he says, shaking his head. "This hill is way too steep. At least they could have cleaned it up."

"That's what I thought. How hard is it going to be to clean up, do you think?"

"Oh, it will clean up fine. You can break it up with a sledge-hammer, use some of it for fill." He echoes Ed's words. "But it shouldn't have happened in the first place."

I am grateful for his sympathy, his mild outrage on my behalf. Over the past several days, one man after another has told me not to worry, that it was no big deal. Even my neighbor, when I explained to him what happened, said, "Oh, that kind of thing happens on every job." Despite these assurances of normalcy, I haven't been able to muster the required nonchalance. In continuing to feel upset, I have come to realize that I am not a full-fledged member of the club I've been trying to join. Not only have I been reminded that I am the homeowner, I have been reminded that I am female—in subtle ways, an inflection, a shrug. As much as I want to be one of the guys on this project, I will never really cross over. I feel some sense of loss in this realization, and a feeling of inadequacy—as if in responding with tears and anger, I have shown myself to be unworthy of the crew. And so I am relieved when Jeff, a concrete professional—a guy, with credentials—tells me this is not normal; this is not acceptable; and yes, this is one big mess of concrete. *

* IN A FEW DAYS, the second set of walls is revealed, dark and solid. The original foreman returns to set the forms, the one who told me that the rocks make the foundation strong. I want to ask him why he wasn't here last week, why his esteemed colleague made such a bad call, and why they haven't offered to clean it all up. But I keep the peace. I watch him set the forms and later I watch his colleague, cigarette dangling from the corner of his mouth, as he wrestles with the hose. I decide it is another occasion for me to learn when to keep my mouth shut. Besides, I have a more important question that I have been waiting to ask. As he removes the forms, I see my opportunity.

"How come the forms don't stick to the concrete? Are they treated?"

The concrete man who gave me keylines confirms my hypothesis. "We spray them," he says.

"With a giant can of Pam?" I ask him.

"Something like that." He smiles, but does not yield his concrete secrets to me.

Seriously nonstick, I think. Maybe a sort of Teflon? Unbidden, a picture of white rice sticking to the bottom of a pan presents itself to me. I wonder if the forms would come off just as easily if my foundation were made of rice.

No good, I think. Mr. Hayden's butterflies would surely eat the rice.

parade route

COTTAGE-MOVING DAY, and it dawns damp with a light drizzle. Hayden's guys were here yesterday, measuring the bolts on my foundation, and I asked them how the weather might affect the move. "Oh, we can move in light rain, but they can't use the crane in heavy rain. Too dangerous." Visions of the cottage slippery, wet, eluding the grasp of the big red crane. We can't have that.

Rain this morning means the cottage will probably spend the night in my driveway. We have the place cleared: a flat resting spot at the bottom of the circle where we can tuck the cottage in for the night. Scotty pruned the low branches on the oak tree and hauled out the midnight broom. The broom have seen their better days, and I know it gave the arborist pleasure to remove them. He has been telling me for years how awful they look, and they do—except when they are in beautiful, spectacular, bent, weeping bloom. I love the yellow sweep in front of the purple lilacs—old lilacs—as old as the house, fifty years.

Last night, Hayden called. He now identifies himself as Bob Hayden rather than Mr. Hayden when he calls, but somehow I can't think of him as Bob. Maybe it is that gruff, matter-of-fact, smoky voice of his, and the image it conjures of a man at the helm of a whaling ship, somewhere in the mid-1800s. He is too crusty to be merely Bob. I don't know that it would be polite to call him by his last name to his face, so I avoid the issue entirely.

"Weather tomorrow," he said.

"So I heard." I have learned not to say more than required with Mr. Bob Hayden. I try not to exceed his word count in replying to his remarks.

"Could hang us up," he continued, and I was pleased that he answered the unasked question.

"How so?" I offered.

"Really heavy rain like they are predicting—we can't be on the road. Too much of a hazard. It's not that we can't do it, but some idiot comes around the corner too fast, poor visibility, and he crashes into us. Then they say, 'What were they doing moving a house in this weather?'"

"Oh." Again, I didn't ask a question and so he answered it.

"Hoping the storm will blow through tonight, clear early. We're set with the cops for 8:30 in Harwich. Call you in the morning."

It is almost 8:00 A.M. now, and the weather is only starting to show up. Harry is already here; Bruce is due to walk off a bus any moment. Tony, who had planned to come, can't make it. Something about work he had to do at Boston College. In that I think this may be the most exciting day of my life, I don't understand how Tony would be willing to miss it. Ditto with most of my female friends who, while interested in the fact of moving the cottage, seem blasé about the act of it. In my mind, they should be gathered along the parade route, waving flags and clapping as we hold up traffic. I figure we will make those drivers' days. How often do you see a cottage coming at you on Buck Island Road? It's a story to tell at dinner, a memory for the kids strapped into the back seat, the perfect and complex excuse for being late to work on this gray May morning.

By quarter past eight, I still haven't heard from Hayden; his machine picks up when I try the office. I wonder if he's already in Harwich, if he forgot to call me. We pick up Bruce at the bus stop and take the back roads to the cottage. We follow in reverse the route that Hayden has plotted for the move. This way, we'll meet the cottage on the way if they have started the move without us. We are just turning into the cottage colony when my cell phone rings. As I dig it out of my slicker pocket, I see my cottage.

"Bob Hayden," he says as soon as I pick up, as if he were the one answering the phone. Before I can ask him what is happening, he tells me: "Postponed the troopers till 12:30."

"I'm in Harwich," I tell him. "It's just starting to drizzle here."

"It's pouring in Cotuit," he says. "Headed that way. Can't move in this; no visibility. Too big a risk." As he speaks, the rain is getting heavier; the storm is sweeping down the Cape. "Have to decide by 10:30 whether we'll do it at 12:30," he says. "The cops need two hours' notice."

"What do you think?" I ask him.

"Hard to say. Could blow by pretty fast. Call you on your cell." ✳

✳ THE WINDSHIELD WIPERS can't keep up. The defroster isn't adequate without the air conditioning blasting too. Harry drives slowly as we head, shivering, straight into the storm. We have decided to go into Hyannis, grab some breakfast, see what the weather does. In Yarmouth, when we turn onto

Route 28, Harry slows down so I can lean out the car window to get a shot of the sign.

May 24
House-moving Today.
Expect Delays.

It's raining so hard that I know the photograph will not come out. But it is a necessary act, nonetheless.

"Expect Delays," I read. Well, we are having one now. And we've had plenty already. Two weeks back, on one of his afternoon visits, Hayden told me about the permit problem in Dennis. "The only town I have to get approval from all the selectmen. Last Friday, I bring the paperwork over for this Tuesday's meeting, and the lady behind the desk tells me, guess what, I missed the deadline. 'You said today,' I say. And she says, 'It had to be in by 1:00; it's 3:00 now.' Couldn't believe it. Every other town, I just need one signature, no big deal. But not Dennis. Wish there was a way to avoid driving through that town." There is exasperation in his voice. Whaling captains never had to file for permission.

I was sympathetic. I remembered my experience in the Health Department. I could imagine a gatekeeper in Dennis who took a secret joy in delaying us for two weeks. But Tom Howes was annoyed. "Hayden blew it in Dennis. We should have been moving this week." Tom's opinion was that Hayden does this for a living. He should know the rules. But I suspect what Hayden knows best is the way around the rules, the side roads that his houses take.

"Expect Delays. It's a good working philosophy for any project, isn't it?"

"Kate gets philosophical," Bruce says to the mike in the video recorder. He's getting a shot of the sign, too.

Harry reads the sign not as a fortune cookie, but as a banner. When I pull my soaked head back into the car for good, he says, "You're famous."

"Well, not me—the cottage," I say. But I do feel a bit like a celebrity. It isn't often that we get a public sign dedicated to an activity in our lives. Go/Children/Slow doesn't exactly count. When my grandmother retired, she got a sign. At the brand-new Holiday Inn in Somerville, Massachusetts. Right out front, right under the green Holiday Inn logo, her name in marquee lettering. "Congratulations, Mary Ford!" the sign shouted on one side, "Best Wishes Mary Ford!" on the other. I was a teenager at the time and not easily impressed. But Nana's name in lights—that was pretty damn cool.

In Hyannis, we head, not to breakfast, but to the Mid-Cape Home Center, my new favorite store in the universe. They have a section called the Bargain Box, where I am spending more and more of my time. Special orders not picked up, doors that did not quite fit, windows that fussy homeowners refused, odd-sized cabinets. I have been shopping for doors and windows mostly, and I want to show Harry a door with frosted glass that I am thinking could work as the back door for the hallway. On this third trip to see the door, I find it a little too formal for my setting, and Bruce suggests that there are security issues with an all-glass door. I decide I won't tell him about the French doors that will lead to the deck, or the full-view door I have in mind to replace the front door of the cottage.

Ten o'clock and no word from Hayden. At the Home Center, the rain is pounding on the aluminum roof. We have to shout to hear ourselves.

"I don't think we'll be moving today," I yell.

"Doesn't look likely, does it?" Bruce is disappointed, because he only has today off from work. Harry, however, has taken two days for the big event, unwilling to miss either the move or the placing of the cottage.

We drive to downtown Hyannis for hot drinks and bagels. It's after eleven now, and we have resigned ourselves to the idea of a rainy day. We split up the *Boston Globe* and decide we'll pass on the bagels in favor of going to lunch at the Indian place in half an hour. "It's letting up a little," I say, my mind not on the paper in front of me. The men grunt in the way men do when they are reading newspapers. Then my cell phone sings. I grab for it, almost missing it.

"It's a go," he says. "We leave at noon."

I am already folding up the newspaper and gathering up my cup of tea. "Noon," I repeat before Hayden hangs up. Bruce and Harry look up from their sections of the paper. I nod and we rush out of the coffee shop, across the street and into the car. It's after eleven-thirty. We repeat the journey we made only a few hours ago, with the same fear, that we will miss the beginning of the move. ✳

✳   WE ARRIVE IN HARWICH PORT as the rain departs. There is that after-rain feeling in the air, which is still thick, but clean, tart. The wetness is shimmery on the grass we cross to get to the cottage. Hayden and his crew are already there. My little cottage, separated from its brethren now, is atop a flatbed trailer that is attached to a red-cabbed dump truck that looks much too small to haul a house. Hayden moves houses of all sizes, some that have to be cut in half, others that require telephone and electric crews to disconnect and reconnect the overhead wires along the way. Moving these cottages is a small project for him, even if it is huge for those of us who will welcome the cottages at the other end of their journey. I've noticed he calls them "shed" moves. On the day he told me he had all the permits, I reminded him that my new addition is a cottage.

"I am not going to all this trouble to attach a shed to my house." I said it with a smile, which he returned in a crooked sort of way. Then he told me he'd arranged for state troopers to escort the cottage on the twenty-fourth of May.

"Saves money," he said. Without their presence, he explained to me, we'd have to pay for escorts town by town, the cottage passed like a baton from one police department to the next. "Two-hour minimum, each town, four towns, a thousand bucks. And a hassle every time we change towns."

The state police cruisers are here today, sleek blue-on-blue Crown Victorias parked on Route 28, their drivers ready. Their presence only reinforces the parade concept in my mind. I think of high school, marching band, high-stepping in black-and-red uniforms. "Knees to waist," our high school band director, an ex–Navy Band man, would shout over his megaphone at our endless after-school practice sessions. We marched for every holiday, and we also marched to every home game, a parade through town every other Saturday, a police car at the fore, blue lights clearing the streets for us. When we reached the field, we'd settle into our assigned places in the bleachers, playing fight songs and marches to cheer on the home team, a team that never, in my entire high school career, won a game. Maybe that's why it was so important that the band look good. At halftime we would wow the fans with our intricate pinwheel formations and our strong sound. We played a new program for every home game, forming letters and making pictures with precise movements, our helmet-like hats bobbing.

Harry takes over the video camera and I snap a picture of the police cruisers, feeling a little like a spy. Then I focus on the red cab that bears the surprisingly elegant logo of Hayden Building Movers on its doors. I want to get a long shot of the house and truck. The start of the journey.

I recognize Glen, one of the men who was messing with the bolts on the foundation yesterday, and say hello. He and another of Hayden's men are in the truck, ready to go. Hayden is moving around, chatting with the cops, going over the route, doing a few last-minute checks. House looks good; headsets are working. Finally he gets into his maroon Volvo station wagon, the grand marshal of the parade. Harry aims the camcorder at Hayden's bumper: "Save a Tree. Move a House." The cops move from the side to the middle of the road, blocking traffic. One of the troopers motions the traffic to a halt while the line assembles: police car, Hayden, police car, truck hauling cottage.

I can hardly contain myself as I watch the cottage turning onto Route 28, but I manage to shoot the departure: the cottage on the back of a truck, state cops with red and blue flashing lights. Even as I have come to understand the possibility of lifting a building from its foundation, even though I saw Tony's pictures of these very cottages, lifted up and away, even though I have visited my cottage several times, grown used to the sight of it up on concrete blocks, I find it nothing short of miraculous to see this tiny house on the back of a truck, zooming away from us.

We shoot until it is out of sight; then we pile into my car. Harry's Nova has been retired, and he has a line on a low-mileage 1987 Volvo wagon, a distant, elder cousin to Tony's new vehicle. Harry is driving, Bruce is in front, now in charge of the video camera, and I am squeezed in the tiny back seat. I am here because Bruce has a back injury and cannot risk the contortions that my rear seat demands, and because I do not want to drive on this big day. I just want to watch. Still, I feel a little annoyed that Bruce occupies the front row while I have to watch from a lesser seat.

We pull onto Route 28 and turn at the lights onto Route 39. No cottage in sight. "We'll see it soon," I say, because I cannot imagine that they are going very quickly on these back roads of Harwich. But we travel a mile, two, three, and still no cottage.

"Could they have gone a different route?" Bruce asks, and we all contemplate this horrible possibility for a few moments. Imagine missing the move. Imagine arriving home to find the cottage already there, delivered, the house-movers ready to call it a day.

"No," I say. "This is the route. They just had a head start." I say it with an authority that I do not feel, and we are reaching a road where we must make a decision. Which way did they go? Either one will work. We hesitate before we choose the road Harry deems most likely, and in another minute, we spot the cottage up ahead. Relief.

For awhile, there is a white SUV between us and the cottage. "OJ," I say—imagining a helicopter photographing us from above. The cops have stopped the oncoming traffic on this narrow road to let us go by. The driver of the Trooper seizes the opportunity to pull a U-turn—no doubt planning an alternate route in his head, glad to drop out of our parade. We are thrilled with this development; now we have an unobstructed view of our cottage. I snap pictures, wondering if they will come out through the windshield, and I take in the view in case they do not. The trees are fresh with new green, and many are in flower, their colors even more bold on this still-gray day. The cottage moves along, and at a good clip.

"They are going thirty-five!" Harry says, and we marvel at the speed and skill of these house-moving men. Every so often, we reach a narrow stretch of road with low-hung utility wires, and we slow down. Hayden hops out and lifts the wires with something that looks like a cross between a rake and the triton of Neptune. As he lifts, the truck inches forward ever so slowly, the wires slipping off the cottage roof. Then Hayden runs ahead, jumps back into his car, vigilant at the wheel, on the lookout for more wayward lines.

We hold up traffic only occasionally, when the road is extra-narrow or curving. By virtue of the declaration on Route 28, however, my house-moving will be blamed for many unrelated traffic snarls today. Everyone looks for a reason for

Cape Cod traffic, especially in those few days before the tourists arrive. We fool ourselves into thinking the roads are still our own, but in truth, the traffic has been thickening as surely as the weather has been warming. As we pass ongoing traffic pulled onto the side of the road, I try to read the faces of the delayed drivers. Despite the driver of the white Isuzu and his obvious desire to escape from his place behind the house, I still imagine that the drivers we encounter are happy to see a house-moving. I imagine that they are taking it all in, rehearsing the story they will tell later. If they are made late for an appointment, I know they will be forgiven when they tell their story. Yes, despite that one impatient driver, I remain convinced that our parade is enriching the lives of these lucky Cape Cod motorists. This view is only reinforced when we encounter Ed, stationed in South Dennis, on the small green by the old church. He is in shorts and a T-shirt, camera poised. He returns our wave and flashes a big grin as we pass in my tiny blue car. Another satisfied spectator.   *

*   ONCE WE FEEL CONFIDENT of the route, we slip away to a side road so we can meet the cottage head-on. The first time we do this, we surprise the movers. They smile, and Glen gives us a big thumbs-up out the passenger window as we shoot the cottage coming at us. We get behind them again and follow until we hit Station Avenue. In order to keep the traffic moving on this stretch of road, the town of Yarmouth has put up construction cones, creating a special lane for the house parade. We take this opportunity to zip ahead again and get some good shots of the house rounding the corner.

"How'd you get there ahead of us?" Glen shouts. We just laugh and point our cameras at him.

Back in the car, we discuss the shot we know we have to get: the house coming around the Airport Rotary in Hyannis. This is the photograph I want to blow up and hang in the hallway that will connect the house and the cottage: the bank's digital readout of time and temperature high in the background, the Welcome to Hyannis sign in the foreground, the confusion of traffic, the flash of police lights, and the cottage, serene, above it all, rounding the curve of the circle. We decide we need to get well ahead of the cottage to set up our cameras; we take a direct route, while the cottage weaves in and out on back roads. Along the way, we see my mother, stationed on the side of the road in West Yarmouth. We pull up alongside her car.

"I was just getting ready to leave," she says with a nonchalance I cannot understand.

"You're LEAVING?" I can hear the uppercase in my voice. "WHY?"

"I thought I missed it," she says.

"No, it's coming! It's coming! I promise. STAY RIGHT THERE." I issue the command, and we depart, flying now, afraid we will lose our lead. We watch for a sign of a cottage in the rearview mirror, and we discuss the best place to park. Wendy's, we decide. "Good, we can have lunch while we're waiting," Harry suggests.

"LUNCH?? I can't believe you would risk missing the house go by just to stand in line for a burger at Wendy's!" The capital letters are still in my voice, and I feel a little bit like a Peanuts character as I speak. Peppermint Patty maybe?

"I'm hungry," he says.

"So am I, but Harry, the HOUSE!"

We get to Wendy's, find our spot by the edge of the parking lot. We have the perfect view. We'll see the cottage as it approaches on Route 28, get some shots while it pauses to enter the rotary, and we'll be able to watch as it travels halfway around, then exits the traffic circle.

"Do I have time to pee?" I wonder out loud. We decide I do, plenty of time. We were well ahead of the caravan, and they have to brave a stretch of Route 28 with no barricades or special lanes. Bruce joins me as I run into the restaurant. Inside the women's room: two booths, a quartet of women, a small child, and a baby in mid-change. I weigh how badly I have to go against the possibility of being stuck inside the restroom while the house goes by. But the line moves quickly. Bruce and I emerge in tandem, and while he contemplates a cup of coffee, I run outside. He passes on the coffee, follows me to the car.

"You missed it," Harry says, and I know he is kidding.

"Yeah, right," I say, making sure my camera is ready.

"No, really, you did."

"Don't even *say* that. It's too cruel. Don't kid about this, Harry."

"I'm not," he says, and I notice he is walking toward the car, keys in hand, that he is not on the lookout for the cottage.

"You're serious?" I ask in a small voice. He nods, solemnly.

"You mean when MY cottage was coming around the rotary in Hyannis, I WAS ON THE JOHN?????" I cannot believe this. Bruce is silent, my outrage enough for both of us.

"I got it on video," Harry says, which makes us start laughing.

We climb in the car, struck by the absurdity of our lost opportunity, before we move back into superhero mode, ready to chase down the cottage. Again it has a lead, a good lead, and we don't catch up with it for several miles, coming up behind it just after the parade turns onto my street. We get some good shots as they back the cottage into my driveway. The traffic is stopped in both directions, but I sense that people are not upset with the delay, not right here in my neighborhood. Indeed, people are climbing out of their cars, gathering around, asking questions. One man tells me he'll be glad to paint the cottage, gives me his number, and asks for a copy of the video for his son. Turning from him, I see Erika and her sister Sara. "My dad wanted to come too," Erika says, "but you know him — too busy with work. Will they put it on the foundation today?"

"Tomorrow afternoon," I say.

For today, the cottage lands on the spot we have cleared for it, and Hayden's men detach the truck from the trailer. People are back in their cars; the cops direct the traffic away and come to congratulate me on the move.

"Thank you so much," I say to them, as they smile for another archival photo. I am effusively grateful to everyone who has made this day possible. I am even ready to call up Mr. Van Buren and thank him, but I remember his words about the "other" house they lifted, and decide to rein in my enthusiasm a bit. I thank Hayden and his men and tell them what a wonderful job they have done, how impressed I am with them and how well they know their work.

"See you tomorrow!" we shout as they climb back into their truck and wave. Imagine hitching a house to a truck and moving it, all in a day's work. Wielding tritons and lifting power lines, wearing headsets and enjoying the spectacle of a two-car police escort. "Good work if you can get it," Ira Gershwin would say. Mr. Hayden gives me a little salute as he climbs into his car.

"Crane'll be here by two," he says. "Have it up in Eastham first thing, then coming to you."

"Two," I repeat. He's already in his car. "Thank you!" I shout after him. *

* HARRY AND BRUCE and Erika and Sara and I approach the cottage.

"Shall we go in? Do you have a stepladder?" Erika asks. I get it from the shed. One by one we climb up and in through the side door, a little worried about the weight of us all. We survey the small rooms, the green-walled kitchen, the purple bed-room. An army of hangers in the bedroom closet, the hole in the wall by the hot water heater.

I am again admiring the Mexican tiles over the kitchen sink when I notice it. "The soap!" They all turn to me. I point to the half-used bar of yellow soap, sitting kitty-corner on the left edge of the sink top. "This soap was in this exact position when the cottage left Harwich Port. And look"— I lift it—"it isn't attached or stuck in any way. But it is in the same exact place, after riding twenty-eight miles in a cottage hitched to a truck!"

This seems essentially marvelous to me, the very definition of a marvel. I begin laughing, almost hysterically. Then I notice the paint cans, also in the same place where they began their journey, and the little jelly-jar light cover, still upside down on the lower counter. "I meant to take those paint cans out in Harwich Port," I say, "because I was afraid they'd roll around and dent the floors, and the light cover—I was worried that might break. But nothing's moved!" It's almost spooky. We decide to take the paint cans and the lamp glass out before the house-lifting the next day. But we leave the soap, exactly as it is and was. Harry got my speech on video, and now he zooms in on the soap. I get a shot as well, documenting its precise location—almost but not quite touching the strip of stainless steel that surrounds the kitchen sink.

One by one we file out of the cottage, close it up. Erika and Sara refuse our invitation for Chinese food, so Harry and Bruce and I set off for our delayed lunch. We are starving. For once, I am not crabby, the way I usually get when I am hungry. But I am lightheaded and silly, and find it hard to contain my giggling in the back seat. The cottage is in my driveway! At the restaurant, we mug with the camera as if we are tourists. We eat well and review the high points of the day. "I think I had more fun today than I have had in my entire life," I say, and although it seems hyperbole, I realize in that moment it is true.

Harry looks at me to determine whether I am kidding, and when he realizes I am not, he says, "It was an awfully good time." ✷

✷ WE HEAD BACK HOME, where we introduce the cat to the cottage. Egypt peers in the window and looks back at me. "Yes," I admit to him, "I am the one responsible for this." He rolls his eyes, jumps down, and sits with his back to me. Cats always prefer the status quo.

Bruce goes on his way, bus to ferry to the island. He has to work in the morning. He wishes he could stay for the lifting, but it is not to be. Back at the house, Harry and I hang out in the living room, chatting. I answer the phone periodically, exclaim over my day to friends who are checking in. While I am on the telephone, Harry spends time looking at the video on the camera's tiny screen.

"Do you want to see it?" he asks when I come back into the room.

"Not yet," I say. No, not yet. Right now, I want to hold the day still, unmoving, a series of impressions, not yet memories. A red truck, gray-white skies, blue lights, a pink azalea in perfect bloom, yellow cones in the road, a strip of red caution tape, my last name in light orange chalk, printed vertically on a cottage trim board, and a pale yellow oval resting on the edge of a white porcelain sink.

lifting off and landing

"I FEEL LIKE I carried that cottage all the way on my back," I tell Harry. "I am so beat." He's already been up and out, and the futon is folded back into a couch. When I stumble into the living room, he is sipping coffee from Donut Works and reading the *Boston Globe*.

"I got you a honey-dipped," he offers. I eat donuts only in the company of Harry or Tony, and I eat only honey-dipped. I regret the act of eating them—always—later in the day, but Harry knows I find it difficult to resist a perfectly glazed donut when it is presented to me.

"Did you sleep?" Harry inquires, and I admit that I did not sleep well, or more accurately, that I did not dream well. For weeks, I've been plagued with anxiety dreams about the cottage. I share the latest in this series. The cottage requires a special traveling lane, and I am charged with making it. This means I must jackhammer the asphalt, take up a portion of every road to expose the dirt beneath the pavement. It is backbreaking work, and the cottage-movers must wait for me to clear the path. As we near my house, I realize that I will have to put all the roads back to their original condition, and I am overwhelmed by both the necessity to repair the roads and the fact that I have not thought of it earlier. In the dream, it becomes evident that the project will cost me thousands and thousands more than I had anticipated. As I think about the day ahead, the warning that Hayden gave me yesterday about my "challenging site," and the waiting foundation that has cost about three times our original estimate, I suspect that my dream-self may be onto something.

The dream loses some of its power in the telling, and the soothing effects of the honey-dipped begin to set in. I am looking forward to the day. It is a lovely morning; yesterday's rain has disappeared and the air is warm when we step outside to check on the cottage at the base of the driveway. It's a good day for liftoff, I think. The sun will do its work this morning, and by afternoon, cottage, crane, and foundation will be baked dry. No slippery equipment or wet surfaces to concern us. The image of that house in Osterville falling apart does haunt me, but I know this cottage is sturdy, well built, and in excellent shape. "It will be fine," Harry says, sensing my new worry as we climb into the cottage, and for the moment, I choose to believe he is right.

My exhaustion doesn't lift, however, and my anxiety reasserts itself as the morning unfolds. To distract myself, I call friends and neighbors to let them know the timing of the great event. The crane is due to arrive around noon. We expect liftoff by two. One neighbor says he might just cut out of work to come watch, and another tells me her grandchildren will be watching from her backyard. "Come on down," I say to her, sounding like the host of *The Price Is Right.* I'm hoping for a landing party, but the only definites are my mom, Erika, her sister, and Harry. And Egypt, who this morning can tell that something is up. He follows us to the cottage, but he refuses to come inside. He sits by the lilacs and waits for us to emerge before he leads us back to the house, to the kitchen, to his dish. He has a little bite before he slips into my bedroom closet for a long morning nap.

Egypt wakes around twelve-thirty to the loud, insistent beeps announcing the arrival of the crane. He is annoyed when I explain to him he must stay put, that he will be safer inside, away from all this heavy equipment. But he's come to appreciate and respect heavy equipment. He'll be fine. This he tells me with a certain angle of his chin. "There will be houses flying around," I say finally. "You just have to stay put." He gives in, turns his back on me, and jumps onto the living room windowsill to watch. I make a quick exit, trailing Harry in the direction of the big red crane.

It is big, and it is red. Immediately, this crane takes a place in my heart alongside those Cape Cod lighthouse cement mixers. It says "Baxter" in white block letters on the boom, which for the moment is settled into the side of the truck. I am struck by the scale of the crane, which takes up the full width of the driveway; even with the boom tucked in, it is tall and imposing. The driver emerges from the cab, introduces himself as Rick, smiles. Instant infatuation. Perhaps because I haven't been in a relationship for awhile, I am lately reverting to schoolgirl behavior in the romance department. I take a minute to figure out the source of my attraction. Rick is handsome in a clean-cut kind of way that usually escapes my notice, but he has a great smile, and a friendliness around the eyes. Not to mention that he has arrived in the crane that will deliver my cottage to its resting place. And it is springtime, after all. In the excitement of house-moving, perhaps I am a little extra susceptible.

I lead Rick down the driveway, explain what has to happen. Of course he knows he's here to lift a cottage, but Rick is clearly a little surprised by how tight it is. He paces the section of the driveway where he plans to park the crane, and I hang back, giving him space to ponder, to plan. I feel a little nervous that we're starting all over again, that John Baxter with his binder and his pencil and his ratios has shared none of his February calculations with the man he sent to do the job in May. While Rick does his rendition of Rodin's *The Thinker* in motion, some of Hayden's guys show up. I tell Glen that I'm worried that John Baxter isn't here himself. "Be glad," Glen says. "He sent the best man for the job. He'll figure it out."

After several more minutes of pacing, Rick has figured it out. Because we've had so much rain this spring, he doesn't feel confident that the bank on the bog will hold up. He wants to pull in close to the hillside so the crane, even with its pads extended, will be on the firm ground of the driveway. That means we need to move the hay bales aside, take down a small scrub pine and a couple of sapling oaks, then dig into the hillside to make a flat surface for the pads to rest. Hayden's guys get right on it. A chainsaw is produced and three trees—sickly, skinny, vine-strangled trees—are out of the way in minutes. They pull up the stakes on the hay bales and shove them aside and start digging. Amidst this activity, Bob Hayden arrives and confers briefly with Rick before he grabs a shovel himself.

I'm thinking of the Conservation hearing, Mr. Van Buren on the dais, glasses in hand, speaking into the microphone. I hope he's busy scaring someone else right now. I don't think we're doing anything we didn't say we'd do, and we did make it clear we would be working outside the hay bale line on the day we moved the cottage. But I worry about those hay bales tossed aside, the fence gone, the digging into the hillside. I have a feeling Mr. Van Buren and his commissioners would be a bit dismayed by the activity. I imagine myself in front of them again, having to answer for this day. But there is a cottage sitting in my driveway that needs to land on this foundation, I would tell them. We can't stop now.

As if he were reading my thoughts, Hayden pauses in his shoveling, shields his eyes with his hand, looks up the hill to find me. "Kate," he yells. "You sure you want to do this?" He's smirking, leaning on the handle of his spade.

"Positive!" I shout. "We can't stop now!"

"Okay," he says. "Just checking." He turns back to the driveway. "I think we're ready for you, Rick." I run down to meet the crane, stopping to say hi to my mother. She's stationed herself on the Adirondack loveseat in the front yard, where she has a view of the approach. She arrived just about the same time as Mr. Hayden. Erika and Sara are just coming up the driveway now, a digital camera dangling from Sara's hand. This has to be the most documented house move in the history of Cape Cod. That reminds me that I'm not sure where Harry is. He's the videographer today, and he's been occupied finding the right angles to shoot the actual lifting.

"Harry!" He's back by the shed. "Come on—we want to get the crane coming down the driveway!" He makes his way down the hill and shoots the crane head-on. I join him with my camera after I get a few shots of Rick raising the boom.

"This is really happening," I say to Harry. I'm nervous. It doesn't feel the same as yesterday. Yesterday, I felt carefree, certain the cottage would make the journey well. Today, any number of things could go wrong. I try not to list them in my head, focus instead on imagining a smooth landing, a cottage sitting firmly on a foundation that is exactly the right size, a cottage resting comfortably alongside its new neighbor, my house. ✻

✻ ONCE THE CRANE is in position and Rick is satisfied that he is on level ground, Hayden and his crew begin the business of backing the cottage down the driveway. They hitch the house trailer to the truck, and yesterday's driver climbs into the cab. They don't have their high-tech headsets to communicate today, so there is a lot of shouting.

"That's it. Now cut to the left!"

"What about that tree?"

The driveway is narrow, and bordered by trees and brush. The big ones must be avoided. For the smaller ones, Hayden has no mercy. "Don't worry about that tree. You're bigger than it. Just keep comin' back."

"Hey! Stop!"

"Stop!"

"Cut left—hard!"

"What?"

"Left!"

"Left!"

"You're going over the bank—cut hard!"

Ovah. Hahd. I try to focus on the distinctly dropped *r*'s that characterize the speech of the true natives of Massachusetts. This exercise helps me avoid panic as I watch the cottage and its trailer list conspicuously to the left—in the direction of the bog.

"Stop! Just stop!" Hayden is speaking now. He stoops down to have a look at the situation under the trailer.

The men walk around the trailer, the truck. I get a little closer, see that the right back tire of the truck is deep in the mud of the driveway, stuck in it the way you can get stuck in a snow bank. The left rear tire is precariously close to being in the ditch that defines the bog. The left side of the attached trailer is leaning into the soft bank of the bog, which appears to be melting under the weight of the trailer and the cottage.

"Try rocking it." I notice they aren't shouting anymore.

The driver obliges, in an attempt to free the right rear tire. If they get that tire onto level ground, there is some hope of righting the load. As he rocks, the tire sinks deeper into the mud. An exact half circle of rubber is above ground now.

Rick has climbed out of his cab and is standing next to me. "You know the house has to be set down facing in exactly the opposite direction as it is sitting on the trailer?" I've reminded Hayden already, but I want to make sure I've said it out loud to the guy who has to do the work. Now's as good a time as any.

"180?" Rick asks.

"Yes." I nod. "The front door of the cottage needs to face the bog."

"Oh, they always give me the toughest job," he says with a smile, that smile. I find myself, even as the cottage heads bathroom-first toward the bog, entertaining fantasies of shared meals with laughing reminiscences of the day he lifted my cottage into place.

"I didn't want a houseboat," I say, turning back to the activity. Rick chuckles. Another one of the guys hears me and repeats my nervous humor.

"You hear that—she doesn't want a houseboat!" Low-level laughter.

They pace. They assess. They mumble. They try pushing the truck, five men at first, before they use a second truck. The cottage tilts first twenty degrees, then forty-five, and now sixty degrees. It's headed straight for the bog.

Harry's on the other side of me now. "I didn't think they'd want me to keep filming," he says.

"Yeah, just let them figure it out."

"Maybe we shouldn't watch?" I know he has a point, but I am not going anywhere. If my cottage is going to land in the bog, at least I'm going to watch it happen. The men are working silently now. No shouts, only murmurs. Another truck arrives with the Hayden Building Movers logo. A jack emerges, more blocks of wood. Hayden crawls under the house.

I hear Harry's breathing. I am thinking about all the calamities I have imagined. A slip of the crane, a house dropped without a parachute; a roof snapped off like the red cap of a Tylenol bottle; a cottage too big for its foundation landing on earth and air. I never imagined that the bog could claim my cottage. The Conservation Commission comes to mind again. I wonder what papers you have to file to let the town know you have inadvertently dumped a cottage in a protected wetland. No doubt the state would get involved, too. Then there would be the matter of getting it out. Which would probably cost a good deal of money—and if the cottage falls face-first, the way it is leaning, that would be the end of it. Leaving me with a big hole in a hillside that currently more closely resembles a sand pit.

Or a money pit. God, I wonder if Hayden is insured. He must be, but $3,000 for a lost cottage won't build me an addition from scratch. I think about how much more the cottage is really worth—the price of engineering plans and permits, of a yellow mini-excavator and a state police escort in the rain, the price of making way, of concrete forms and pump trucks—the cost of my commitment.

As I calculate my losses, the men work to right the cottage. It is slow going, and it takes all of seven men, two jacks, lots of wood blocks, a shovel, a ramp along the bog bank, and two red-cabbed pick-ups. Finally the truck and trailer are once again on level ground, edging down the driveway. Rick moves away from me and toward his crane. The cottage is coming.

"Stay right," Hayden says to the driver, as if the driver would consider doing anything else. "Away from that bank. Too damn soft."

Slowly, the cottage, unharmed, sitting up straight, closes in on the crane. Harry resumes his camera work. Erika and Sara move to the backyard to get some shots from there. I move too, but slowly, like the cottage. I think we are both feeling a little shaken. ✳

✳ WHEN THE COTTAGE is within ten feet of the crane, Hayden's men begin the next stage of preparation. They thread two long straps—a slightly wider, stronger version of the kind you might use to tie down a canoe on top of your car—under the cottage. Then John lowers the boom and they grab for the cables that swing down. They hitch the ends of the orange straps to each of four cables, creating a harness for the cottage. The cables themselves are connected to two steel bars, which hang on another set of cables that connect everything to the crane. It is a hoist of elegant geometry: parallelogram to double triangle to single point where the arm of the crane hooks in to lift its load.

While his colleagues prepare the cottage, Glen circles the waiting foundation with a sledgehammer. Four swings send the wood blocks flying, revealing the four openings where the straps will land. Satisfied that the cottage is secure, Hayden's men step back. Two stay with the house and the rest move up the hill, stationing themselves around the perimeter of the foundation.

Harry decides the best place to shoot the video is atop the shed, and he scrambles up to get into position before the action begins. I have a camera around my neck, but I'm unconvinced I'll shoot much more film today. I want to see this with my own eyes, not through the lens of a 35-millimeter. Sara and Erika promise to take lots of pictures for me. As I move away from the group, my mother warns me not to get too close to the foundation.

There is no countdown, and the liftoff is almost imperceptible. A tightening of the cables, a stretching of the strapping, the subtle rise of the boom. The men straighten the strap, lend a guiding hand. A minute passes, and another before the cottage appears to be levitating. Hovering, just a few feet above its trailer. It is the strangest thing to see. Slowly, it rises, and even though I know the ascent is controlled by the crane, by the crane operator, it is hard not to imagine the cottage has supernatural powers all its own.

The house is seven or eight feet off the trailer when it begins to turn. In order to avoid the big spruce, the cottage must approach the foundation sideways. The ninety-degree rotation is graceful and smooth, and for another minute I allow myself to be impressed by my knight in shining armor at the controls. I take some photographs of his excellent work, marveling at the miracle of a house in midair. The cottage moves up, up, and in, swishing past the spruce tree, bending back the tips of a few branches. When it is almost over the foundation, the cottage begins another slow rotation. I watch the tiny bathroom window move away from me, and watch the side door come into view.

"Oh, that side's cute with the little door," my mother says. "Are you going to leave it that way?" She is referring to the bright blue section of vertical pine siding. The side door of the cottage once led to the screened porch, the porches that were lopped off by Hayden's men before they moved the cottages the first time. My guess is that when they added the porch, the owners must have replaced the white cedar shakes with the pine boards. Personally, I have always thought these out-of-context blue planks should be the first thing to go, but I see what my mother means. From this angle, the blue door is sweet and appealing, and the planks hardly bother me at all. It's remarkable what a little altitude and a sense of presentation can do.

"This is amazing, Katie," she says. My mom hasn't always been impressed with what I have accomplished, or more accurately, she doesn't always say much about what I do. It isn't that she doesn't care, but rather that she just expects me to do well in the world. But this cottage move. This is a surprising achievement, and strangely, she credits me with it, even as she has seen the men pass by with the house on the back of a truck, even as she has viewed the near-miss, the save, and the cottage liftoff.

"It's too bad Barbara isn't here to see this." My mother knows I miss my longtime neighbor.

Since my first sight of the cottage, I have felt the urge to share the adventure with Barbara. I can imagine how intrigued she'd be with the project. I know that she would have taken a proprietary interest in my adding on. In so many ways, the house is hers, her father and mother's, as much as it is mine. I've thought of her often, but have visited her only twice, unable to rouse her on either occasion. I suspect they keep her sedated. Barbara, who suffers from chronic depression and chronic impatience with the idiocy in the world, can be difficult. I understand from her attendants that when she is awake, she demands to go home. Busting her out for a day to watch a cottage-landing—though it is exactly what I would like to do—would probably be more cruel than kind.

"They said it would be too much for her; that it would upset her."

"It probably would." I know my mother is trying to make me feel better. "Wow. Look at that," she says now, turning the conversation and our thoughts back to the midair activity.

The cottage is almost parallel with the house now; Rick has achieved about 178 degrees of the required 180-degree turn. It's high in the air now, suspended and motionless in this moment. We are silent, all of us—even the house-moving men. This dislocation of object and place requires our beliefs to extend at least as far as the arm of the crane. I remember many years ago, when I worked in a bookstore, looking out the plate-glass window at just the right moment. There was a truck stopped at the light, hauling a dozen post office letter boxes in its open cargo area. I remember feeling giddy seeing all those blue boxes—destined to be bolted down to side-walks—riding free in the back of a truck, as if they were having an adventure.

I stare hard at my cottage now, and I can't help smiling. I take advantage of the pause in the action to take a shot or two. But I am pretty sure I won't need the pictures for reference. The image of a silver-shingled house floating against a backdrop of blue sky and treetops has imprinted itself in my mind—I am pretty sure—for life. *

* THE DESCENT IS SLOW, careful, punctuated by directions from Hayden and his crew, who communicate to Rick mostly with a combination of shouts and hand motions.

When the cottage is only about two feet off the foundation, the men move in close. Rick waits for further direction. Glen and Hayden are positioned on the far side.

"Ease it down, now."

"Okay, take it up."

"Up."

"Down."

"Up again."

"Down, easy. Okay, up."

This series of small lifts and lowerings goes on for about ten minutes as Hayden's crew attempts to line up the bolts in the foundation with the holes they have predrilled in the sill of the house. They work one side at a time, Rick lifting and lowering again and again, Hayden's men drilling a new hole where the old one isn't quite lined up. Finally, they are ready to work all four sides at once. Rick lowers the cottage within inches of the foundation now, and Hayden scurries with the drill, makes a couple of last-minute adjustments. The men resume their positions, Hayden on the side closest to us once more.

"Want to help with this part?" he asks me.

"Sure." I don't know what he means, but I'm game. It's my cottage, after all.

He produces a roll of bright pink foam, a little wider than packing tape, and hands one end to me. "Sill sealer," he says. Leaning in close to the foundation, I work with Hayden, unrolling the thin layer of pink and pressing the adhesive side up onto the wooden sill on the bottom of the hovering cottage. Through the pink, my fingers touch the house, sturdy and prepared for its landing. No houses falling apart here, thank you.

The sill sealed, we step back and Hayden signals Rick that we are ready.

He lowers the cottage far-side first, Glen and his partner adjusting, righting it, just a couple of inches away from the waiting bolts. Next our side, then the front, and finally the back side. Everything is lined up. Rick lowers again, in the same sequence; the men guide and right the cottage before they step back, section by section. I hear the sound of the bolts sliding into place. The rear section—the wall closest to the house—is the last one to find its position. When the men step away from that section, Rick lowers the house all the way. I hear a series of squeaks as the bolts squeeze all the way into the sill and then one long, deep groan. It is a satisfied groan, a groan that is almost a sigh, the sound of a cottage that has found its home.

The straps are unbuckled and Rick pulls back the boom. Hayden's guys gather their tools and begin packing the trucks. Erika and Sara say their good-byes, promising to e-mail me some pictures soon. I offer the men something cold to drink. "Beer? Ginger Ale? I have to warn you. It's got real ginger in it, and it's kind of strong." They laugh at me. Rick and Mr. Hayden decide to brave the ginger ale. The rest of the crew, house-moving done for the day, opt for beer. I deliver the drinks to the bottom of the driveway, where we lean against the crane and drink.

"Hey, this is strong," Rick says after his first gulp.

"I usually cut it with seltzer," I offer. " Want some?"

He nods and I fill a glass halfway with seltzer. "For you?" I ask Hayden.

"No," he growls. "I'll drink it straight." This doesn't surprise me.

We recount the day, the bog crisis, the lifting, the landing. There is a lot of head shaking and laughter. "You guys were all so great," I say at last. "Thank you so much!"

The party breaks up. First Hayden's men depart, taking the empty house trailer with them. Next Rick, whom I thank one more time as he climbs into the truck. "That landing was so smooth," I say. "I could tell the cottage was in good hands as soon as you picked it up. You really know what you're doing. I'm glad you were here—especially after the bog adventure." He laughs, accepts my thanks, and does not start up his truck. I ask the question I've been wondering all afternoon. "What does it feel like to lift up houses?"

"Well, whenever I have a project with Hayden, I know I'll get a rush."

"You like it?"

"Oh yeah, I like it."

"I suspected as much. Hey, is it true this is the biggest crane on Cape Cod?"

"It is today. But we're getting a bigger one—next week, I think." Before he starts the engine, he tells me a little more about cranes, about the German heritage of this red crane, and of John Baxter's preference for Krupps products when it comes to heavy equipment.

"Thanks again."

"Sure. Good luck with the rest of your project. See you."

My infatuation has not yet ebbed, but already I know he will not see me, nor I him, unless by happenstance, and certainly not over dinner. Still I respond in kind. "Yeah, thanks. See you."

I walk back up the driveway and climb the front steps. My mom is on the Adirondack loveseat again, and Mr. Hayden is still poking around in the basement of the cottage. "Concrete blocks will take care of these holes," he says to me as I walk down the hill to meet him. He means the openings in the foundation we made to accommodate the orange straps. I nod. "Went pretty well," he offers. "Only lost a half hour." He is referring to the bog incident.

"I was a little worried," I say.

"So much damn rain this spring." I find I can read between the few lines Mr. Hayden offers me. I am following him. The rain made the ground soft; the soft ground made the truck get stuck. The stuck truck made the house tilt. The tilting house made me worried.

"Yeah," I say.

"Perfect today, though."

"Perfect day to land a house." We walk companionably down the hillside onto the driveway.

"Oriole," he says, just as I am wondering if that is the call I hear. We turn toward the sound, try to locate its source. But the trees are in leaf now, and the bird is well hidden. The orioles don't stay for long on the Cape. They pass through in May, and if you're lucky you'll catch a glimpse of one or two in your backyard. Half an orange nailed to a tree trunk will sometimes bring one into view. "Saw one yesterday in Cotuit," Hayden says.

"Oh—I haven't seen one yet this year," I say, and he can tell I am impressed that he has. The bird calls again. "Now it sounds almost like a robin. I wonder—"

"You must have a book, book lady."

I nod.

"Go get your book."

By this time, we are at the bottom of the steps. My mother and Harry are sitting together on the bench now. Harry takes in our approach and I know what he is thinking. Yesterday—following the house, watching Hayden wield his wire-rake, listening to Bruce narrate as he filmed the progress—I said, "In the movie version, I'd fall in love with Mr. Hayden." Harry grins at me now.

"Go—get your book," Hayden repeats. I follow his instructions and emerge with a Peterson's guide. We hear the bird again and follow the sound back to the driveway. "What's it say in that book?" he asks me.

I read the syllables that Roger Tory Peterson has assigned to the oriole's note. "Hew-li." Conveniently the bird calls again—from a different location.

"An oriole all right," Hayden says. He is looking up again, and pointing. "See'm? Way up there." I lean in, and follow his finger. I see little more than a speck, way up in the treetops. I stare hard, trying to confirm the oriole-nature of the speck. And then he flies, down, closer, close enough to see that, yes, he is an oriole. At that moment, he calls again, a series of hew-li's in a piping song.

"Well, now you've seen your first one this year."

Indeed I have, and I have seen the oriole—dressed in brilliant orange and black-tie black—on the day the cottage landed. It seems a blessing and another omen, another good omen.

I walk with the house-mover to his maroon Volvo wagon. "Thanks for everything," I say. He's already in the car.

"I'll come by," he says through the window. "Check progress."

"I hope you do," I say just before he starts the engine. He gives me a quick wave and pulls out of the driveway. I watch him turn onto the street. *Save a Tree. Move a House.* I wonder where I can get one of those bumper stickers.

the history of concrete

IT IS EARLY JULY. The cottage has been sitting beside the house for the better part of six weeks. I have been here watching nothing happen for three of those weeks. For the other three, I was away—far away. In Paris. I'm working on a novel that is set there, and depending on cash flow, project schedules, the balance on my Frequent Flyer account, and—most important—Tony's ability to cat-sit, I sneak away once or twice a year. I love my Paris sojourns—time to be away from the daily demands, time to be a full-time writer—but I wasn't as excited to make this last trip, leaving only ten days after the cottage landed. I'd made my travel plans last October—long before I knew I'd be expecting a cottage.

I was hoping to see some progress before I left—most notably, the final bit of concrete work. We need to build a foundation wall running from the left back corner of my living room to the right front corner of the cottage. A little bit of orientation might be helpful here. My living room juts out about four feet beyond the rest of the house, in the direction of the bog. In that four-foot jog, there was once a door, which I replaced with a single pane of glass that looks out onto the patio and the backyard. Now that the cottage has landed, you can still see to the backyard—through a narrow four-foot alley, the distance between house and cottage. Your more immediate view is of disturbed earth. Although the cottage is lined up with the corner of the living room, it sits about fourteen feet back, roughly even with the rear wall of my kitchen. A four-foot concrete block foundation wall will bridge that fourteen-foot expanse. On top of that foundation, we will build a new exterior wall, which will eventually mark the boundary of my expanded kitchen. Our plan is to get everything connected and sealed up before we break down the stretch of the existing load-bearing wall that now encloses the kitchen. Then you'll be able to step from the kitchen through French doors to the deck.

The weather didn't cooperate before I left for Paris, and I resigned myself to missing some of the action. But nothing happened in my absence. The plumbing company didn't come to give an estimate. Stan the electrician didn't come to review the long list I'd left with Tony. The lack of response from plumber and electrician is minor in comparison to the absence of the concrete forms men. Nothing can proceed without this stretch of foundation wall.

"Brecht must have been inspired by a construction project," I write in an e-mail to a friend who asks how things are going. I check in with Ed and John, and they promise to push Ronny, to let him know we'll go elsewhere if he can't pull it together. But it is high season now for concrete men; the loss of my small job is of no consequence to Ronny's business. We should probably threaten him that we will never give the job away, that it—and we—will haunt him to the end of his days. Maybe then he'd think of coming.

We wait. Ronny cometh not. He has been not coming for almost two months now. I attempt to blend calm with perseverance. I also watch the calendar, and I wait for Mercury to move forward. I have an abiding interest in astrology, a subject

I have studied since I was a teenager and stumbled onto *Linda Goodman's Sun Signs* at my aunt Rosemary's house. I was babysitting; my cousins were napping, and I stretched out on the flowered couch to read about the Libra Woman. I remember one passage in particular that made me feel as though the author were reading my mind. I wasn't yet a woman, and certainly not everything she said applied to me, but enough of it was exactly on target.

Music school and studies in Western philosophy sublimated but did not extinguish my interest in astrology, and my first job in a bookstore served to reawaken the budding astrologer within. The assistant manager warned me that customers could be difficult on the full moon. They made wacky demands— for books we'd have to order—and they wanted everything right away. They often left unhappy and without placing an order. Over time, I discovered that the new moon brought us customers who were equally odd, but in a much lighter way. Their requests were bizarre, but they were consistently good-natured, optimistic. They placed orders and were willing to wait. I returned to astrology, learned about the influence of the moon passing through each sign. More months and more moons in the store, and I began to notice the small fluctuations, each few days, in moods—and in requests, too. I was hooked.

Astrology at its best has wisdom and a sense of humor. Three times a year, Mercury provides the laughs, and the opportunity for learning. According to astrologers, when usually quick-moving Mercury is "retrograde," life slows down. A good thing if we are vacationing, or if we are seekers focused within, but an often frustrating phenomenon if we are living in the outer world. Communication is tangled, breakdowns of all sorts are routine, and delays are to be expected. It isn't a time for new beginnings, but a good time to revise and rethink, redo—often those very things you might have rushed into the last time Merc was in a tailspin.

With the backward motion of Mercury in mind, I call Ed or John every third day to report that Ronny has not arrived, but I don't really expect him right now. We are well into the retrograde; it is best to wait it out. I am slightly annoyed, sure, but somehow not so worried about the lack of progress at the moment. I make a call to the plumbing company, reminding the receptionist that I am overdue for an estimate, but I don't try to pin her down to a time. And the message I leave on my electrician's answering machine is equally unemphatic. "Come when you can," I say. "I expect construction to begin by the end of the month." In two weeks, Mercury will move forward in the heavens once more. I'm willing to bet we'll have some forward motion down here, too.

I am cautious about revealing my interest in astrology. In my working life, I have discovered that a handful of clients find an occasional astrological insight to be helpful, but most clients, I suspect, would be prone to firing me if they knew I was a serious star watcher. In my personal life, there is a similar divide. While even skeptical women friends have commented that my astrological bent is just an indication of my complexity, men—at least some decent proportion of them—seem to see it as an indication of a deeper personality disorder. They flee.

I smile now as I imagine talking astrology with Mr. Hayden. I don't think so. Or even Ed, John, Dave. Dave, Erika's father.

He would be a runner, I bet. That quiet engineering mind. No, it was best not to mention Mercury to Dave, even while he worked on our application in the last Mercury retrograde. Better for me to expect delays, to double-check every document before we sent it out, and to double-check the double-check. We got through that cycle okay, and we'll come out of this one, too.

While we wait, Egypt and I establish our routine. Every night we walk over to the cottage, walking out our front door and making a right—away from the cottage—circling around the house and into the backyard. You cannot approach the cottage directly yet. Stepping out the kitchen door, you would drop into the ditch between the two buildings.

I have created makeshift steps out of concrete blocks at the side entrance to the cottage. I use the steps. Egypt jumps up and over the threshold in a single leap. We walk from room to room, patrolling. It strikes me that this is just the way a cat would add onto a house. Get another house. Set it beside the old one. Rub up against the new doorways, head-butt the corners of things, scenting the place, claiming it as yours. Connect them later—only as a convenience for winter travel across your territory.

While I was away, Tony painted the little bedroom yellow, and most of what will be my office is now a deep, lovely aquamarine. The little Mexican tiles are still up in the kitchen, and the sink is still there, the tiny gas stove, the hot water heater, the homemade kitchen cabinets. Between client calls, I wander over to the cottage, where I pry off the tiles one by one. That wall will be disappearing soon. It will be the six-foot open entryway to my office. I imagine my office; in my mind, I place the furniture that Harry will build me. The desk, we have decided, will have a cherry surface, and the legs will be made of wide copper pipes. It won't look like anything I have in my house already—not that a common theme could be identified, except perhaps yard-sale chic.

It isn't hard for me to envision what the house will look like when it is finished, but as I receive visitors I realize that most of them do not see what I see. I give them the tour, tell them what wall will come down, what doors will be replaced, what the roof will look like, and what I hope to do with the inside hallway. At some point, they inevitably say to me, "What a lot of work!" My neighbor to the rear said pretty much the same thing after she saw the cottage tucked in place. Or more accurately, she said, "It needs a lot of work, huh?" I realized in that moment that she did not see what I saw, not at all. And these echoes of my neighbor's remark tell me I am communicating process well enough, but I am not able to share the visuals that I carry with me in my mind's-eye. It is a lot of work, sure, but what I can already see motivates me, propels me forward. ∗

∗ MY UNCLE JACK surprises me one Saturday with a visit. He and Jane were on the Cape for the weekend, and he decided to take a drive. I answer the door in disarray, wishing he had called first, even as I am touched that he took the time to come over.

"I thought I'd come to see your project," he says, and makes no mention of my strange attire, my lack of makeup, my general dishevelment.

I invite him in, offer him a cup of something—not sure that I have coffee (another reason visitors, especially morning visitors, are wise to call ahead). He accepts a cup of tea, and I fill the teakettle and set it on the stove. We walk to the cottage while the water is heating. I give him the tour, tell some stories about the landing, point to where the roof will be, explain the hallway.

He listens carefully, nods, asks an occasional question. He stares down the alley between the houses. "It's beautiful," he says, and I note the tense. He is seeing it finished.

Back in my kitchen, he pulls up a stool to the counter, sips his tea, and tells me that his kidneys are in trouble. I'd known through my mother that he was having some tests, but I didn't know what Jack is telling me now. "The doctor says I'll be on dialysis within a year's time." He says it matter-of-factly, and I try to be matter-of-fact in turn. I know it is what he wants from me.

"What will that mean?" I ask him, and he speaks of home dialysis versus hospital dialysis, the differences, the pros and cons.

"I'm lucky to have some time to investigate my options," he says. He talks about the possibility of a donation, and lets me know as if he is talking about the weather that he is already on a transplant list. He tells me about the special diet he is on now, and what he can and can't eat. We sip our tea.

When he is ready to leave, I give him a big hug, thank him for coming by. I don't know how to say more than that out loud to my uncle. But when I close the door behind him, I find myself standing absolutely still, contemplating the enormity of what he has just revealed to me. Jack, sick. Jack, very sick.

He has always been the healthy one in the family. Sure, he's not far from seventy, but until a few months ago, he was playing basketball—a champion in the senior league. It's been easy to ignore the fact that Jack has been getting old, even as I have watched him these last few years grow into a man who resembles more his uncle than mine. I wonder about this blow to his body, this sapping of the physical well-being that has always bolstered his emotional strength. Jack has always been the one who comes through when you need him. Now, it seems he may start needing us. I can imagine the house complete—and so, I am pleased to know, can Jack—but I cannot imagine my uncle weakened, old—or gone.

That afternoon, I go for a swim. The beach is at its best late in the day. The water is warmed by the all-day sun, and the wind that comes up earlier in the afternoon has usually died down. Best of all, almost everyone has gone home, their body clocks set to some internal timer that goes off at 4:00 P.M. On some days, the beach is entirely my own.

It was my father, my stepmom, and his second family who initiated me into the secret society of late-day beachgoers. We would vacation, many years ago, just past the elbow of Cape Cod. For a couple of weeks each summer, I would morph from only to eldest child, playing endless games of Sentence Scrabble and Silly Poker with my stepbrothers and looking after my much-younger sisters. My father would bring a huge stack of paperbacks with him, spending a good portion of every day on the deck, catching up on his reading. He passed his books along to me as he finished them. They weren't books that would appeal to me under other circumstances—his favorites were fat novels by James Michener and mysteries by

Alistair MacLean—but sipping lemonade and talking with my dad about them made the read worthwhile. My reader-father could not be coaxed to the beach until the late afternoon, where, once in the water, he was as happy as I ever saw him. He was a strong swimmer; his long body and muscled limbs worked in a graceful synch. But he was willing to play with us kids, too. He would horse around with the boys, and my younger sisters would vie for rides on his shoulders. He taught me how to float the way he did—as if he were sitting on an invisible lounge chair, carefree, fully at ease in the world.

I find my solace in the water as well. My father died young— at forty-eight—and yet I think of him almost every time I float and paddle and ride the waves. When my mom was sick several years ago, I came to the beach, religiously—every after- noon—swimming away the hours at the hospital, the con- cerns, the unanswered questions about her future. Sometimes I think it is that feeling of being immersed in something much bigger than ourselves that gives us the comfort we seek. The ocean is much more than the sea of our troubles.

Today, I think of Jack. I focus on his matter-of-fact way with me this morning and recall how he, as much as the ocean, helped me through my mother's illness. I realize that in some ways, Jack has morphed into my father figure. I've always imagined that if I were traditional enough to be given away in a wedding, Jack is the one man I would ask to do the honors. That settles it, I think, as I let my worries be carried away by the tide, Jack is staying on the planet at least long enough to perform that ritual. And at the rate I'm going, that means he'll need to stick around for many years to come. *

＊ ONLY A FEW DAYS LATER, I wake in the very early morning to a clanging sound outside my bedroom window. I reach for the tiny clock by my bed and squint to read the time: 6:20 A.M. Egypt yawns, but rises with me to look out. We see a man in pale green shorts and a gray T-shirt, hauling a bucket. A concrete man? At this hour? It has to be! I am instantly awake, and astrologically astonished. This is the very first day out of the retrograde. Is this project that closely attuned to the cosmos? I am hopeful.

Outside, I introduce myself to the man. Frank is not one of Ronny's men, he tells me, but a subcontractor that Ronny called to do the job. "The truck is due at seven," he says to me, "and I am prepared for every contingency."

I can't say why, but his words do not inspire confidence. Maybe because in this short while, I have grown used to men who don't say a thing about what they plan to do, but just do it. Is it possible I have grown mistrustful of words? I brush away my misgivings, but I do ask him how he plans to do the job. He is convinced he won't have to pump, he tells me, and my heart sinks. I point out that we have had to pump everything except the lower footings, that the hill is steep, that Ronny was planning to pump. He repeats that he has planned for every contingency, and I wonder (cruelly) whether he has recently learned the word. "What will you do if you can't pour?" I ask.

"Wheelbarrows," he answers, and he points his shoulder in the direction of two cement-caked wheelbarrows. Next to them, some buckets, shovels.

Maybe I am wrong, I say to myself, maybe he really is prepared for every contingency.

The truck arrives shortly after seven, and with a sense of déjà vu, I watch this man named Frank botch my job. When he leaves around nine, the wooden forms that Ed and John built for the retaining wall are swollen and curved with the weight of unevenly poured concrete. The upper footing to connect house and cottage is still empty—save for a few shovelfuls that missed the forms.

I feel sick, but oddly calm about the whole episode. I call Ed, and I do not cry. I am not even close to tears this time. There is what astrologers call a "shadow"—about two weeks on either side of a Mercury retrograde period—when the fleet-footed messenger is barely creeping through his celestial errands. Surely this morning's disaster is the natural result of moving too quickly in the shadow. And to think I fooled myself into thinking the early-rising Frank was right on schedule.

"Don't worry," I hear Ed telling me at the other end of the phone. "I'll find someone else to do it. Maybe Vito." Vito is the mason who has been waiting to build the wall on top of the nonexistent footing. "I just spoke to him yesterday. He's busy next week, but he can come the week after."

"Vito. In two weeks." *Perfect timing.* ✳

✳ THE ASTROLOGY IS GOOD on the morning of July 25. Vito is due at eight-thirty and Ed and John have promised the mason will do the job right. I have high hopes even before Vito makes his way up the hill to introduce himself. I am in the side garden, and he is beneath me on the bank when he extends his hand to shake mine. I know from Ed that Vito is not his real name. "All the guys at the station have nicknames,"

Ed explained to me. "His real name is Bobby." I'd asked because Ed often referred to a mason named Bobby, and I was not 100 percent sure he was the same mason John called Vito. "One and the same," Ed confirmed. Bobby a.k.a. Vito works for the same fire department from which Ed is retired.

"How did he get the nickname?" I asked.

"Something to do with *The Godfather*," Ed said. "Bobby is Italian, and the guys were kidding him about it, decided to call him Vito. It stuck."

I am one of the six adults over age forty in America who have not seen *The Godfather*, but my sense is that most of the characters are not nice people.

"You'll like Vito," Ed said, possibly reading my mind. "He's a nice guy."

"Does he mind the nickname?" I had asked. It seemed to me that a nice guy wouldn't claim a mobster namesake, that an upstanding, firefighting Italian American might not appreciate the stereotypical associations. "And which name should I call him?"

My question is answered this morning: "Hi, I'm Vito," the mason says as he shakes my hand.

After my string of bad-luck no-name concrete men, I am so struck by Vito's confident presence that I can only manage, "Kate."

A moment later, Jeff, the concrete-pumping man, makes his way up the hill to say good morning, and reminds me we have already met. "I was right here after they dropped all that concrete. Remember?" I do remember him, but in fact the memory of the botched job, the concrete all over my hillside looms larger than Jeff's face, friendly and inquiring, doing the job right a few days later.

"Right," I say. That was the first concrete screw-up. Then the 6:20 wonder who thought he was prepared for every contingency. I still can't believe that guy tried to do the job without a pump. Ronny knew we needed to pump. Didn't he tell the sub? Or did the sub just decide to try it on his own? "Good to see you again," I say to Jeff. "You seem to be the one who comes to the rescue."

Jeff shrugs off the white-knight-in-a-pickup-truck role. "You just can't do this job without a pump," he confirms.

"We're ready to go as soon as Obie gets here," Vito says, using John's firehouse nickname to conjure his truck, which pulls into the driveway at that moment. We walk down to meet him. Vito shakes his hand, claps John on the back. Jeff introduces himself. John perches on the truck's back bumper to pull on a pair of fireman's boots.

"Yours?" I ask, and he admits that because he has to work later, he didn't want to mess his own up. He grabbed a spare pair from the station. He looks a little guilty about this.

"I'll wash them off," he adds. Vito tells us he found his boots at a boating store over by Kmart. Vito's boots are not as tall or as sturdy-looking as John's rugged footwear, but they will do for sloshing around in concrete when he makes the basement floor. Jeff's boots are standard-issue work boots, caked with dried concrete. He'll be pumping rather than working in the basement, but he admires the rubber boots of his coworkers. I feel a little bit like a spy from the other side, listening in on these men talk about shoes and shopping. After a moment, I recognize their conversation as a variation on a business ritual: small talk. The chatter before the chore, the patter that precedes the pitch. A verbal warm-up for the task at hand. ✳

✳   THERE IS A FAIR AMOUNT of setup work before the concrete will flow. This time, instead of a crane, Jeff has a smaller pump that is hitched to a pickup truck parked high in my driveway. The barrel-shaped pump has heavy hose attachments, which are spread from the driveway to the basement, crossing through the bed of daylilies. The orange tiger lilies are transplants from the wild and almost impossible to kill. Still, the sight of the trampled lilies, in bent bloom—and some of Barbara's transplanted irises, too, not as hardy— makes me sad. I remind myself that I have saved as many plants as I possibly could, and that I cannot maintain the respect of these men if I am always asking them not to step on my flower beds. I let the lilies lie.

The cordless phone in my pocket rings, and I run inside to take the client call. Maine calling. This one will take awhile. I am disappointed that I have to miss the flow of the concrete, but I am back outside in time to watch John and Vito and Jeff inside the basement, working on the floor, moving around in their boots. Soon enough Jeff cedes the job to the better-booted John and Vito; not long afterward, John gives over the finish work to Vito. "This is what he likes to do," John says to me. We sit inside the frames for the cellar windows, the entry point for the concrete this morning, and look in on Vito.

Vito swirls the concrete, levels it, swirls and levels again. He is on the upper section of the basement, kneeling on a board, working with his hands. John leaves me to remove his heavy boots, and I stay to watch, snapping a picture of the deep gray floor against the pale gray walls. How can a concrete floor look so beautiful? But it does. Perhaps the long wait for my basement accessory item enhances my appreciation of concrete beauty, but more likely, I am taken with the fine workmanship that the mason brings to the job. While he works, Vito tells me the names of the tools they have been using: trowels, floats—the big one a "bull float"—and the funny number that looks like a bicycle handle, called a jitterbug. I repeat the words, hoping to remember them, holding them in my mind like another set of lucky pennies.

When Vito moves from the basement to the footing for the foundation that will connect house and cottage, I move with him. John joins us there, now wearing regular work boots. I watch the two of them, working closely, silently. As if by secret signal, John gets up to help Jeff load some of his equipment, once again leaving the finish work in Vito's hands. Stationed in the ditch between house and cottage, I watch him, or more accurately I watch his back, his blue T-shirt moving with the motions of his arms.

"I wonder who figured out concrete." I say it almost without realizing I have spoken aloud.

Vito is leveling the footing, using his hand trowel, and he responds immediately, "Oh, it was the Romans." He gives me a brief history of concrete. He talks about sand and a beach in Italy, and he tells me that the concrete in ancient times was much stronger than the kind we use today.

"Really?" Inane, but all I can think to say.

"Yes," he says. He speaks of grades of concrete for a moment. "The strongest grade we use—to hold up skyscrapers—isn't even as strong as the concrete they used in ancient Rome. Think of the Colosseum," he says.

"It's still standing. Because of the strong concrete?"

Vito smiles, nods.

I am afraid to look into his big brown eyes, afraid to return his smile with my own. Afraid that I may fall in love with this man. A firefighting mason who does such beautiful work, a man who can tell me how the walls were built in ancient Rome, a man who answers questions I wasn't even aware I'd asked. ✳

✳   BY THE TIME Vito finishes the footing, I am nursing a full-fledged crush. My inner cynic congratulates me on the eight-week interval since my last infatuation. But my inner romantic believes this is more than just fifteen minutes of fascination. I can imagine dating Vito. But I cannot imagine that Vito is unattached. He's too handsome, too sweet. He has to be taken. Katrina says that is a defeatist attitude. "Any wedding ring?" she asks me.

"No, but how could he wear one in his line of work?"

She gives me that much. But she is convinced, in her romantic way, that I will meet a man on this project. Perhaps that man is Vito. For moments at a time, I allow myself to believe that could be true. But even if he is available, I'm pretty sure he is a lot younger than I am. This argument gets nowhere with Katrina; Ruben is eleven years younger than she is. "Flirt a little," she tells me.

Flirting is not my strong point. And I don't exactly believe in it, either. At least I don't believe in it as a means to an end, or as a casual activity among strangers. I don't deny the energy that flows between heterosexual men and women who have something—for example, this cottage project—in common. I know that if I were male, my interactions with John and Ed and Mr. Hayden and Vito and all the rest of the men on this project would be quite different. I am aware that they are aware I am female. I think back to the woman in the Health Department, and how I wished she were male. (She probably would have been happier if I were male as well.) It's tricky, this geography of gender. On one hand, I hold dear the feminist principles of equality, fairness for all, and I remain ever-grateful to the strong-hearted women who made possible my life as a self-employed, home-owning, cottage-moving female. On the other hand, there is what Erika calls "eye softening," a perceptible warmth that creeps in around the eyes when two people like each other. I am pretty sure there would be a lot less of that if I were just another one of the guys.

When Vito returns a few days later, he has a helper and he also has a dog. A big dog, part German shepherd perhaps, who immediately settles into a comfortable hole beside the bird feeder. Egypt and I look through the screen door in the kitchen in an attempt to categorize the nature of this threat. Egypt puffs himself up and, looking large, moves away from the door. I stay a moment longer and contemplate the end of my crush. I don't think I could ever date a man with a dog big enough to swallow my cat whole.

For the next few days, Vito works in a vibrating fog of concrete dust. He must cut the blocks to fit as he builds the wall.

The saw, he tells me, is designed for masonry. The blade is diamond-tipped. His helper moves between the cutting station and the wall, using an old wheelbarrow to haul the concrete blocks, while Vito layers block upon mortar upon block. The wall grows day by day, a beautiful perfect wall of gray and gray. Apart from its function—to connect house and cottage—I love the wall for its form, and for the steadiness and skill that hold it up. When it is complete, Vito tells me he needs a few days to think about the final connection, the bridge between the wall and the cottage foundation.

"I'm thinking of using a sonar," he says. We are staring at the point where the walls meet. "You need something—to prevent water from getting in, that sort of thing."

I don't say anything. I am thinking that sonar is something like radar, and I don't understand how sound waves will keep the water out.

"I've done that before," he says, "and it worked really good. Here I'd use a half-round or maybe a quarter. Just cut the form."

Ah, a form. A concrete form. A round concrete form. A half-round concrete form. I get it. "You'd put it right here, and pour into it?" I ask. He nods. "Well, a sonar sounds good to me," I affirm, as if I'd known all along exactly what he was talking about. He nods, and takes me seriously. Then he calls his dog—her name is Violet, and despite her fearsome size, she is calm and gentle.

"I'm lucky with dogs," he says. "She goes everywhere with me."

For a moment my heart leaps. A man with a calm dog. A man so attached to a calm dog named Violet. Maybe such a man is not married after all? ✳

* SONAR, I LEARN, is really *Sono* with a south-of-Boston accent. *Sonotube* is the name on the form, the brand name of the cardboard tube into which Vito will pour the concrete. He cuts it into something close to a three-quarter round and fits it into the corner between the two foundation walls. "Perfect," he says. I agree that it is an elegant solution. The job is finished. Vito comes into the house for the first time ever. He comes in the front door, mindful of his muddy boots, his shorts and T-shirt dusty with concrete remains. He stands in the center of the tiny entrance rug, pen and invoice pad in hand. He pulls himself in tight, as if an elbow outside the perimeter of the rug would disqualify him in some way.

"Don't worry," I say. "Have a seat and I'll get my checkbook." He protests, but I insist until he sits cautiously and begins to write. He is perched on the very edge of the futon couch, still afraid to leave some trace of himself or his work behind.

"So many books," he says. The living room is full of books, it's true. Fiction A–Z encircles the room on the high shelf the Bog Boys built, and there are four tall bookcases of nonfiction in this room as well. I hope to move some of them out when I have the hallway, the office. I'd like to open up this room a bit.

"My business," I reply. It is my standard response, and probably better than admitting to incurable bibliophilia.

He picks up a book on the coffee table, *A Garden in Tuscany*. "I just finished *Bella Tuscany*," he says.

"Frances Mayes." I respond. It's an automatic response. Title-Author. Like many in the business of bookselling, I am a small catalogue of only occasionally useful information. We "know of" a lot more than we know.

"Did you read it?" he asks me.

"No, I haven't." I admit. "Did you like it?"

"I loved it."

"Well, you might enjoy this one, too. There's some buzz on it already. It's by a new writer," I say, slipping into another bookseller habit: the if-you-liked-this, then-you-might-like-this. "Why don't you take it?"

"Oh, no," he says. " I can buy a copy. I'll write the title down."

"It's not out yet. That's an advance reading copy. You can't buy a copy. Just take that one."

"Oh no, I couldn't take your book."

"Borrow it, then. I get them sometimes. Really, you'd do me a favor by reading it. I won't have time to get to it; maybe you could let me know what you think." With this, I imagine a date, a dinner date. Vito tells me what he has learned about Tuscany, and I sip a crisp white wine. Better yet, the wine is red, and we are in Tuscany. We are seated across from each other at an outdoor table with a view of an Italian hill town. I am wearing a black linen dress. The waiter arrives, refills our glasses; Vito orders in Italian.

Are there hills in Tuscany? I need to get my hands on one of those Frances Mayes books. I reel in my imagination, and set about the business of writing a check. We chat a little longer about books, and I wonder if I will ever see him again. I've given him the perfect opportunity: a borrowed book to return.

"I want to build you a fireplace for that new cottage," he says suddenly.

"I hadn't ever thought about a fireplace there."

"Well, think about it," he says. "I'll make you a really nice one."

"I'm sure you will." He stands. I stand. Thanks are exchanged.

"You've got my number," he says, as he opens the door to leave. "Call me when you are ready to build the fireplace." He smiles; his eyes dance one last dance, and—I am pretty sure—they soften as he says good-bye.

MY HOUSE: *white picket fence and arbor, cedar shakes, yellow shutters. Note the peaceful feeling. The house has no idea the cottage is coming.*

THE COTTAGES: *all in a row, waiting to be adopted. They have been moved from their original locations and rest on blocks, awaiting transport to their new homes.*

THE DAYS OF DIGGING. *Notice the raingear and hats on the men, who are excavating awfully close to the house. Right about now, Egypt is convinced I'm really nuts.*

THE ONLY PART *of the foundation we are able to pour: the first set of concrete footings. The angle of the truck and the length of the chute show why we can't pour the walls.*

HERE, THEY ARE *getting ready to pump concrete into the forms that will make the walls of the foundation. I can barely fit the crane-arm of the pump truck into the frame.*

THERE'S THE COTTAGE *up ahead. We're stuck behind the Isuzu, at least until the driver gets impatient and pulls a U-ie. Then, we're thrilled to have an unobstructed view of the action!*

THE COTTAGE NEARS *the end of its journey: my driveway, where it will rest for the night. All traffic is stopped in both directions, and people are getting out of their cars to watch.*

EGYPT CONDUCTS *one last inspection of the foundation and certifies its readiness.*

THE COTTAGE, *coming in for a landing.*

THE INIMITABLE BOG BOYS: *Tony (left) and Harry (right), removing the sink from the cottage kitchen. (I saved the bar of yellow soap.)*

BACKS AND BUTTS. *I'm not saying who is who.*

THE CAT-IN-CHARGE *checks the scaffolding to be sure it is safe for the guys.*

THE WELCOME DEMISE *of the kitchen wall. This strategy session takes place before the small problem with the big beam.*

THE SPACE BETWEEN *house and cottage that will one day be the hallway. Note the lovely connecting wall of concrete block, still in progress.*

THE HALLWAY, FINISHED: *looking in, from Barbara's extra-wide door. You can see one of the new bedroom windows on the right, and the outdoor lanterns I chose to light the hallway.*

THE HOUSE AND *cottage, happily married. We have taken down the picket fence and the arbor to open up the front yard and to show off that gorgeous deck.*

MY OFFICE, *the right-handed version. By reversing my chair and Harry's handmade desk a few days later, I feel much more comfortable, and in possession of a larger view.*

KATE AND CAT, *looking out the bathroom window of the cottage. Harry snapped this one. Egypt looks impatient to get on with his next inspection.*

progress

THE FOUNDATION WALL is beautiful; the concrete blocks are held together as much by Vito's care and attention as by the perfectly smooth mortar. On our daily cottage walks, Egypt and I survey the wall; he scales it and sits atop, lending the mason's work his official seal of approval. This wall will disappear from view once the hallway and the deck are built, and though I will miss it, I am ready to give up my daily sighting in the name of progress. But alas, there is no sign of progress, no sign of Ed or John. I leave messages for Ed, and receive no return calls. After ten days, I call John. I reach his wife, Margaret, who advises me to page him. John calls back within minutes and informs me that Ed is on vacation. Until mid-September. It is now early August. *Six weeks.*

"John," I say, "I will be very unhappy if I don't move into my office in October." This is a polite understatement. I am unhappy now. The cottage has been in place for more than two months, and still it sits unconnected to the house. The yard is a disaster of sand and stones. I've been patient. In fact, I don't care so much about the October deadline, but only want to feel some movement, some forward momentum, the sense we are going *somewhere.*

John mentions he will be finishing up a roof and a siding job in the next week or so. Depending on weather. The only weather we can depend on this summer is lousy weather. Rain and more rain. "The weather's been killing me this year," John says.

As we lament the bad weather, I realize that on some level, I am a little leery of working with John. Although I have gotten to know him better through the excavation, my real connection is with his father. I know John is smart and full of energy, but I think he is more interested in results than process. This job is a process job. Not to mention that I have always suspected John thinks I am a little crazy to move a cottage, that he thinks it would have been easier to build from scratch. I would much prefer to work with Ed in charge. But I want to get going, and I do not want to wait until mid-September.

"Would it help if I made a list of everything that needs to be done?" I expect John to pooh-pooh the necessity of such a document, but he surprises me.

"That would be great. Can you do that?"

I am pretty sure I can. It seems to me that my mental list is activated with every evening stroll. I see what needs to be done, and I even have a pretty good idea of the order in which I would like it completed. I am thinking that most of all I want some of my yard back, or at least somewhere to walk that is not sand or, alternatively, mud. I figure I can walk outdoors to get indoors for some time to come, but I'd like to walk on something—the deck. I want John to build it before we do everything else. I'd run this idea by Ed months back, on an earth-moving day. He told me he built the deck on his house before they finished the addition. "That way Susan could still enjoy the summer weather," he said. "and it meant we tracked a lot less dirt into the house." This summer's weather hasn't been terribly enjoyable, and I've all but given up on the dirt around me. It doesn't need to be tracked in; it floats in through the windows with every ocean breeze. Still, I want a deck, and as soon as possible. I imagine having friends over, being able to walk from the front to the backyard once more. Not to mention that having a deck around the cottage will certainly make the roofing job easier.

John suggests we meet on Saturday to review the project. In the meantime, I spend three whole evenings with my laptop, creating pages of indoor and outdoor building tasks. For each item, there is a column for estimated time, timing, and date of completion. When I am finished, it is the punch list from hell. But I don't think I have forgotten anything. Thanks to the high estimate I finally got from the plumbing company, I have a pretty detailed list for the next plumber to price for me. While I am at it, I outline the electrical tasks as well. When I reach Stan, he too seems relieved at the prospect of a list. He asks about my progress. "We're starting the building next week," I say, stating my hope rather than what I suspect will be reality. *

＊ AT ELEVEN O'CLOCK on Saturday morning, I am dressed in a camisole tank, low-slung harem pants, and a purple coin belt. I barely hear John's knock at the side door over the sound of oud and naay and Middle Eastern percussion. I feel idiotic and exposed, tugging on my top to cover my belly as I answer the door. This outfit, I think, will not help the already tentative nature of my relationship with Ed's son. What if he thinks I am trying to impress him with my sweaty dancing body?

"Let me turn down the music," I say, and I make a dash for the living room, take off the coin belt, pull up the harem pants to meet the jersey top while I crank down the stereo, then thinking better of it, turn the music off entirely. "I thought you were coming at one," I say, returning to the kitchen. "I don't usually dress like this. I was practicing."

"One?" he says, and I nod. "Oh no." He consults a little card he is carrying. "You're right. I'm supposed to be at another client's right now. Can I use your phone?"

I watch John drive away in a little white Miata. I thank God for small favors; for John's error this time, not mine. Enough dancing for one day. I shower, make myself presentable, and when John returns a little after one, I am appropriately and conservatively attired. We make no reference to the Egyptian dancer who answered the door earlier. I harbor some hope he will take me seriously.

John says no thank you when I offer him a cold drink. I remember back to the days of digging, how John would never say yes to coffee, would drink it only if the coffee appeared before I asked. He never used the bathroom, either. None of the guys did, not in long chilly days of operating Bobcats and drinking coffee. Even though Ed had told me to spread out some old towels inside the front door to catch the mud from their boots, their boots rarely came inside. Most questions were answered across the sill of my office window; no need for Ed or John to come indoors to chat.

I pour John a seltzer when I pour mine. "Just in case," I say, and he smiles.

We go through the list. When I propose we begin the outdoor construction with the deck, he listens, but he just doesn't see doing it first. He tells me the order of the project as he envisions it. "First frame the hallway, then lay the floor joists for the hall. Put in some insulation, then the hallway decking." By this he means the plywood subflooring. "Next frame the roof." John is worried about getting that right, and he knows it will be a challenge to connect the two rooftops.

"I have drawings," I say, rustling through the green binder I have been using for all things cottage.

"Until I'm up there on the roof, we won't really know how it will all work out," he says. He has no interest in the drawings. Part of me understands his thinking, but part of me also believes I know *exactly* how the roof will look. But I cannot build it. John's probably right.

I submit to his judgment on the deck, and we rearrange the list. He looks over the plumbing estimate and agrees it is too high. "Plumbers," is all he says when I ask about any subs he has used recently, but there is a telltale roll of the eyes coupled with an exhalation that tells me to forget using any of those guys. "Ask around some more," he says, "and I will too."

"Thanks for coming over today," I say as he stands to leave.

"No problem. Thanks for making the list. Let's see. I'm not sure yet which day, but I'll see you next week."

"You'll start then?" I ask. I'd been afraid to ask when he could begin.

"We'll start with the hallway," he confirms, a step outside already.

"See you then," I say in my most casual voice, resisting the temptation to jump up and down, to cheer—to dance. *

＊ LESS THAN A WEEK LATER John arrives. He introduces Peter, who will work with him on the project. Peter is John's right-hand man, I learn. Another firefighter, Peter also answers to his nickname, Cappy. While I watch John and Peter together, I am struck by the contrast. John is trim and clean-cut, and he moves quickly. He has a little bit of gray in his black hair, but he keeps it cut so short, you wouldn't notice unless you were sitting across the counter catching secret glimpses while you reviewed a project list. He's somewhere in his thirties, but he could pass for a younger man. He's slight, wiry, and angular in his movements.

Peter, on the other hand, is pleasantly blurred around the edges. He has the kind of looks that don't change much between thirty and fifty-five. I'm guessing he's quite a bit older than John, mostly based on his thinning gray-blonde hair and his manner, but I can't be sure. Who does he remind me of? It bothers me for a few minutes while I watch him walk the wood over to John. Peter ambles, I realize, while John strides. They are a good team; already I can tell by the shorthand conversations and the steady work they do together. Who is it? This is going to drive me crazy. Then I realize—he is Charlie Brown! Charlie Brown all grown up and somewhere in the middle of his life. Although one could argue that Charlie Brown himself is middle-aged.

Peter might not wish to be compared to a cartoon character, but I have a deep appreciation and an abiding respect for the characters created by Charles Schulz. Especially Charlie Brown, who is kindhearted and low-key, and creates peacefulness around him. Still, Snoopy is my favorite, and not only because I got to play him once in *You're a Good Man, Charlie Brown*.

When I was just out of college and cobbling together a living, I wrote greeting cards for Hallmark. Most people don't know that a freelance writer puts the words in their speech balloons when the Peanuts characters appear on a Hallmark card. In those days, you had to type your submissions on little three-by-five cards, giving the greeting card equivalent of stage directions—describing the character, pose, and situation to appear on the front of the card, as well as indicating what words would appear where. If Hallmark picked one of your submissions to publish, you received the handsome sum of $76 per card, and they received the right to put your words in the mouth of the character you indicated—for life. I haven't submitted a card idea in almost twenty years; I imagine it happens electronically these days. But one card of mine—in the "missing you" category, featuring Linus in the pumpkin patch—shows up in card stores every Halloween. I'm thinking Hallmark got their money's worth on that one.

As the men work in the ditch between house and cottage, I receive guests in the living room: Bruce, who notes it is exactly three months to the day since he was last here—on cottage-moving day—and two friends of his, a couple who are in the midst of planning their own building project. They're not bothered at all by the construction noise and the flurry of sawdust drifting in the open space where the full-view window was about three hours ago. As we sit in the living room watching John and Peter, Bruce's friends tell me they have been flummoxed by regulations, expensive septic estimates, and a house design that is not at all what they had in mind. They bemoan the slow and slower response times they have experienced in all facets of their planning.

"This is great, " she says. "You're really moving right along."

It would appear that we are. By the time they arrive, John and Peter are deep into their work and the first bit of framing for the hallway floor is under way. Seated on the couch, my guests have a perfect view through the opening and into the ditch between the two houses where the guys are working. John has set up a sawing station over by the rhododendrons. Peter measures; John cuts and carries the board to his helper. Then he scrambles over Vito's wall and into the ditch, where together they position and attach the supports into place. We speak over the intermittent buzz of John's table saw, the sound of compressors, the hard snap of nail guns.

In the midst of all this activity, it is hard to convince this couple that my project has been stalled out for most of the past three months, to remind myself that it has been eight months since first sight. Still, I persist in telling my story, in an effort to tell them to take heart. I hope they will find encouragement in my experience. Steady progress matters more than speed, I want them to understand. But they remain convinced that I have done something that they have neglected to do, that there must be some key to unlock their own project. When I tell the story of the list, they are sure that is the secret.

"They're here today because of that list."

"Yes, but—" I don't kid myself. The list helped, and yes, I did gather up my impatience and put it to some good effect in these past couple of weeks. But I also believe this project, from the very beginning, has had a life and a life cycle all its own. I think that is true with any project, really. Or maybe— if I get philosophical—about almost anything we do. Which is not to say we can just sit back and wait for life to happen, or even for the astrology to be right. But I do believe that we benefit if we tune in a little more—to our own human rhythms, to the pace of the seasons, the movement of the stars. Push when needed and when helpful, pull back when to push will only frustrate and deter progress. But I can't say this out loud. It makes me sound like some sort of self-proclaimed construction guru, and that I most certainly am not. Here's what I can say, though, and here is what I really believe: The work is beginning now because this is when John can do the work. There is no magic to it. Only luck and good timing. I just happened to push him at the same time he was ready to begin. ✻

✻ OUR LATE-AFTERNOON COTTAGE WALKS take a more direct route. Now Egypt and I can walk out the kitchen door, and instead of a four-foot drop, there is a plywood floor, the beginning of what will one day be the hallway. At the end of the almost-hall, we jump to the ground, walk another ten or twelve feet, and take a right to reach the cottage door. Egypt prefers this route, but sometimes I still take the long way around. Instead of following my lead, he races down the hallway and dives to the ground when he sees me coming around the corner. There is no mistaking the fact that he is showing off. No doubt he pities my stupidity, the fact that I cannot seem to remember there is this new way of getting from house to cottage. In truth, I kind of like going the long way, and I love to meet a kitty in midair.

John and Peter have been here on a regular basis since that first burst of activity last week. They have framed the connecting section between house and cottage, the only completely new construction on this project. The shed roof over that section is framed out too. The plywood decking they put in while Bruce was visiting is protected by blue tarps attached to the exposed roof beams. Farther down the hall, the tarps are anchored on the parallel rooftops. The light travels more slowly through the blue plastic, creating an odd feeling—not quite day and not quite night—in the passageway.

Today, John will tackle the new roofline, bridging house and cottage. Although he has now looked at the drawings that Harry and I have made, John has held to his original position: "We won't really know what we'll do until we're up there, figuring it out." I can tell he is looking forward to this bit of engineering, the challenge of making the gable work visually as well as structurally. He has peeled away the tarps, and he is up there now, calling out measurements to Peter, who is at the saw. Peter cuts as instructed and hands the wood up to John, who works slowly, methodically, section by section, roof beam by roof beam. I watch the progress, the lines of wood across the blue sky. I think of flying buttresses, cathedrals soaring into clouds. My tiny cottage is nothing close to a cathedral, but still this roof inspires awe. I love watching it appear, board by well-placed board.

At noon, John asks me about the skylight. "If you want one, now is the time. I need to plan for it in the framing." I know I'd love a skylight, but I am not sure I can afford one. I suggest I take a trip to the Bargain Box.

"It's worth checking," John agrees. "Otherwise we can pick up one that fits tomorrow." He does not add, "at full price." John encourages me to look for a light that opens, dismisses as mythology that there is any greater propensity of a venting skylight to leak. I set off in search of the perfect, venting skylight. And miraculously, I find it. It is nestled between the twenty or thirty boxes of kitchen cabinets, an entire kitchen that has been returned. Why? I wonder, but I don't spend too much time imagining the circumstances. (I can go against type when I am on the trail of a bargain.) Instead I find the manager to get me a price. $150. A deal. But the width is an eighth of an inch above the max John gave me. They let me use the phone at the desk to call him. I read John the specs.

"Rough opening?" he asks, and I confirm that is what it says on the box. "It will work," he says. "That's a very good price," he adds, and I feel proud of my bargain-hunting prowess, perseverance coupled with sheer good luck.

"Can you fit it in your car?" Not easily, it turns out, but yes. Beach chairs and jumper cables loaded into the back seat, the skylight out of its box and wrapped in towels, the trunk tied down to protect my precious cargo, I take the back roads home. ✳

✳ TONY AND HARRY arrive in separate, matching Volvo station wagons on Saturday morning. Tony's Volvo is several years newer than Harry's, and more pewter gray than silver. It is also a more expensive model, he tells me. He tracked it down just as his Wish Angel said he would, and he is quite proud of it. Tony comes bearing donuts, and there is coffee and conversation before we start the day's work, followed by a tour of the progress. The new roof is framed and covered with plywood now, and the skylight is in place. Two blue tarps protect the exposed wood from rain. Harry looks up at the roof-line. "Huhh," Harry says, a downward inflection. It means he is thinking, taking something in. It is a very Harry sound. After a moment: "It isn't exactly what I pictured."

"But isn't it perfect?"

"Very nice work," he agrees.

Thanks to a window that has been removed, there is now a narrow opening into the cottage from the hallway, which means we no longer need to go outside to get inside again. We slide sideways through it, landing in the cottage living room. There is repainting to do in the yellow room. In my rushed departure to Paris, I'd passed the wrong paint chip to Tony. I returned to Crayola Mellow Yellow, not mellow at all. Buttercup was what I wanted, bright but not so screaming yellow. Tony stayed an extra day when I got home and painted one wall Buttercup. I think the new color will work. I'm a little nervous, though. Yellow is such a difficult color to get right.

"It is a little much," Harry agrees about the three walls that are still the brighter shade.

"Especially in full sun," I tell him. "You know, I didn't realize it right away, but I painted my bedroom this sort of blazing lemon yellow when I was a teenager."

"Really?" Tony asks, "and you remember?"

"It was a hard color to forget, especially against the hot pink shag carpeting."

"Very seventies," Tony says.

"And very fourteen. Do you think the new yellow is okay?" I ask the guys.

"Yes," Harry says. "I even like the old yellow. But I can see where it might be a bit much. And I'd take a pass on the pink shag this time." He grins.

I move back into the office. "I like how it looks from here, the blue wall and the yellow wall in the distance," I say. "And I like to stand in the yellow room and see the yellow shutters on the side windows of the house. It looked great when the primroses were in bloom in the side garden."

Tony leans in to look. "That is nice," he says. "Buttercup?" he says, lifting up the new gallon of paint. I nod. "I'm on it," he says. "I'll put a coat on, then I'll join you guys in the hallway."

We leave Tony to the painting and slip back into the hallway. "What's with this light?" Harry asks, and I point to the tarp covering the skylight.

It's a funny space, this hallway, the blue filtered light and the combination of being both indoors and outdoors at the same time. There is no door yet at the end of the hall, and the section of hallway where the French doors will be is wide open to the elements. On both sides of the hallway, the walls are covered with wooden shingles, red cedar on the house side of the hall, white cedar on the cottage side. The shingles make the hall-way feel narrow and uncomfortable, and disheveled in the way you feel when you really need a haircut. This feeling is reinforced by the asphalt shingles on both roofs, more out-door materials that have found their way inside.

The view outside isn't much better. If you look down the hall-way to the backyard, you see trash barrels and an expanse of dirt where there was once a lawn. If you stand where the French doors will one day open to the deck, the stretch of sandy hillside beneath you is decorated with construction debris, the odd lump of concrete.

As we begin to strip the wooden shingles off the walls, I envision the hallway with the skylight open and lots of knotty pine boards on the walls, doors leading to the deck. It's a bit of a stretch to hold this image as we pry and yank and sweat. At first Harry works with me on the walls. We try working at different levels to stay out of each other's way, and on different sides of the hall. But we keep bumping into each other, sometimes mid-yank. After awhile, we decide it will be better if he works on stripping the roof while I keep working on the walls. He climbs up the ladder on the house side. I work low, peeling shingles from the cottage wall.

One coat complete, Tony joins us, climbs up to the cottage-side roof, begins to strip roofing. "There's two layers over here," he says.

Harry moans. "One layer's bad enough." Tony hands down a sample for me to inspect. Under the layer of light gray are what may be the original shingles; they are brick red. The shingles on my house are the same aged color. I point this out, excited. Another piece of evidence for the "separated at birth" theory of house and cottage, or at the very least, another indication of their innate compatibility. One of the next items on John's agenda is to reroof both house and cottage. He's been after me to select a shingle color, and I've been leaning toward a red roof.

"I've never done a roof in red," John said when I told him. He's done lots of roofing in his construction lifetime, and it worries me a little that none of his customers have requested this color. "It'll be a first," he said.

"Am I making a mistake?" I asked him.

"Not if you know that's what you want." A sensible, non-committal reply. I am pretty sure he thinks I'm nuts to make my roof red.

"When do you need to know?"

"Next week," he told me. That was early this week, and in the past few days, I have observed rooftops as I have never done before. Well, I did stare at rooftops quite a bit when I was thinking how the cottage might be attached to the house, but then I was looking at form, structure. Now I am obsessed with color, contrast. My unscientific survey has revealed that many houses on Cape Cod have pale gray roofing, pretty similar to the shingles Tony is peeling off the cottage side. Some bigger homes have mixed-color shingles, grays and blue-grays, to look like slate. You need a big roof to make that work, I decide. Same with the odd-shaped asphalt designed to look like wood, or wood itself, which is rare in these parts. I notice a lot of newer rooftops sporting light brown-tan shingles, including one just down the street that John sends me to see. I don't mind the color, but I imagine it blending in with the red cedar shakes. If I wanted the roof to disappear, that would be the color to choose. I'm thinking I want the roof to show, to be a feature in the landscape of the house. I see a number of black roofs. Hot, I think, like having a road on top of your head, and don't give those another thought.

In my travels, I don't see another red roof, not one.

Through the years, the original red roof on my house has darkened with age. It is closer now to a burgundy color, and in some places it could pass for almost gray-black flecked with red rather than the reverse. The new roof will be conspicuously red by comparison, close to brick red. The roof slopes down in the front of the house, and is very visible as you approach the front door. When I return from my roof-browsing, I climb the steps and stare at the house, imagining that expanse of red. I come to one certain conclusion: It will look awful with the yellow shutters. If I make the roof red, I may need to restore the shutters to their original deep green, the color they were when Barbara's father painted them. The color of the front door. Will it look too much like Christmas? I think of going with a deep, warm red for the shutters and the door, but then I remember the lifetime exterior finish on the Marvin doors I found at the Bargain Box: hunter green. Back to the Christmas problem. I think of the cardinals at the dark green feeder. Certainly there will be additional greeting card photo ops. But the cedar, the white trim, they will tone down the feeling of red and green. I've come pretty close to deciding that the roof will be red, the shutters green when Tony hands me the shingle from the cottage. That clinches it. The new roof, the roof that marries house and cottage, will be red. Mine will be John's first red roof. ✳

✳ IT'S A HOT DAY for early September, and it is hot work. It is also very messy. I sweep and sweep again, gathering the piles of shingles, wood and asphalt, dumping them into the empty barrels that John left for us. Tony gets another coat onto the walls and begins some gentle demo in the cottage. We need to lose the kitchen counter, under-cabinet, stove, the hot water heater, the kitchen sink, and several panels of wainscoting. There is also a very rough built-in that looks like it might have housed a stereo that needs to be removed. When the light gets low, we quit for the day and eat cake before we go to the beach. Harry and Tony celebrated their birthdays earlier this week; they were born just two days apart. They are tickled by the cake, chocolate with butter-cream frosting and green lettering: HAPPY BIRTHDAY BOG BOYS! I snap a photo as they lean in, side-by-side, cheeks puffed out, poised to make two wishes.

the day of doors

THE DAYS TAKE ON a new rhythm as the summer becomes fall. We rise early, earlier than my hour of coherence. It's hard for me, this early rising, as I have trouble adapting my bedtime to reflect the morning requirements. The man whom I loved on the basis of his voice—did I mention he was a musician?—once said to me, "The best part of being a grown-up is you get to stay up late." When he heard the near-dawn rumble of city garbage trucks, he told me, he knew it was past his bedtime.

Except for that brief period during which I kept something closer to his hours than mine, most nights I am in bed by midnight. Now I am aiming closer to 11:00, even 10:30, and I set the alarm for 6:30. Still I am not ready to face John by 7:00. For exactly one and a half hours after rising, I am a zombie with flyaway hair, sleep in my eyes, and the creases of my pillow imprinted on my left cheek. I relinquish my vanity and my reputation for natural intelligence, and I settle for being awake when John knocks at the front door. He needs my car keys some mornings, and every morning he needs to plug into the outlet underneath one of the living-room windows. I open the door, hand him the keys, leave the door ajar so he can return to get his electricity set up for the day. He laughs at my early morning self and at the fact that it is clearly, truly difficult for me to be up, alert, when he arrives. Sometimes, but not often, John has a question for me, and I must make a decision in my pj's. Generally, though, he learns to wait an hour, until I have showered, shampooed, and made every effort to be in the world again. When Peter arrives at eight, I arrive with him.

Today, Ed shows up a few minutes after Peter. He is ruddy and relaxed and full of stories of his cross-country drive. With him is an older man, Howard. Tall, with strong features, Howard smiles his hello, shakes my hand, but doesn't say much. He's new on the crew. Sometime this summer, Ed spotted Howard mowing a neighbor's lawn. Ed introduced himself, they got to talking, and by the time Howard finished his lawn mowing, he had himself another job.

"You planning to do any work today, Dad?" John is smiling as he approaches.

"Thought we'd work first on freeing up those doors."

"Be good to get to them today while we have four guys."

They are talking about the double doors that will lead to the deck. Doors with a story. After many trips to the Bargain Box in search of the perfect set of French doors, I had come up empty. I decided to go to the full-priced version of the Mid-Cape Home Center to see what they had to offer. I cruised through a variety of doors and windows, mostly Andersen products, not seeing anything I liked enough to pay full price. Then, at the very rear of the department, I found a set of doors that had been pushed apart from the other models— hunter green on the outside and a beautiful natural maple finish on the inside. Elegant brass handles indoors and out, triple-paned glass; the doors opened easily and sealed tightly, quietly. Marvin is an expensive name. These probably cost a fortune, I thought. But they were exactly what I had in mind. Maybe I'll splurge on the doors. It can't hurt to get the price, I reasoned. I walked over to the desk for contractors. Ed had told me to ask for Del.

"Can I help you?" asked the man who told me Del doesn't work on Saturdays.

"Maybe. I'm working with Ed." When I mentioned Ed's name, he nodded in recognition. "I'm wondering about those Marvin doors, the ones at the wayback—green exterior? Do you know anything about them?"

"Well, I know they're a great product, but unfortunately I can't sell them to you. As of today, we are no longer a Marvin dealer."

"You're kidding." Now that I have found my dream doors, I can't buy them? After a moment of disappointment, it occurred to me: "What are you going to do with the display doors? Will you send them to the Bargain Box?"

"Could. Or we might return them."

"Why would you return them if you aren't a Marvin dealer anymore? What would you do with the credit?" My retail training coming through.

"I don't know." He spoke thoughtfully, as though I might have made a good point.

"Well, instead of going to the trouble of shipping them to the manufacturer, or even to the Bargain Box, can you sell them to me—" I paused, smiled, "cheap?"

"Well, it isn't my decision," he said, "but give me your name and number." My heart skipped. "I'll ask my boss on Monday."

I called Ed on my cell phone as soon as I walked out of the store.

"Listen," he said. I've noticed Ed says that a lot. He has a soft speaking voice, and his imperative is more invitation than command. When Ed says, "Listen," it is his prelude to a plan. As he spoke to me, I felt like a happy co-conspirator. "I'll call Del first thing Monday and tell him we're interested in those doors. I'll see what kind of price he'll give us and I'll let you know."

Two days later, Ed left a message on my machine. "Kate, the retail on those doors is $2,800. We can have them for $850, in the display case. I'm assuming you'll want them, so I told Del to set them aside for me. It's a really good deal," he said, as if he needed to convince me of something.

That was right after the cottage landed. The doors have been propped up against the trunks of two old pine trees in my driveway ever since—covered with tarps to protect the indoor portion of the doors from the elements. More than once, I have peeked under the tarps, allowing myself a moment of satisfaction at my good shopping, admiring the doors, stroking the smooth wood before I replace the tarp, tucking it in carefully, protecting my investment. ✳

✳   IT TAKES THE BETTER PART of the morning to liberate the doors from their laminate display housing. Ed and Howard work carefully, so as not to hurt the doors. When the doors are finally free, Ed rounds up John and Peter, who are building the steps down to the basement. Together, the four men lift the doors off the sawhorses and carry them to the side of the house where they will be installed. I stand back with my camera, take some shots: a man on each corner, the doors parallel to the ground. They are very heavy and it is not an easy trip up the hill. On their faces, I can read the strain, the determination. When they reach their destination, they lean the unit against Vito's foundation wall and plan their strategy. After a few minutes, all four men lift the unit up and into the opening. I shoot this picture: the backs and butts of four men wearing tool belts, arms up, as if under arrest, holding the doors in place.

Some adjustments are needed in the opening. They lift the doors down and hold them parallel to the ground once more. In a little dance, John gives up his corner while Ed, Howard, and Peter regroup into a triangular arrangement. Then John scrambles up the wall and into the hallway, positions a ladder inside, climbs up. He goes at the offending edge of the opening with his Sawzall. In my limited experience with this tool so far on this job, it has lived up to its name. I'm thinking I'd like to own one of those Sawzalls. It seems to be the best way out of all sorts of jams. In this case, it takes two trips up the ladder with the Sawzall before the doors fit flush in the opening. John works to secure them while the men hang on. At last, the doors are in place. At last they can let go. They step back, and I step forward; the doors look funny in their unfinished surroundings, especially since they go nowhere until we build the deck. Still, we admire them, all of us feeling satisfied with our roles in the triumph of the best bargain yet. *

* IT IS A DAY OF DOORS. Once the French doors are permanently in place, John and Peter install the basement door while Ed and Howard begin the process of moving my kitchen door to the end of the hallway. It's an odd-sized, extra-wide door, another door with a story. Years ago, when I decided to replace the big window in the kitchen with a door leading to

the just-built patio, I mentioned my plan to Barbara.

"I may have a door," she said. "Let me check the cellar."

The next day she called me up. "Katie," she said, "Why don't you come up and have a look at that door? I can't remember where it came from, but I don't have any need for it. See if you can use it."

I was a little worried when I climbed the hill, afraid to insult Barbara if I didn't like the door. We made our way down her basement stairs and she turned on a light right over the door. It was more window than door, nine large panes over a single bottom panel, and painted green, just like my front door. It was a great old door, and I told Barbara so.

"Well, it is all yours, Katie," she said. "Come and get it when you have some help." Then she shut off the light overhead, and heaved a sigh before we climbed back up the stairs.

A couple of months later, Harry enlisted the assistance of another carpenter friend, and the new kitchen door was installed. The exterior stayed green, and the inside turned a deep wine-red, to match the kitchen. I have a special fondness for this door, partly for its history, partly for its design, and I was hoping to save it. After much measuring and discussion about the arc of such a large door, the challenge of trimming it on the outside, the aesthetic from the inside, Ed and John and I decided just this morning the old door could be relocated to the end of the hall. *

*   IN THE EARLY AFTERNOON, I slip out for an appointment, and when I return, I don't even go inside the house. I

drop my stuff on the Adirondack bench and walk toward the basement. The cellar door is hung, and the windows are in. As I round the corner, John is attaching trim pieces.

"Wow! I say, you guys are really cooking!" I have to say I am loving having all these men focused on one job today—my job.

"Just do me a favor," John says, smiling, "and go see how far my father and Howard have gotten with their door. Let them know we've got the door *and* two windows all done already."

He knows the older men have the more difficult task. John and Peter installed a brand-new prehung door to the basement. Ed and Howard have to build a frame and install a threshold before they can hang the oversize door in its new location.

"Your son asked me to check up on you," I say to Ed.

"Oh did he now?"

"Yes, he says to tell you they have a door and two windows in already. I think he might be giving you a hard time."

"Wouldn't be the first time," Ed says.

"Is this door a real killer?" I ask him.

Ed doesn't answer right away. Howard nods in the direction of the nine-paned top of the door. "We'll have to replace that pane." I notice that one of the lower windowpanes is missing. I don't ask how it happened, but the missing pane answers my question. The door is a killer, but I also know they'll get it right.

"You tell Johnny if he wants to trade jobs, he can have this one," Ed says, and we both laugh. Howard, in his newness, isn't entirely sure of the joke. His smile is hesitant.

"Do you have some cardboard around so we can cover this?" Howard asks. He speaks with a strong accent: "Do ya have some cahhhdboahhhd ahhhrouhhnd so we ken covahhh this?" Despite the dropped r's, his accent doesn't strike me as Massachusetts. Farther north, I think, or, as he would say it, "fahhtheah nowwwth."

"I'm sure I can find some," I tell him. "That door will be great there," I say to no one in particular. Ed is messing with the threshold. Howard leaning in to help. I mean to be encouraging, but they are not listening. I slip away in search of a cardboard box. On my way back to Ed and Howard, John flags me down. He's gluing the old patio slate onto the tops of the pressure-treated boxes to make the cellar stairs.

"What do you think?" He has two steps in place already. They are not what I imagined. "I tried to match 'em up as close as I could," he says.

That's exactly the problem. I'd envisioned steps that blended blues and grays and purples and reds, and he has created steps all of a neutral green-blue. But I'm not sure how to say that politely. I dive in. "Oh, I like them—but I'd imagined the colors mixed."

"Oh," he says. A pause. "I thought you'd want to match 'em up."

"Yeah," I say.

"You want me to take them up?"

I think about it. "No," I say, "let's leave them. We can make the top step with some colors, and make a little landing that blends the colors too."

"You're the boss," he says. "If you want me to take them up—"

"No, let's just use more color on the top step."

Near the end of the day, John finds me. "You're the color person. You tell me how you want that top step."

I lift and position the stones while John watches. Peter is nearby, Howard too, and soon Ed. Everyone watches me with the slate.

"This is just like *This Old House*," Peter says, "except without the budget."

Everyone laughs. I feel good in the middle of things. I don't even mind they are looking—and laughing—at me.

Howard chances a remark. "She has the camera, too."

"Yeah, but what she really needs is a video," Peter says.

"Whaddya think?" I say, stepping back from my arrangement. They all crowd in, and nod.

"I'll glue 'em into place," John says. He steps in, and I step away. The camera is still around my neck so I sneak a shot of all the men, looking down at the slate. Peter and John complete the landing while Ed and Howard clean up for the day.

"Stairs look good," Ed says a little later.

"And the door," John says, "—and the windows?"

Ed smiles. "You want me to pick up stone tomorrow?" he asks John. "I can have 'em load it in my truck. We don't need that much. Bluestone okay?" He asks me.

"Bluestone? Is that the color?"

"Yeah, you have your choice. There's bluestone, which is darker, more blue-gray. Or I can get a lighter gray stone if you like that better."

I'm thinking redstone, but I don't say anything. "It will go at the bottom of the stairs?" I ask him. He nods. The blue will look good with the slate, I decide. "Blue sounds good," I say to Ed.

Ed will pick up stones, Peter some lumber. John will be a little late; he's working at the firehouse all night. Howard will be here first; he'll start stripping the blue boards on the back side of the cottage. Arrangements are complete. There's a pause.

"What a day," I say. "We really got so much done. It was great."

"My first day back," Ed says. "See what happens when I'm on the job?" He smiles at me.

John grins at him. "You think you'll finish that door tomorrow or the next day, Dad?" Ed laughs. Peter and Howard are smiling, too.

I am happy. I am happy with my French doors, and happy with my basement door and windows, happy with my steps, which almost look planned, and happy at the prospect of bluestone tomorrow. I don't even care if it takes Ed and Howard two more days to get that door in perfect place. I am happy, most of all, with the feeling of movement. Four guys again tomorrow, and talk of starting on the roof next week. And the timing seems just right: the cooling days after Labor Day, the start of the new school year, a time of renewal and of preparation too, a time to ready ourselves and our homes for the coming winter, a time to harvest what we have sown: in this case, a tiny cottage planted on a sandy hillside late last May.

birthday deck

THE ROUTINE BECOMES ESTABLISHED. Most mornings, John arrives first, followed by Howard, then Peter, and Ed, usually last. The schedule at the fire station affects attendance on my job. When John works a day shift, only Ed and Howard are here. If John works an overnight, Peter will get things under way before John pulls up and climbs out of his truck, looking beat but determined to get on with his day. He likes to work back-to-back shifts at the station to give himself more time for the construction business, and I cannot say that his work seems to suffer. Just this spring he was recognized as best EMT of the region, and on the building side, he has many return customers. But I worry he will make himself old and weary ahead of his time. "Do you get any sleep?" I ask him one morning after he's just finished up a double.

"We usually get a couple hours on the overnight. Maybe four or five on a good night. It's always better now, after Labor Day." That makes sense, fewer people on the Cape, fewer calls. "They do some crazy things in the summer," John says, letting me know it is not simply quantity of people but their inclination toward mischief that subsides when the tourists depart.

Thanks to John and Peter, I have a new interest and awareness of the fire station in Hyannis. Now when I drive past it on my way downtown, I peer into the parking lot, looking for John's little white Miata. Sometimes I see it, and once or twice, I have spied his big paneled truck, the truck that has been spending many days in my driveway, the truck that a couple of days ago, Egypt inspected thoroughly. I snapped some photos of the cat detective from the rear before he turned around and faced me, annoyed at the intrusion, but willing to pose for a few more shots: silver-gray cat, tail up, gold eyes glowing in the darkness of the truck filled with tools; bumper sticker in the foreground suggesting voters vote Yes to a ballot question that will affect the funds allocated to emergency services.

I find myself thinking about John's day job—which he often performs at night. I wonder about the matter-of-fact way he says, "I won't be here tomorrow. I have to be a fireman." I wonder how it feels, being a fireman. Answering calls that could be a matter of life and death, placing yourself in danger in order to help others. Another member of the band that I play in—an excellent trumpeter—is the head of Emergency Services for the Cape Cod region. The other night at rehearsal, his beeper went off. He apologized for the interruption, saying, "Don't plan on a medical emergency tonight. Cape Cod Hospital is full and now we have to take everyone to Falmouth. If they fill up, we'll be trucking patients off-Cape."

The next morning, when John came into my kitchen, I knew he hadn't had an easy night. In our town, all firefighters are also certified as EMTs, and the fire department responds to all 911 calls. John has explained to me that there is a rotation, that whether you respond to fire alarms or work as an EMT varies shift by shift.

"Heard Cape Cod Hospital filled up last night."

"Yeah, what a nightmare."

I can only imagine the daily courage, stamina, and strength of character that John's job requires. But I am learning something about the kind of men who choose his profession. Now that the red roof is under way, two more colleagues from the station, Eric and Paulie, have joined the crew. Eric is blond and broad-shouldered; he's the youngest man on the job so far. Paulie is quiet and polite, with dark hair and a dark mustache and wire-rimmed glasses. As the roofing crew works overhead, I hear snatches of their conversations. Much of it is related to the task at hand, but especially when Eric is working, I catch some firehouse gossip. He likes to talk more than his coworkers, and the older men are patient with him. They listen, and on occasion, I hear their gentle corrections—both of his work on the roof and of his youthful assessments of their work at the station.

As a consultant, I move from workplace to workplace, always the outsider looking in. I can get a lot accomplished that way, but sometimes I miss that feeling of belonging, the ability to talk shop with a trusted peer. I know my friends with nine-to-five jobs envy me my freedom. Indeed, I do not miss the office politics. But this workplace on my roof. It seems free of petty grievances and corporate intrigues. As the project progresses, I am struck, again and again, by the easy camaraderie of my firefighting builders. They work together, joke together, rely on each other. And that leads me back to thinking of their jobs as firefighters. Any one of these guys trusts any other with his very life. It isn't the sort of bond you forge in just any workplace.

More than one person has told me, "You are lucky with your builders." But I think the truth is we are lucky with our firefighters. I can't figure out if every one of them is a genuine, nice guy who became a fireman, or if they were just average guys who got nicer on the job. In either case, I feel safe and certain when I hear their heavy boots move across the roof and their light voices drift in through my office window.

"Firemen," I say to Harry one day on the phone, "are the last American heroes."

"Huhh," he says. Harry has a full-time job now, doing programming for a financial services company. I'm not sure if he is thinking or just biding time while he works on a computer operation. I dive in anyway.

"Think about it. We don't trust our leaders anymore, not like we used to. Politicians are not heroes. And we aren't at all sure how to feel about the military. We want them to defend us, but we feel uneasy about the whole military thing." I pause, wondering if Harry will require a better definition of "military thing." He says nothing. "The police, it's the same deal. We want them to protect us; we depend on them to catch the crooks, but we sure don't like them when they pull us over for speeding. Not to mention there's that same follow-the-orders kind of aura around them, too. We don't really trust the cops either."

"It's true," Harry says. I guess he's finished whatever he was doing on the computer.

"But firefighters. They don't enforce rules or kill people in the line of duty. They save people's lives. That's their job. Rescue people, animals. Put out fires. Stop heart attacks. I mean, these are men and women who place themselves at risk every day to save the lives of strangers they don't even know."

"So you like having all those firefighters around, working on your house?" Harry has distilled my speech to its essence.

"Yes," I say, "I do." *

*   THIS MORNING, Peter arrives at 7:20 A.M. I hear him moving ladders from the back to the front of the house. Yesterday, it was John who woke us up, around seven in the morning, as he clomped on the roof over the bedroom. Egypt looked at me, made the final determination that I was the craziest human he'd ever known, jumped off the bed, and headed for the door. "Out," he said, "I want out. Now."

Today the wake-up call is a little easier to take. Peter isn't walking on our heads in his boots. Still, Egypt believes it would be best to go out before breakfast just to make sure Peter is doing his job. After ten or twelve minutes of covert operations, the Cat-in-Charge decides it is time to come home to eat; he bangs on the bedroom window, requesting that I lift the screen. While I am making Egypt's breakfast—half a thyroid pill, half an antibiotic pill ground up and sprinkled in Max Cat chicken— Howard appears at the new side doors, the bargain French doors that cause me sinful pride. I unlock the left-hand door to let Howard climb up and into the house.

"All I need is the Tyvek."

"Ah, the mysterious Tyvek," I say, because yesterday afternoon, he and Ed had searched everywhere for it, never thinking to look in the hall. Perhaps because it is not yet a hall.

"The worst thing is," Howard says, "I think it was me who put it here." I like him even more for this small admission.

Howard is, I would guess, in his late sixties or early seventies, possibly older. His work is slow and steady, and he is a perfect partner to Ed. Now that I have watched the dynamics of this building crew for awhile, I have learned not only that Ed and Howard can be trusted with the small details, but that John has a good sense about who should do what on any given project. He knows his father and Howard won't cringe when I say I want to save boards, move a window, or reuse a door. My recycling makes sense to them, and they don't mind small jobs.

John, on the other hand, much happier with a big job to do, issues a warning whenever I say I want to reuse something: "Whatever you save, you're gonna end up spending on labor." He says "laybah."

I've learned to stand firm with John on my recycling impulses. Last week, we moved a cottage window from the section of wall that will be removed to make the opening to my office. "It has to go," I told John. "And a window in the eastern corner of my office will give me morning light and a view of the holly tree from my desk." John agreed an east-facing window was a good idea, but suggested a new unit would be easier to install. "The window I want in that spot is the old window, the window that matches all these other windows," I told him.

John smiled, shrugged, and put Ed and Howard on the case.

Today Ed and Howard are applying the Tyvek to the formerly blue-planked section of the cottage, in preparation for a coat of red cedar shingles. And you can bet we saved every blue board. Howard and Ed and I are sure they will come in handy along the way. They are pine tongue and groove, and in perfect shape on the side that isn't blue.

When I go outside to say good morning, Ed asks if he can come in to use the phone. "Better get a building inspector over here," he says to me. "Time to start talking to them about that deck." Ed reaches voicemail, gives my address, and asks the inspector to stop by, have a look at the deck—or the imagined deck, to be more precise, the deck we hope to build.

I have always envisioned a deck providing the outdoor connection between house and cottage. On the plan we submitted to the town, we drew a twelve-by-twelve square. But now that the cottage is in place and the hillside is reassembled, it's clear that the deck not only needs to be as wide as the cottage—sixteen feet—but also to wrap around the cottage, providing access to the backyard. I figure we're good with the Conservation order so long as we don't extend beyond the boundaries of the cottage, but how do we handle the wraparound walkway? In that Conservation deals in land, and intrusions into the earth, I have informed Ed and John that the walkway needs to float. We need to use airspace rather than groundspace to support it.

Ed invites me to move outside to have a look. We move through the opening in the kitchen wall where the door used to be and out into the hallway. It is enclosed now and the double doors are in place, but it is unfinished: vertical stud walls, plywood floors, sheets of pink Styrofoam between the exposed roof beams.

To get to ground level outside, we must climb down a pallet base that leans at an angle against the French doors. I've mastered using the slats to come up and into the hallway, but I am still nervous going down. I tend to sit and scrabble down on my butt. Ed, even with his bad knees, makes it down easily and reaches his hand out to me. I am brave; I take his hand and descend standing up this time. This it what happens when you spend enough time on a construction site. I am becoming *machisma!*

We move down the hill to the front corner of the cottage, the edge of what will be the main deck and the beginning of the wraparound section. We plan to cantilever the walkway around the cottage, and that seems pretty straightforward. With a four-foot walkway, we need an eight-foot supporting board, running under the cottage.

"The support will probably need to be a 2 by 10," Ed says, "and what you have here are 2-by-6 floor joists. It means we'll have to cut out a section of the 2 by 10 to get around the sill."

I'm pleased that I am following him. He is saying that the boards that support the walkway will be too thick to fit through the opening between the cottage and its foundation, that he will need to trim down the supporting board, notch it out. "On either side of the sill, we'll have the full ten inches, right?" I ask him. Seems sound to me, but I guess we need the building inspector to tell us for sure.

"He may want 2 by 12's," John says. He's come up behind us to join the deck discussion.

"It can work the same way, can't it?" I ask, and he nods. We move on to figuring out how the walkway will connect to the main deck; we need to determine where we will place the step that will connect the upper deck to the walkaround deck. The step is moved several times, and for at least a few minutes, it resides on the main deck. I like the elegance of it there until I realize just how much of the main deck will be eaten up by a single stair and a landing. We decide to let the deck turn the corner at the upper level, then step down for the walkway. We play with it some more until we are sure we all understand the concept, John drawing a plan with his forefinger in the dirt, me modifying his plan in the air. Finally, we have it. We think we have covered all the bases. We are ready for the building inspector, hoping that he will not require a supporting pillar at either end, hoping that our deck can float, as I imagined, in the air. If the deck can't float, it will mean another trip to Conservation, probably another hearing, and definitely another delay. And it also means the aesthetic won't be as clean. Now when I see the deck, I see it free of pillars, a long balcony in front of the cottage. A balcony I can enjoy by stepping out the full-view door to my office.

"Problem is these are twenty on center," John says as we step into the basement to imagine the internal support system. Oh, he is taxing my newfound knowledge now. At the start of this project, I learned what "on center" meant. But what is he saying now? I look for visual cues, and realize he is talking about the floor joists again. But I don't piece it all together until he says, "And we need to be sixteen on center. We'll have to shoot inside and outside of every one."

Ah—I get it. The deck supports will run side by side with the floor joists, a 2 by 12 on the inside and then on the outside of each joist. "How many?" I ask.

"Every three feet," he answers. I had no idea it would take so much to support this small walkaround deck I have dreamed up. I see the ceiling of my basement filling up with boards, working boards, and I like the image. *

*   A FEW MORNINGS LATER, we have the go-ahead from the building inspector, and John tells me it's time to make some decisions about decking materials. I'd already told him that I didn't want to use pressure-treated lumber. There is a lot of deck, and it will be very visible. I knew I would be bugged forever if I went with that green-cast chemical-infused lumber. Plus, it splinters. I'd end up having to seal it once or twice a year. The same with white cedar, it turns out. I wasn't thrilled with the idea of having a working relationship with my deck. I wanted the deck to be a place of pleasure, of relaxation. I did not want to be sitting on the deck thinking always of the next deck-related task to be done.

"I'd like red cedar," I tell John. In the spring, I'd seen some cheap at the Bargain Box, a brand name that Harry said was very good. He'd remembered it from his woodworking days in Westchester County. It would match my red cedar shingles. I've always liked the fact that my shingles are red rather than white cedar. The red have a larger reveal, and they weather a dark gray-brown rather than a feathery light gray. And when they are new, as they are on the section that frames the doors to the deck, they are a beautiful pale brown with a distinct reddish glow. Unfortunately, the red cedar decking at the Bargain Box is long gone.

We discover through a series of phone calls that red cedar isn't used for decks on Cape Cod. It's too soft, according to one lumberyard. Would white cedar be any harder? And why would all those wealthy homeowners in Westchester County want softwood decks? Too soft didn't sound like the real reason, but red cedar decking was an outrageously expensive special-order item at all the lumberyards John called. "More expensive than mahogany." He laid down the results of his research on the counter for my viewing.

"Hmmm," I say. "White cedar is an option, but I really don't want to have to seal it every six months."

"I tell you, if you want maintenance-free, you should really consider Trex."

Trex. The name had come up before. As I understood it, it was a plastic decking, made of recycled materials, and required no maintenance. I liked the thought of reusing old trash rather than creating new wood waste. But I wasn't sure a huge expanse of plastic decking connecting my very wooden cottages would work.

"Go see some," John advises, and he gives me directions to a house where he built a deck last year. "We used one product on that deck," he says, "but there are others. See what Shepley has, and look at the white cedar and the mahogany. See what you like best." Shepley's is a lumberyard usually open only to contractors, but where John assures me they'll allow me a look around. The fact that this plastic stuff is actually more expensive than mahogany is only a small issue at this point. We always pay more for recycled and organic, and as the chorus of men assures me, I'll save on maintenance. ✳

✳   AT SHEPLEY'S, I tell the guard at the gate I am here on my contractor's orders, and he waves me in. I make my way inside a huge barn of wood and eventually locate white cedar decking. I find some mahogany on my own, too, though it is not the wider, 5/4-inch boards that John has specified. A worker spots me, asks if I need help, and dutifully, I ask if they have the recycled product on hand.

"Oh yeah, we have some. It's outside." He leads me out back. I follow silently, thinking maybe it doesn't all look as bad as the stuff I just saw. Not only did I find it unattractive, but the deck I saw was shedding gray slivers, which did not strike me as a maintenance-free feature. I'd be sweeping it compulsively if it were on my deck. Which would be torture in itself because the stuff feels fundamentally all wrong beneath your feet. But John told me the product they used on that deck had been discontinued. Maybe they have an improved product now. It's important to keep an open mind.

"Here we are," states my guide, as he motions to the pile ahead of us.

The pile of plastic decking in front of me looks even less appealing. "It is sooo ugly!" I say, before I realize he may have a deckful of the stuff at home.

"It's awful," he agrees, wrinkling his nose in distaste. "You know they make it out of recycled garbage bags or something." He's a little vague on the origins, and it's clear he doesn't want to bone up on the subject. "It looks it, doesn't it?"

"God, yes," I agree, relieved to find someone who shares my disdain, if not my guilt over my inability to embrace the stuff for the sake of the environment, the rain forests—probably even the right whale would be happier if we all had Trex decks. "I mean—it's a great idea but why can't they make it look better? Why is it this awful rubber gray color? It looks like car tires."

"They might make it out of car tires, now that you mention it. Though it comes in a sort of tan color too."

"Does it look any better?"

"No." He smiles.

"Ugh," I say. "You know I just saw a whole deck done in this stuff," I tell him.

"Really? How'd it look?"

"Horrible. Absolutely horrible," I tell him.

He nods; of course it would. "Can you show me the 5/4 mahogany?" I ask, as we move toward the barn.

"Now, mahogany," he says. "*That's* a deck." ✳

✳ THE YOUNG MAN who delivers the mahogany is alone in his truck. He asks me where I want the bundles of red wood boards, and I direct him to the side yard. They should be as close as possible to their destination, the deck, and not too far from the sawing station the guys have been setting up by the rhododendrons. He's careful with his delivery, making sure that he doesn't lay the boards directly on the ground. He scouts around for some scraps of wood, and makes a little bed for the mahogany. Then he hoists it, bundle by bundle, off the back of the truck, onto his right shoulder. I stand by; he has politely refused my offer of help.

I think of the deliveries I have had these past couple of months—stones for the walls John has built, red shingles for the roof, bundles of insulation, and wood, so much wood. And not to forget the beautiful, outrageously heavy French doors, in their display housing. Ed said it took seven guys to load them into the truck at Mid-Cape. Heavy. Awkward. Two guys delivered them, but they'd called ahead, and Ed was there to meet the truck. I helped with the unloading, holding up a corner. Still, Jimmy did the bulk of the work. He was big, huge next to his tiny and aging partner, Bob. Jimmy reminded me of a sumo wrestler. He looked like someone who could pick up a piano and pitch it if he felt like it. But he was genial, joking, hardly a grunt. It wasn't until we got the doors positioned between two tree trunks that Ed and Bob began swapping stories of their heart attacks. It's something guys do, I've learned. Still, I found their timing a little disconcerting.

My favorite deliveries are the crane trucks. Have I always harbored a special fondness for cranes, or has it come from watching the cottage landing? Or the concrete pumped up the hill and then down into the concrete forms to make the foundation walls? I'm not sure, but I love it when the big deliveries come from the Mid-Cape Home Center and Drywall Masonry. The driver pulls alongside the hay bale fence, climbs out of one cab and into another. Then he lifts my delivery up, up, and over the fence. He extends the arm a bit and places the pallet halfway between the fence and the house. I don't know why this fascinates me, but somewhere in the mix is my respect for the deep-thinking, practical minds that figured all this out. Forklifts, cranes, pump trucks.

Now when I hear that beep-beeping that signals a large vehicle backing up, I run outside to see who is coming down my driveway. Sometimes the beeps are not for me—heating oil for one neighbor, a load of mulch for another—and I laugh at my own disappointment. Still, my interest does not begin and end at my cottage doorstep. I notice heavy equipment and big trucks wherever I go now. When I see a Lawrence Ready Mix truck traveling off-Cape one day, I feel as though I have spotted an old friend. I wonder where he is headed, if he has a full load—and if he has already delivered his concrete—whether they were able to pour, or whether they had to pump. Then there is my heightened interest in the Big Dig, the giant traffic rerouting that is in its who-knows-how-manyieth year in Boston. I've always been awed by the scope of the project, but now I count the cranes. So many dot the skyline that you can never count them all unless you are in a giant traffic snarl. Forty-seven, I managed once when someone else was driving. Yellow, red, gray, blue.

Color is another aspect in my infatuation with heavy equipment. The little mini-excavator: yellow with a bright red fire extinguisher attached to its cab. The Bobcat: orange and white and black. The crane that lifted the house: red as a fire engine, and at least as big. The concrete mixers with the red-striped lighthouses and blue skies that twirl round and round.

I realize this fascination means I have a lot in common with the three-year-old boys who sleep with their trucks, but I can't kick it. It isn't as though I missed something growing up as a girl. For a good chunk of years, my best friend was my next-door neighbor, Bobby, and in terms of toys, my early childhood was equal opportunity. I possessed Matchbox cars and Little

Kiddle dolls in equal numbers. Perhaps it is the very fact that I have played with trucks that makes this equipment so appealing. Or maybe it is my respect for the ingenious functions packed into the cool designs and blunt colors of cranes and tractors and cement mixers. Or maybe three-year-old boys have an appreciation for the earth-moving world that we grown-ups lack.

Today's delivery is low-key and personal, and the truck is ordinary, white with a dark green logo. It isn't that he couldn't have used a crane to save his shoulder, but this young man was hired for strength, and he is using every ounce of it as he hauls, then carefully deposits each bundle. We talk as he moves between truck and side yard. He asks about the cottage and I tell him the story, that it was moved here, that it was lifted by a big crane. "Cool," he says. When he finishes his work, he looks up at it, and takes in the skeleton of the deck. "It will be a nice deck," he says, and I agree. I try to tip him, because he has worked hard, and I have noticed Ed or John occasionally tipping deliverymen. But he refuses. "That's what they pay me for," he says, and he climbs into the cab and gives a wave as he pulls away.   ✳

✳   I DO CONTEMPLATE my role in deforestation of the planet as I watch the men laying down the decking. I wonder if the conservation effort of moving a cottage cancels out my ecologically incorrect choice of mahogany or whether the reverse is true. If I am not entirely comfortable with my choice from an environmental point of view, I am certain that I have made the correct aesthetic choice. The mahogany looks exactly right next to the red cedar.

Today is my birthday. I've given myself the day off, and am happy to observe the progress of what feels like the perfect birthday present. I realize as I think about my choice—my expensive choice—that I might have settled for white cedar if I'd made the decision a few months ago. But all grown up or not, I still feel a sense of entitlement when my birthday rolls around. I allow myself small luxuries in early October every year. I treat myself in some way or another on my self-declared day off. If the weather is good, I take a long walk on the beach, letting the gratitude for another year, the pleasure of Cape Cod, the sheer luckiness of my life mingle with the slight melancholy that birthdays carry. This year, my luxury, my treat, is not small. It is this gorgeous deck of hard red wood, silver nails glinting as the sun moves around the house. I dread the bill that will come at the end of this month, but today I almost let myself believe it is a gift.

I watch the men moving quickly, efficiently. John and Eric hammering down the decking, Ed at the saw, Peter ferrying the planks to John. They are using stainless steel nails, a must with mahogany, John tells me—a little pricey, but otherwise rust can leach into the wood. The planks are butted up tight against each other, no space between them. John and I made that decision earlier this week. "It will feel more like a room, almost like a wood floor," John said. "The disadvantage is that you'll have to shovel it if we get a really heavy snow, and you may get puddles in the rain."

We'd purposely matched the deck to the floor level of the house, rather than the cottage. Step out the double doors, and you need not step down. I want the deck to feel like an extension of the kitchen. He told me the planks will shrink a bit over time anyway—less shoveling. In the same conversation we resolved the problem that the pressure-treated underbeams present.

"I don't want to see them," I said to John.

"We can dress 'em with cedar." To dress, in this case, means to cover the offending beams with a cedar board. Another handy construction term for my growing glossary. He showed me how it would look, holding up a plank. Perfect. Nothing like a well-dressed deck. *

*   AT THE END OF EACH DAY, the men gather around John's truck to review the day's progress over a beer. I observe this ritual, and am intrigued that much of the conversation is about their work; it strikes me how happy they seem to talk about what they have accomplished, to consider what they will do tomorrow or the next day they'll be on the job. Sometimes the conversation drifts to the station house, or to a recent softball game, but mostly they speak of what they have accomplished today, and what they will do tomorrow. For this reason, I am not entirely excluded from the end-of-day gathering, though I do try to give them their privacy. Still, when I am invited to stand around the back of John's truck, I feel as though I have been admitted to a very special club. I am not a beer drinker, but I drink in their conversation, their humor. We laugh and chat and then as soon as they have each finished one beer, they are on their way.

I invite the men to have their end-of-the-day beer today on the first section of decking they have laid, and they accept the invitation. After all, it is my birthday. Eric toasts me and jokes that tonight, when my friends arrive, I can have my first legal drink on my brand-new deck. He's been teasing me all day about my age, trying perhaps to guess it, but I do not reveal that I am exactly twice the legal drinking age. Instead I tell the story of being carded, just this summer, in a Chinese restaurant. I hadn't a clue what the waiter wanted as he kept saying, "ID? ID?" When I finally produced my driver's license, I tell them, the waiter squinted to make sure he was reading the date correctly. Then he handed it back to me as if it were made of hazardous materials. "So sorry, so sorry!" he said. No problem, I wanted to assure him. You made my day, my week, my year. But before I could say a word, he had rushed off to the bar to get the glass of white wine he'd almost refused me.

The guys laugh and nurse their drinks. We admire the view, their excellent work, and the conversation turns back to the project. Tomorrow, the kitchen wall comes down, John reminds me. I'll have to clear out the cabinet tonight, be prepared to move the fax machine, relocate the phone. John outlines the plan for tomorrow; he and Peter will pick up lumber in the morning—cedar for the dressing, and the giant beam we'll need to hold up the ceiling once we open up the wall. Ed and Howard will start early in the kitchen, taking out the window, exposing the studs. Everyone else will be on the deck until it's time to put the new beam in place. I'm thrilled to be working from home again tomorrow; it sounds like another action-packed day. We appreciate the deck in silence for a few more minutes as the conversation winds down. The sun sinks low in the western sky; the beers are finished, and we are done for the day.

opening up

TODAY, THE LAST WALL between the houses will fall.
Already the kitchen window is gone, and the spice rack that
Harry and Tony built me a few years ago is on its way out.
Next, the kitchen cabinet I unloaded last night; then, piece by
piece, the wall. John and Ed had an extended discussion this
morning about how to hold up the ceiling before the new
"header" is in place. I followed most of it. Essentially we need
to keep the house standing while almost fourteen feet of structural wall comes down. "Lolly columns," Ed says, and pleased,
I add another word to the magical new language I am learning.
It seems we will have pillars in the kitchen and a temporary
suspension system between roof and ceiling. I don't fully
understand how it will all work, but I decide to just wait and
see. John and Ed seem tense this morning; we are all a little
nervous about this important opening. I do my best imitation
of an affirmative, manly grunt when John asks me if I am okay
with the plan. I have learned this year that there are times to
ask detailed questions and times to grunt; it's clear to me this
is a grunting moment.

Ed and Howard are working indoors, one on either side of the
diminishing kitchen wall. "Easier on the old guys," John says
jokingly about his dad's indoor location, but in truth this is
the tougher project today. Paulie, John, Peter, and Eric are at
work on the walkaround section of the deck, while Ed and
Howard mastermind the "demo." It is apparent to me that

Howard enjoys demolition, smiling in at me from the hallway as he saws through a section of wall and unveils another stretch of studs. I don't know how they feel about me staring at them like this, taking the occasional photograph, but Ed and Howard are patient, jovial souls. Even if they wish I were elsewhere, they put up with me. Still, midmorning, when I have to run out for a haircut, I suspect they are not sad to see me disappear for an hour. "Will I make it back in time to see the beam go in?" I ask, and they assure me I will see it. I dare not ask them to delay on my account, but it is exactly what I hope they might do if I run late.

I take another look at the beam on my way out. It is stretched across the bench on the deck. It's a huge, gargantuan thing, six inches deep and ten inches high, made of composite lumber, scraps of wood all glued together. "It's stronger that way," Peter assures me, sensing I might be worried. It does look strong, though it isn't very attractive, this glued-together wood. But in its heft, the beam is beautiful to me. It makes me feel safe, secure, certain that my roof will stay up. I want everyone to see it. I imagine visitors marveling at the span and scope of such a structural member, and for a moment consider leaving it exposed. But the impulse leaves me as I imagine it hanging, its dark patchworked nakedness imposing in the kitchen. Touching the beam, I pause for a moment, and say a little prayer of thanks to all the trees mixed up inside that timber. I step down the untrimmed stairs, marveling at the miracle of the emerging deck, and I am on my way.

When I come back, I enter through the front door, sensing commotion in the hallway. My hair is shorter and redder than it was when I left, but no one mentions it. They are too busy struggling with the header. As I enter the kitchen, I take in the lolly columns: poles with boards atop them and cloths atop the boards to protect the ceiling. They are stationed in front of the sink, and the men are in the hallway. I have arrived just as they are hauling the beam from the deck to the kitchen. It takes four of them to lift it—Ed, Howard, John, and Paulie. They maneuver it carefully through the doors, executing a sideways turn into the hallway.

"Okay," John says. "Now." Their movement is synchronized, a slow-motion choreography of forward march, stretch, and lift. They push the timber up, up into place. Their faces are red with effort. I think about heart attacks happening when men have their hands over their heads, and push that thought away. Have to get this on film. I snap a photo; they lift, maneuver, lift and hold. In the glare of the flash, we all realize: It doesn't fit.

"Too long," John says. The words come out in an exhalation.

"No," says Ed, patient. "It fits. We just need to get it into place."

"Too long," John repeats. He is sounding exasperated. "Who measured it?" He knows his father and Howard did.

"Who cut it?" asks Ed in turn, smiling at me. From his grin, I know that his son was at the saw.

"Let's take it down and take a half-inch off of it," says John. But no one moves.

"It will fit," says Ed.

"Here's the problem," says Paulie, who is at one end. "There's a tiny jog right here, about halfway up. If we can just get past this, it will go right into place."

"Cut off half an inch," says John; his voice is starting to strain. His face is at least as red as his father's now.

"A half-inch!" says Ed. Clearly this strikes him as a dramatic measure; yet he is yielding on the issue of shoving the beam into place.

"Paulie," John says, "can we angle around that jog or is this beam too long?"

"Too long," Paulie says.

"Thank *you*," says John. In silence, the four men ease the beam down, angle it out the doorway.

"You'd never make it as a framer," John says to Ed after they have deposited their load back onto the bench.

"But it's wide by maybe an eighth of an inch, tops. A half—"

"A half will make sure we can get it the hell up there this time. This is rough carpentry. It isn't a problem."

Ed shrugs and John has his way. But I can see the tiny, invisible gap bothers Ed. If he had his druthers, he would eliminate the one-sixteenth inch of wall that is in the way, and then lift the perfectly measured, accurately cut beam into place. John's right; that half-inch will not matter, not in practice. But in principle, Ed's old-world carpentry ethics have been compromised.

They are in the kitchen again, and the tension is palpable as they lift the beam into place for the second time. It glides right into position. John smiles. Quickly, they begin securing the beam. I snap photos in time with the nail gun. In minutes, the beam is holding the weight of the roof, the ceiling, the house.

The men are standing, looking up at their work. They are silent. Then Peter walks in. "Hey, that looks great," he says, his comment as easy as a sunny day. He is oblivious to the drama.

"Go back outside if you know what's good for you," Paulie warns. "It's thick in here."

Peter shrugs, "Really opens up the kitchen," he says to no one in particular as he goes back out the double doors.

Paulie smiles first. Then Ed. Finally, John, looking right at his Dad. Howard grins too, the newest guy on the crew taking his cue from the others.

"I love it," I say.

"But who was right?" Ed asks. "Did it fit? Or not?" He knows I had the best vantage point.

"Paulie was right," I say. "There was a tiny jog. If you could have gotten past it, the beam would have fit, so you were right. But John was right to make a second cut, because you'd have had to tear up the wall otherwise. So you are both right. You're a good team."

John rolls his eyes at my obvious, though truthful, diplomacy. But Ed soaks it in: "We are a good team, aren't we?" He winks at me as John slides past him, moving outdoors where the air is cooler and where a sixteenth of an inch carries much less significance. *

*   STAN THE ELECTRICIAN shows up in the afternoon to work on some wiring. He's impressed with the new look of the kitchen. "Great view," he says to me. "What a difference."

Neither Ed nor Howard volunteers any information about the events of the morning, and I follow their lead. "I love it," I say for the second time in a day.

I met Stan about twelve years ago as a young homeowner in need of a new furnace. He came to hook up the thermostat. He looks a lot like Neptune, with longish blond hair and an even longer blond beard. The Neptune image is only reinforced by his surfing habit. I haven't seen him emerge from the sea, but I can imagine it without difficulty, surfboard as triton, wet suit as godly regalia. He lived in California for a long time, and that shows in the aviator sunglasses he wears and the laid-back approach he takes to life and work. It isn't that he doesn't work hard, or that he doesn't do an excellent job. He's just hard to track down sometimes, and it's hard to pin him down once you reach him. Getting him over to estimate the project took several phone calls. But when he's on the job, Stan is smart, capable, and an excellent problem solver. Just what we need for this quirky little project.

With his West Coast roots and his golden Santa beard, Stan isn't exactly one of the guys. On the first day, he was working outside with his ladder set up by the electrical connection to the main house. He hauled a wooden box onto a plank below him that became his base of operations. When he opened up the box, there was a stereo inside, tuned to the local all-folk station. I wondered how this would go over with John's crew, who were working on the skeleton of the deck. I've learned something of their musical tastes. Peter prefers easy listening while he is working. John and Eric listen to the rock station when Peter isn't on the job. Ed requires no music at all, while Howard is a whistler who plays whatever comes to mind.

What happened next was interesting. The men noticed the music, but more, they noticed the box Stan had built to house his music. "Great idea," John said, coming over to inspect the unit.

"Yeah. It keeps the boom box from getting banged up with all the moving, especially when it's in the back of my truck—which isn't always real well organized." Stan smiled.

Peter came over, touched the handle of the box. "We ought to make one of these," he said to John.

"Pretty basic building," Stan offered. "Is the music okay?"

"It's great," John said before he returned to the deck.

In the days that follow, Stan is indoors and out, joking and laughing with every member of the crew. Everybody likes him. They respect his work, but they also like his easy manner, the way he connects personally with every guy on the job. He is welcomed into the fold. I think the guys are doing their best to welcome the plumbing crew, too, but they are keeping to themselves so far.

"Who's their boss?" Ed asked me yesterday, referring to the two apprentice plumbers who have been installing almond baseboard in the cottage all week.

"A guy named Kevin. He came recommended by a friend." The friend is Katrina, who vouched for Kevin's honesty. He had done some work around Katrina's house, had started his own business after working for several years for the company that gave me the original estimate, the one I hoped to cut in half.

"Haven't," John said, when I asked if he'd heard of the plumber. "But that's a good thing."

Stan said much the same thing. "Plumbers," the same downward inflection John had used, the word itself almost a sigh. Stan smiled. "I know one good one, but he's all the way in Sandwich and he's way booked up. I haven't heard anything bad about this guy. Can't hurt to call."

Kevin arrived a few days after my call in a lime green van decorated with pipes on an overhead rack. He moved quickly as I walked him through the house and cottage, and he asked the right questions. Did I know where the gas line came in, where the water hookup was? This seemed promising, as did his attire: a T-shirt and jeans. The other guy did the estimate in a white shirt and tie, dress slacks. Mr. Dress Slacks had done lots of measuring for baseboard heat, but showed no curiosity about where the heat might come from, or where it was now, and he barely glanced at the cottage bathroom, assuming (incorrectly) that I would want all new fixtures, all new plumbing. I showed Kevin the little back hall where the furnace and the hot water heater reside, asked about moving the furnace to the new basement. I showed him the cottage bathroom and the hot water heater in the cottage kitchen and asked about moving that as well.

He looked critically at the hot water heater in the cottage. "Doubt this even works," he said.

"People were living in this place just a few months ago. I'm sure they had hot water."

"It's old," he said. "It isn't worth moving. The thing to do is get a new one, bigger, put it downstairs. Get rid of both of the ones you have." I wondered how much money he would make on a big new hot water heater.

"I was thinking I'd keep one on each side." I'd thought about this, inspired by the hot water arrangement at the place I stay in Paris, where there are separate water heaters in the kitchen and in the bathroom. During a plumbing crisis two trips ago, I was able to take hot baths even when the heat wasn't working, and when there was not a drop of hot water in the kitchen. This struck me as a very practical arrangement.

"No point. You only need one. One good-sized unit."

"The one on the house side is new, still on warranty."

"Yeah, but it's way too small. Fifty-gallon. You need a bigger tank for two bathrooms so you don't run out of hot water. Don't know why they even gave you that one new," he said, enjoying the chance to deprecate his former employer. "I never put in a unit that small. Or hardly ever. Maybe for some old lady living alone." He paused.

I looked at him. Kevin is tallish and very thin. His dark hair is cut close to his head. He has a sprinkling of freckles, barely there, across his *Family Circus* nose. He looks fifteen. Maybe seventeen. I felt like an old lady next to him. Or at the very least, I felt on the verge of becoming an old lady, an old lady who lives alone and only needs a fifty-gallon tank. "Price it both ways," I said. "Same with the furnace. Give me an estimate for leaving it in place and plumbing everything over here, and an estimate for moving it to the cottage basement, plumbing everything over there. And tell me if it would be cheaper to just heat the cottage separately on a completely separate boiler."

We moved back to the little closet again, where he studied the boiler. He approved of it, said it would handle the increased load no problem. "No reason to make a separate system unless you plan to rent it out separately or something. That would add a few thousand to the price. Best thing is to use this, and move it over there. It isn't that big a deal to move. You'd be without heat, probably for a day. That's all."

His outlook intrigued me. It was the opposite of the feedback I got from the well-dressed estimator, who seemed to think moving the boiler was indeed a big, expensive deal. I asked a couple of questions, which Kevin didn't really answer. I noticed that he didn't look at me straight on when he spoke, that his eyes were always cast slightly to the side—shyness? He also rushed me, lacking the patience of Ed or John or Stan, or their ability to imagine I may know what I am doing. I got the sense that even if he hadn't classified me as a fifty-gallon old-lady customer, he had labeled me as "lady." "Oh— you don't need to know that," he said in answer to one question I asked after he told me to call the gas company. "It's just terminology."

Oh, but I do need to know, I wanted to say to him. All the words are mine to learn. But I let it pass. I remembered Hayden's skepticism when we began working together. I figured it would be another case of having to prove my worth as a consultant on my own project.

If I had my doubts about the child-plumber (Katrina swears he's in his thirties), I felt good about his estimate, which was much lower than the first quote. When I had followed up with the owner, he almost admitted it was padded. "It's that crawl space," he said. "You never know what we'll run into under there. We gotta plan for that." He wasn't willing to shave anything off the quote, and what's more, he wanted half up front.

The biggest problem with plumbers, according to John, is that they just don't show up. I knew the original company was reliable, would show up as scheduled, but I wasn't sure how much that was worth. I called Kevin and said it was a go. A few days later, he came by and I gave him a check for $1,500 for materials. He hadn't asked for any cash up front, but I figured it might get things rolling. I felt pretty good when, a few days after that, Kevin appeared with two assistants. They unloaded a lot of almond-colored baseboard from his van and stacked it up in the basement. Then Kevin disappeared, and has not been heard from since.

In his place, there are two men who show up at odd hours and stay for indeterminate lengths of time before they disappear as they arrived, unannounced and unexplained. In the past couple of days, I have taken to following them around and asking them what they are doing. Today, I also ask one of the guys when I can expect to see them tomorrow.

"It all depends on Kevin." That, I have learned, is a standard response to many of the questions I have asked. "He's the boss." Somehow this is of little comfort to me. The next day, I call the boss, inquire when he might stop by to check on the work of his assistants.

"Lyle's okay." That is Kevin's response when I tell him I'm not feeling very confident in the crew. I would agree that Lyle is the more competent of the two men, and he is certainly more verbal. I note that Kevin supplies not even this half-hearted defense of the unnamed guy with the glazed expression who follows Lyle around on his mysterious errands, a man I like even less because he had the chutzpah to light a cigarette when he was working in my basement.

"When can I expect to see you?" I ask Kevin. "I'd really like to have you check what's going on here."

"Soon. Got a lot of no-heat calls. This early cold snap. Everyone's turning on their heat. You know?" It doesn't occur to me to tell him that I have no heat in the cottage either; now that everything is opened up, it is damn cold in the house. I'm wearing four layers of clothing as I speak to him on the phone. "They're fine with the baseboards. Don't worry."

He cedes nothing to me on the phone, and I hang up frustrated. I curse myself for giving him money up front. Now I'm stuck with him and his motley crew at least until my $1,500 runs out.

The day after I finally speak to Kevin, Okay-Lyle shows up with a new sidekick. Smaller and neater, he projects an air of—what?—not exactly confidence. Determination? After watching him for half a morning, I know what it is—compulsion. Or am I jumping to conclusions based on the latex surgical gloves he never removes? Like his predecessor, he leaves the talking to Lyle, and I can't help but notice Lyle is doing more of it recently. He makes little jokes and grins at me. I notice, too, that he looks at me for several seconds longer than necessary in every interaction, and I feel acutely and uncomfortably aware of my gender in his presence.

"New Jeff," Stan says to me after they have left for the day. The plumbing surrogates have been dubbed Mutt and Jeff by the rest of the guys, who do not approve of their lack of supervision.

"Yeah," I say. "I guess he's an improvement. He can solder." The new guy had spent most of his day in the hole between house and cottage. John had left one plywood four-by-four section of the hallway floor unattached so that the plumbing and electrical connections could be made there.

"The gloves are a little weird, though," Stan says. We laugh, and I feel grateful for Stan's easy presence.

"You know, I don't know about Lyle, either. I think he means well, and he seems to know what he's doing, but—uh—it's the way he looks at me sometimes."

"What are you saying?" Stan's tone is serious now.

"I don't know. It's hard to explain. But I feel vulnerable having these guys in the house, uncomfortable in a way that I haven't felt with anyone else on the project."

"Okay," Stan says.

It's just one word, but I hear reassurance in it. And I am not disappointed. On Monday morning, Howard pulls me aside. "They never get here until ten or ten-thirty at the earliest. So I'm gonna take out this shower stall right now, and dump it out front. When they get here, I'll tell them you and your boyfriend pulled it out over the weekend, and they need to take it away."

And just like that I have a boyfriend. He lives in Boston and he comes down on weekends and some weeknights. And just like that Stan starts arriving with the late shift and staying until the plumbing crew departs. And now when Lyle makes his little jokes, I feel stronger. I learn a little about his life, which includes an ex of unclear marital status, a school-age son, and an abiding interest in playing pool. Bolstered by Stan and Howard, I realize that Lyle is a nice enough guy, and probably lonely and unable to express himself well around women.

Lyle outlasts his neatly gloved partner, and for many days, he is the lone representative of the plumbing team. I grow used to him, and he grows used to my questions, which he answers more directly now, without referring me to his disappeared supervisor. As he moves from installing the baseboards to replumbing the cottage bathroom, I realize Lyle's okay, just like his boss told me he was. But it isn't simple to befriend a man who looks at you a certain way. I feel guilty, gender-bound, and confused. I try to be not only nice, but also kind to the almost-plumber. Still, I place the counter between us when he comes into the kitchen to say so long for the day. ✳

✳ "HOW MANY MEN TODAY?" Katrina asks me.

"Nine," I say proudly, ignoring her double entendre. We have reached the peak of activity: six builders, one electrician, two plumbers all at work on the project. I love the progress and the process, the questions, the conversations, the decisions. My bookstore-making background has primed me for this house-marrying project. As I work with my clients in California and Maine to create their spaces, I contemplate the compromises I don't need to make on my own project. I am the design team. I am the owner. I have freedom, and direct access to the contractors I have hired. I don't often have that on my work projects. On some assignments—the bookstore in Maine, for example—I do have a sense of collaboration, but even in that case, I am collaborating with other conceptualizers. Here, I can huddle with Ed or John or Stan—or recently, Lyle—and come to a decision that works, both in concept and in building reality. How can I not enjoy myself?

I assess our progress. The deck is nearly complete, wrapping all the way around the cottage, enclosed with mahogany verticals beneath a wide flat mahogany rail. Soon John will be moving inside to work on the ceiling for the hallway. "Do you have time to talk about it now?" he asks me when I run into him on the final stretch of deck. We move inside, and with my hands, I sketch what I want to do with the ceiling in the hallway. I want to follow the beautiful rooflines that John has made. On the house side, I want to follow the plane of the once-exterior wall, extending it upward in a straight line to the new roof. That's no problem. My vision for the cottage side of the hallway is more complex.

"I want it open on this side," I try to explain. "Jutting into the old cottage roof."

"How far in?" He climbs up the ladder.

I locate the wall based on the new roof's rafters.

"We'll have to cut into the old roof beams."

"Is that a problem?"

John doesn't say anything. He's thinking. "So you want a knee wall right here?"

Knee wall. I like that expression. "Yeah, maybe with doors to get into that attic?"

He smiles at me. We are both beginning to understand that in conversations like this, we add layers of complication as we go. "Doors."

Ed has come up behind us. "Two doors on either side. That would look nice. Good access too, as long as you have a ladder."

John looks down at his dad. "Who invited you?" He knows he's overruled. He's not sure about this plan of mine to follow the roofline, but he's willing to figure it out. He and Ed talk about whether to cut into the original rafters.

"Do you mind seeing them?" Ed asks me. "We can take off the sheathing and leave the roof beams intact. I think that's best."

I'm trying to visualize the roof beams now, beneath the de-shingled roof. "You know, I don't think the roof beams will bother me at all. They'll hardly show from this angle."

"That's right," says Ed. "They'll just be like dividers on this shelf we'll be making. You can put books up there and use the beams like bookends to hold them up." He's right to figure I always need more space for books, but I am pretty sure I won't shelve them up there.

"I can dress them, too," John says, "if you decide you don't like the way they look."

"You want light up in that attic?" Stan.

"Can I have it?"

"You surely can. I'll even give you a switch for it so you don't have to try to find a string in the dark."

Stan, Ed, John, and I stare at the old roof, some recalcitrant shingles still attached. I don't know if they see what I see, but I'm convinced it will be perfect when we're done.

"Maybe we should talk about those back steps," Ed says, interrupting my reverie. "You want me to call Vito?"

Vito. I can't stop the butterfly from lighting on my heart. Vito's taken, I've found out in the interim. In a big way. Married. With children. I found out one afternoon in September, when John called him from my kitchen. He wanted to use Vito's account at the masonry supplier to charge some interlocking stone for a retaining wall in the hillside. I stood nearby as he dialed. "Amy?" he said.

Amy? I heard. Oh no.

"Vito home yet?"

Home. Oh no.

As John joked with Amy, I felt my hopes deflate. No Italian hill towns. No dinner, no wine, no Vito charming the waiters with his perfectly accented Italian. It wasn't that I ever believed in my fantasy, but I hadn't entirely given up on the idea that maybe I'd see Vito again and we would talk about that book I'd loaned him. That maybe—*Amy.*

I crossed the kitchen, picked up a phone book. Flipped to the M's. There they were, Robert and Amy. Married. Why hadn't I thought to check before? *Idiot, Kate.*

Vito. Call Vito. Do I want Ed to call Vito? Ed is smiling

through the pause. I am pretty sure he knows I had a crush on Vito. Ed's perceptive, and I bet every woman who meets Vito ends up with a crush on him. Poor Vito. *Poor Amy!*

"You know," I say, wondering how many beats have passed while I was occupied with my review of crush and crash of crush, "I don't think I can afford the steps right now. Can we wait till spring?"

"Well, you might wanna check with him before you decide for sure." For a moment, I think he means Vito, but when I follow Ed's glance, I see Egypt has come to sit just behind me. As the construction has progressed, the Cat-in-Charge has taken his title even more seriously. The cat who still runs from the house at the very sight of a vacuum cleaner is now completely calm in the face of compressor motors, nail guns, electric saws. Even as the weather grows cooler, he insists on at least daily inspections. He's investigated John's truck inside and out, scented Stan's boom box cabinet with a swipe of his head, and walked the scaffolding in the front of the cottage. As more of the work moves indoors, he likes sprawling out on the kitchen floor to keep an eye on the guys. Stan calls him the Pharaoh, and Egypt rewards Stan for his show of respect by paying even closer attention to his work.

"Okay to wait on the steps?" I ask Egypt as I lean down to give him a rub behind the ears. Egypt doesn't answer, or maybe he does. He turns tail and heads toward the doors to the deck.

"Hey, it's the Pharaoh. On your way out?" Stan asks him. "Just a sec." And in the manner of any good subject, he puts down his tools to open the door for the King.

Watching Egypt depart, I realize my answer to Katrina's question this morning was incomplete. Eight men on the job, I should have told her—plus one woman, and one Cat-In-Charge, in charge of us all.

finish work

WHILE THE COTTAGE was waiting to be adopted, no one thought to turn off the water. No heat, one good cold snap, and all the pipes burst. We find this out only when we try to send water through them, creating a small-scale flood in the bathroom and basement below. It is not my favorite day on the job. I'd hoped to slap a coat of paint in the bathroom and call it a day. Fix it up later, over time. But now that I need to replace the plumbing, it makes sense to replace the hideous, uncleanable shower stall, the faucets that don't turn off all the way, and the toilet, which is ancient and leaky at the base. And why not tile the floor with the eighteen dollars' worth of pale blue and cream ceramic tiles I found at the Bargain Box? I'm saving the porcelain sink, though. It isn't beautiful, and I haven't been able to remove all the green copper stains, but it is original. Same with the medicine cabinet, which, though rusty, sports an etched mirror and a little slot inside for disposal of razor blades. Whenever I open the cabinet door, I wonder where those forty or fifty years of razor blades are now.

This bathroom renovation, unplanned, is not in whatever is left of a budget. I'm more than a little worried about the money. The equity line is all used up, and I have been using those checks that the credit card companies routinely send in the mail. The interest rates are low for six months, and I figure I will refinance the house by the time they rise, but the monthly payments are a little daunting in the meantime. I sit down with paper and pen and invoices and estimates and attempt to come up with a financial plan. When I opted for mahogany decking, I knew I was entering a whole new realm of cash requirements, but I hadn't counted on spending $2,000 on the cottage bathroom, or sending another $2,500 to Hayden Building Movers.

Mr. Hayden had told me—even before we almost lost the cottage to the bog—that he'd underestimated the challenge of the site. On the day of liftoff, I'd forked over another $1,500, bringing the total paid to $3,000. "Take me awhile to figure it all," Hayden had said when I gave him the check, "but this covers my costs anyway." When I didn't get a bill in June or July or August, I wondered if he'd decided we were settled for the amount of his original estimate, or if he was still figuring. My answer arrived at the end of August, when I received a detailed bill for a total of $5,500.00. Balance due: $2,500. I thought about calling, protesting, and then thought of his growly machine. I wrote him instead. I told him that I understood the difficulties of the site, that I remain impressed and grateful for his excellent work. I also told him I was stunned by the final bill, by how far out of his original $3,000 ballpark we had landed.

"Therefore, it is with the utmost respect, and appreciation of your work and your word that I propose we settle this bill for $4,500," I wrote. "If you can live with this compromise, I would greatly appreciate it. If you cannot, I will live with your decision, and will be able to pay you the balance at the end of October." I wondered, as I reread the letter, how a man might handle this situation—write, call, let it go? Did Hayden assume I wouldn't question him—because I was a woman? I thought about how our relationship had begun: He was Mr. Hayden and I was Kate. And I remembered his mentioning he'd have his "girl" type up my bill. Was there gender bias buried in this balance due? As an independent contractor myself, I know some jobs just turn out to be bigger and take longer than you expect. You end up charging more than planned. I was sympathetic to that possibility in this case. Certainly, Hayden hadn't planned on extra men—and trucks—to save the cottage from the bog. But this was such a large discrepancy. I sighed, unsure if I was being paranoid, or merely smart to protest. I enclosed a check for $1,500, sealed the envelope, and hoped for the best. A week went by, then two before the call came.

"Bob Hayden," he said when I answered.

"Hi. You got my note."

"Look, this is what I ask people. Is there a quarrel with the work?"

I realized he was asking me. "No quarrel at all. Like I said in the letter, I appreciate all your work—"

"No quarrel with the quality of the work?"

"None."

"It got done."

"Yes."

"Satisfied?"

"Very. You guys were great."

"Need to pay me, then."

"Okay. I said in the letter I'd abide by your decision."

"If you're short on cash, pay me when you can. This month, next month, by the end of the year. I don't care when, but I need it all. That's what the work cost."

"Fine. I just wasn't prepared for this bill, hadn't planned on it being so much more than the original estimate. Everything else is adding up, too."

"I knew when you started this thing you were in way over your head."

I decide not to bristle, because I want to accept his offer of a payment plan. In the pause, he changes tone. "How's it going?"

"Well, it *is* costing me more than I planned. But it looks great. You'll have to come by sometime and see it when it's all done."

"Got some pictures of your move. I can drop 'em by."

"That would be great." Another awkward pause. "Are all the cottages moved now?" I venture.

"Oh yeah. Done. Lady had a hell of a time with the Historic people on that last one."

"Was her move as dramatic as mine?"

"Oh, nothing like yours. Short ride. Did it all mechanically. Easy site, no crane. Could never have done yours mechanically. Hill was way too steep."

"Tell me about the steep hill." I was thinking of the failed concrete attempts. "Hey, I saw that old house on East Main Street getting set up to be moved. Is that your project?"

"No, some off-Cape outfit. They sent out for bids. Guarantee you they won't make any money on that move. Just as glad it isn't me."

I noticed we had circled back to the issue of paying Mr. Hayden what he is worth. "It's a huge house," I offered.

"Three stories."

"Will they have to cut it up?"

"Oh no, it's just going across the street. Can get it that far in one piece."

"You're kidding—across the street? Why?"

"Yeah, next time you go by, look down that driveway behind that other big Victorian; you'll see the new foundation. They're putting in a heart center where the house sits now."

"No wires in the way then?"

"Plenty of wires just to get that far. Electric, telephone. Bet on one big traffic jam that morning. Not a long move, but it's complicated with a house that size."

"I'd like to see it." Moving my cottage has piqued my interest in all house-movings. I have a fantasy of bringing all the cottage-movers together for a roving picnic, each of us showing off our relocated cottages. I find myself checking out the Move of the Month on buildingmovers.com.

"Watch the paper," he advised. "They'll announce it." Another pause in which I realized this was the longest call I'd ever had with Mr. Hayden. Despite the awkward origins of the conversation, I found myself enjoying our telephone small talk.

Mr. Hayden, I suspect, is more complex than his shorthand sentences—which, I have noticed, are replete with subjects and verbs when he isn't in a hurry, inspecting a job site, or calling out instructions to his crew. There's no Hollywood romance here, but I think there is a fondness between us. Even though I questioned his bill, I respect and admire his work, and I am pretty sure he knows that. And if it weren't for Mr. Hayden, there would be no cottage addition. I am grateful, and I am willing to pay, and I am also willing to trust his judgment. Still, I am not unhappy that I wrote the letter about the bill. Funny thing is, I don't think he is either. ✳

✳ I'VE TYPED ALL THE INSTRUCTIONS about Egypt's meds, the phone numbers of John and Ed, a neighbor, my mother. I've recorded a message on my office line saying I am away for the week, and I am more or less ready to depart with Katrina for dance camp. Except I'd rather stay home, watch the walls and ceiling appear. Before we reach the highway, I feel nostalgic for what I will not see unfold. In my mind, it is nothing short of miraculous, this progressing project. That word, *miraculous*—it keeps coming up. From the day of the cottage-moving to the day of liftoff—and again and again, as I have watched the building process. I know miracle is not the right word for what is conceived in imagination and created in our human reality. When it is written down, we call it fiction; when we see it in a gallery, we call it art; what we can hear, we call music. I think about how much creativity it takes just to get through an average day, producing no tangible, earth-moving results. It strikes me that we are very limited in what we describe as imaginative.

Aren't there a million different kinds of imagination? I can walk into an empty bay in an unfinished shopping center, stare at the concrete floor and metal studs and various HVAC-related items dangling from an exposed ceiling, and imagine a bookstore. To create that reality, I need to be able to communicate that vision so that others—men like Ed and John and Peter and Howard—can build it. They need to see it too, to imagine it in three dimensions, to consider details and implications that are beyond what I can visualize. I think of Ed, gently steering me away from a bad design decision, or of John asking me what I think about an idea he has. What do you call this? Shared vision, collective imagining, standing in a sandpit, drawing pictures in the air, seeing a deck? Then making it—that is what I admire most of all. I think of John and Ed, their crew, Stan, and lately, Kevin and Lyle, men with vision linked to skill, men who make something from nothing every day of their lives. A day's work to them, something like a miracle to me. Maybe we need a special name for the kinds of miracles mere humans perform.

While I am away, Sandy is taking care of Egypt and the house. She is a Jungian psychotherapist and a colleague of Katrina's. Tiny and blonde, she wears little tortoiseshell glasses and speaks with a Texas accent, using words like Honey and Girlfriend in the way that only a Southerner can do with authority. Sandy's gestures are large, like her home state, her enthusiasm contagious. When I met her—just last week— she told me about herself, her work, her recent move to New England, and her book project. As she spoke, I felt sure I could trust her with my kitty and my house-in-progress.

On my second day away, I checked in, and Sandy reported on

the progress. "You have walls in the hallway, and you almost have a ceiling now. It looks great. You're gonna love it when you get home."

She was right. The hallway is gorgeous. The wood is warm; the angles are dramatic; the combination of horizontal and vertical lines is perfect. I've chosen tongue-and-groove pine to cover the walls and ceiling. The lower boards are wider, with the groove running up and down. At the point where the roof used to begin, the boards run side to side, with a smaller interval between the grooves. The plywood floor looks like hell, and the holes in the cottage wall need attention, but the hallway is gorgeous. I think back to the late summer, remembering the roof appearing beam by beam, my feeling that my ceiling touched the sky. Now November is closing in, and the light is changing seasons. The sky is steel blue, but the ceiling still soars toward it, unafraid to touch the coming cold. John is pleased and Ed is ready to leave for Florida again. "I'll be back around Christmas," he says to me. "We'll probably finish up a few odds and ends then."

Indeed, we are down to the odds and ends. The big John-jobs are done. "I gotta work on a roof before the weather gets really cold. But on the rainy days, I'll be here. Change out that bedroom window, make the closet you want in the bathroom. All the small stuff. And the floor, when the boards come in. Howard will finish the painting meanwhile." John's referring to my most recent list: Painting Tasks, Interior and Exterior. We'd talked it over and decided Howard was the man for the job. There's just too much on the list for Tony to do it, especially now that he has a full-time job. Howard has already painted the ceilings in the cottage; his work is careful, neat, thoughtful.

We decide he'll start with the exterior painting, which must be done before the weather turns even colder. Howard begins work on the cottage windows, which require reglazing. I did a round of reglazing when I first bought the house; it came out fat and wormy. Even as I gained on-the-job training, my capacity to make the glazing smooth and unobtrusive did not improve. A few years later, when Harry and Tony painted the trim, they redid my work, most of which was cracked and missing already, a consequence of weather and lack of storm windows—and the horrible mess I'd made of it the first time.

Howard knows exactly how to glaze a windowpane. I watch him with the putty knife and the glazing compound, and wonder how he makes it look so easy. I've noticed that his hands sometimes shake with age, yet his touch is steady, sure. His strips of glazing compound are smooth and just wide enough to do the job. Watching Howard, I tell him about my bad job, confessing that the glazing was actually visible from the inside, that it was wider than the wooden mullions. He laughs, but does not share his secrets. I am grateful for his age and the experience he brings to this job. New windows do not require glazing, and I imagine that Howard's will soon be a lost art. I think of John, who has declared his open hostility to painting. I cannot imagine him mustering the patience for this painstaking work.

Howard has all the patience, and all the time in the world. After he completes the glazing, he suggests a coat of oil-based exterior paint to protect his work, followed by the latex I've chosen. I'm not a fan of petroleum-based products, but he convinces me that this is the good old-fashioned way, that the glazing and window trim will hold up much longer in the face of the elements. "You're in charge," I say after some discussion, and he sends me to the hardware store to pick up what he wants.

We settle into a routine. Howard arrives every morning promptly at eight. He'd come earlier, he says, but he doesn't want to get caught in the hospital traffic when he crosses Hyannis. I am glad for this logistical slow-down. Those seven o'clock mornings with John have taken their toll. By eight, I am up, showered, presentable. I'm usually in the kitchen making breakfast when he arrives. Egypt is out on patrol, and the side door is unlocked. Howard taps twice, lightly, on the French doors, and lets himself in.

"Good mowhning!" His voice is loud enough to rouse me if I am not in the immediate vicinity. He has a true Yankee accent, and I love hearing his dropped *r*'s and extended *ohh*'s. He sings his morning greeting more than he says it, and I find myself answering in kind. "Good morning, Howard," I reply, a five-note response to his musical call. ✳

✳   IT IS QUIETER NOW. There are no more compressors or nail guns, no radios, only the sound of Howard whistling between brush strokes. I miss the activity, and I consider how strange it will feel to live alone again, to live without the project that has absorbed me for so many months, to live without a crew of men around the house. I'm glad that Howard is here for awhile longer. I'm glad that there are still decisions to make, paint colors to mix. I am not ready to become a woman without a project.

Stan is still finishing up—installing the smoke alarms and the light fixtures in the hallway. They are outdoor lights, weathered copper with little panes of glass. I have chosen them as a tribute to the once-exterior walls that now enclose the hallway. I want to create a visual reminder of the outdoors coming in, the two houses becoming one. I selected two more fixtures with the same finish, one to replace the fixture over what was once the kitchen sink in the cottage, and one for over my kitchen sink, where I've never had quite enough light.

Stan and Howard are an unlikely pair, but it is clear they enjoy each other. Stan always gives Howard a full-voiced good-morning and Howard smiles a big, broad smile whenever Stan turns up. Last week, Howard asked Stan about plastic molding to cover wires, wanting to know where he could find some that he could paint to match his daughter's living room. She wants to cover up the stereo wires, and, Howard tells Stan, her husband is hopeless when it comes to even the most minor home improvements. Very smart and a good provider of course, but hopeless with a hammer and nails. Howard has mentioned his daughter's husband to me before. Though I can tell that it puzzles him that the younger man would rather hire out than learn how to do a job himself—I think it disturbs his inclination toward thriftiness—I suspect Howard likes coming to his daughter's rescue in the area of home repair.

Stan knew exactly what Howard was looking for, and he arrived the next day with more than enough wire molding, for which he would not let Howard pay him a penny. This small favor sealed the bond between the two men. "Are we expecting Stan today?" Howard asks me, and I can tell he hopes for his company. *

✶   I HAVE HEAT NOW, and hot water. I followed Kevin's recommendation to get a bigger tank on the hot water heater. With one hundred gallons of warming water, and my soon-to-be-installed second shower, two people will be able to shower at the same time. The fact that Kevin mentions this as a selling point reassures me he doesn't view me as one of those fifty-gallon old ladies—not yet, anyway—and gives me hope that I may not grow into one.

After the hot water tank was installed and the pipes were laid, the furnace was moved from kitchen closet to cottage basement without incident. Maybe because the weather was colder, or perhaps because I was uncomfortable following the plumbing crew into the confines of my back hall closet, I didn't watch the move with the same deep curiosity that I have brought to many of the other aspects of this project. I provided a garden hose so they could drain the boiler, and I took a few shots of the shiny debris they tossed into the yard as they worked in the cramped back hall: nuts and bolts and tubes and pipes and screwdrivers and odd bits of wire. I also got a shot of the relocated boiler connected to an array of gleaming copper pipes in the new basement: a labyrinth of indoor waterways, some carrying hot water up to the new cottage baseboards and over to the not-yet-installed shower and the ancient sink, others moving warmth across the basement, through a hole that once held an orange cottage-landing strap, traveling under the hallway and over to the house.

I'm grateful for the heat, especially when I am sitting at my desk, and I think Howard is glad for it, too. It helps his paint dry, and it means he doesn't have to wear so many layers when he's working inside. As Howard stains and paints and sands and spackles, I begin clearing space and moving furniture in the living room. Much earlier in the process, Erika sent me an e-mail: "I dreamed about your house last night. It was beautiful. It felt so spacious and full of light." I am determined to create exactly that reality. I start with the books, sifting through, boxing up what I don't need to own. I go through paperwork that I have tucked away in odd places. I clean. I clear. I breathe. I've finished up both of my big consulting projects and I can focus on the house, claiming my space and my winter place. It feels good.

In the stark December light, I contemplate my increased wall space. I dig out unframed prints I've had buried in closets for years, and I make several trips to the frame shop. I know the framing will add a few hundred dollars to the mounting total for this project, but I have resolved to stop worrying about the money. I'll end the year with no spare cash on hand, and a lot of bills to pay, but I will also end the year with a new home. It will cost almost twice our back-of-envelope estimates, but my banker assures me adding on has doubled the value of my house. That means in terms of equity, I've made a significant net gain. And more important, it means it's more likely they will approve a new mortgage to pay off all my construction debts.   ∗

∗   ONE RAINY MORNING, John shows up. Howard spots the white truck out the bathroom window at the same moment I hear the familiar beep-beep-beep. "Is that John?" Howard asks me, excitement in his voice.

"I think it is. He said he'd be here on a rainy day." There is a thrill in my voice, too. We're like two kids, which I guess puts John in the odd position of favorite uncle. You know, the one who stirs things up—who tosses the babies up in the air, who lets you order a double-dipped even if it's before dinner, the uncle who likes the same radio station you do, who takes you to your first PG movie.

Peter's truck pulls up behind John's. Two of them, I think. We'll get a lot done. And we do. They stay late into the evening, hauling out my bedroom window and replacing it with two windows that Peter has donated to the cause. The window we installed in the cottage bathroom came from Peter, too. "You should see his place," John said to me once. "He has so much stuff! Don't know how he finds anything, but he does!" I imagine a basement filled with discarded windows, doors, shutters, doorknobs. A couple of sheds out back, all filled up too, according to John. I can relate. I've been saving windows and doors and all manner of things on this project myself. If I were on a different job every day, the temptation would be great to take home the castoffs. In the meantime, I am glad for Peter's hoarding tendencies, which have brought me the two four-over-fours that will grace my bedroom wall.

John's plan for today didn't include this installation. But when they finished installing the fir flooring where the cottage sink and stove used to be, and were all done building the bathroom closet, it was only three o'clock. John decided to yank out the old window while he had Peter on hand to help. Once they got it out, they were all revved up, even though it was quitting time. With no discussion, they made the new opening for the second window and framed and fitted both new windows into place. They look great from the hallway, where I have been documenting the process with my camera. We all move to the other side, into my bedroom, to get the full effect.

Oh.

God, they look awful. This is a case where what I imagined and what I am right now staring at are not the same. I don't say anything. Could I have made such a really horrible design decision? I stay quiet, because I don't want John to know I think the chocolate-paned windows look like hell.

"They need a windowsill," John says. "I was thinking one long sill. Maybe a little deeper than your standard sill, so it would be more like a shelf."

"Yes, that sounds good." A sill, I realize, will make a huge difference, and so will trim, and most of all, a few coats of paint. I think more than anything, the dull brown of the mullions against the peach on the bedroom walls looks like hell.

"I'll come back tomorrow and trim it all out. And I'll do the trim on these other windows too, if you want." My bedroom windows suffer from clamshell molding—a mistake I made as a younger homeowner. I want to change it to the simple flat pine that matches the rest of the house and cottage.   *

*   HOWARD RECYCLES the piece of drywall we removed to insert the second window, using it to fill in the space left when we took out the original longer window. It takes a lot of joint compound and paint, but it's better than tearing down all the wallboard and starting from scratch. It looks okay—not great, but passable—by the time he is through. The windows,

on the other hand—joined by a single sill, trimmed out and painted in Coconut Milk white—the windows do look great. John has rounded both ends of the sill ever so slightly, a perfect touch. I stare at the two windows, joined by a single white sill, and think back to my hopeful New Year's wishing. Wishing for a cottage, wishing for a man. Hoping the man would come if I made room for him.

Two old windows, not looking their best, a wall twice-broken to accept them, reinforced to support them. New paint and a pathway built between them. Some trim to enclose them, and a good washing. I push my bed against the patched wall under the windows and contemplate the intimation of Bedroom Future. The one that will not have my desk staring at me when I lean up against the new headboard the Bog Boys have made for me. Egypt joins me. I reach for him and give him a pat as I lie back. Up through the windows, I see the new pine boards of the hall ceiling and a patch of sky. I kneel to take in another view. Across the hall is the tiny French-style window over what used to be the cottage kitchen sink—both panes swung open, deep blue against the bare wood walls of the hallway; beyond that, the office-to-be, empty now, the floors refinished, gleaming. I stand to see beyond that—the full-view door to the floating deck; and beyond that, the treetops of the bog. I move my fingers across the smoothness of the sill before I join Egypt again on the bed. This is a version of exactly what I want: a connection with a view, a union that invites light.

moving in

OFFICE-MOVING DAY is set for December 17. Tony and Harry are coming to help.

Howard and I have already moved the Bond—a huge oak kitchen cabinet from the early 1900s, the British equivalent of an American Hoosier. The unit is about six feet tall and four feet wide. Designed to store all manner of pantry items, the Bond features a white enamel fold-down counter ideal for rolling out piecrusts, but it lacks the built-in flour-sifter that some Hoosier cabinets have. That's just as well, because I use every inch of available storage space in my Bond to hold office supplies, files, and reference materials. I bought it several years ago, and it was delivered by a husband-and-wife team, he American, she British. I'd given directions replete with land-marks, including my standard, "Slow down when you see the Blessed Virgin Mother."

When they arrived with the Bond, they told me the story. "I missed the turn," he said. A common enough error. It's some-times hard to see Mary in the dark, especially if she isn't lighted up. The Catholics are erratic in their attention to the BVM. She's down the hill from the church itself, and perhaps the priests don't have occasion to drive by Mary that often. They don't notice when the spotlight burns out, leaving her blasphemously in the dark. I cannot explain how much this annoys me, more than for the sheerly practical reason of losing a directional landmark. I consider the Virgin's presence a benediction of sorts, and not just because I am a long-lapsed Catholic. I am equal opportunity when it comes to blessings, saints, and masters. Just a stone's throw away from Mother Mary is a large statue of Buddha. He sits high, in the middle of a brook, on another part of the property originally willed to the Catholic archdiocese, and subsequently sold off to fund the building of the church. I've always wondered what the priests had to say about Buddha when they discovered him, large and content, the water flowing around him. I take it as a sign of their respect that Buddha remains, though now he is on private property. A bit of a shame. Still, taken together, the Buddha and Mother Mary are a very strong spiritual team. I like living nearby.

The Bond-delivering wife interrupted my silent reverie on the neighborhood saints. "We saw the statue of Mary, but he didn't think we'd gone far enough."

"It didn't seem like we'd driven that far, and I didn't remember seeing the general store you mentioned," he put in on his own behalf.

"He keeps driving until I say, that must have been it. But he is sure we haven't gone far enough. 'For God's sake,' I say to him, 'how many bloody Virgin Mothers do you think there are in this town?'"

I couldn't help laughing at her exasperation and conceded she had an excellent point. He just shrugged and asked me where I wanted them to place the Bond. In the bedroom, I told him, on this side—the side of my bedroom that has been my office for the past five or six years. For the five or six years before that, my office was on the other side of my bedroom. I've rearranged more than you'd expect given my limited options, always attempting to make the office feel a little farther away.

This weekend, we'll move the office out of the house entirely, and into the cottage. This is the moment I have been waiting for, the reason for all the chaos of the past six months. The cottage is ready; the office is lovely, the walls, blue above and Kate and Howard's custom-blended stain on the wood below. The floors have lightened with refinishing. They catch the shadows of the six-over-sixes when the winter sun pours through the windows. I can hardly wait to move into this new and glorious space. I cannot imagine what it will be like to have elbow room, to be able to move from one project to the next without clearing everything off my desk to start all over again. And I am especially looking forward to the morning commute, the distance we have created between home and work. *

* THE WEEKEND BEGINS on a Friday with the arrival of the Bog Boys in their Volvo station wagons. Shortly after they get here, Harry and I take off in his car for some off-Cape shopping. "Sorry—no heated seats," Harry jokes, a reference to Tony's newer vehicle. Tony is very proud of this feature, and also of his working air conditioning. Harry says he'll sweat, which is easy to say in the wintertime. I've told him he should fix it now, just so he has it; after all, the car only cost him $1,500. But he reminds me that he drove around those last days of his Toyota-Chevy without AC, and he survived. I'm convinced that if he had hair on his head, air conditioning would be more of a priority for him.

"Besides, the heat works great," he says.

"That's what you said about the Nova," I say, "on the day we went to look at the cottage." We both smile. It's just ten days shy of a year since we first saw the cottage, my cottage. So much has happened in a year's time.

We're going to the Wal-Mart in Plymouth, where I intend to buy a little futon for the yellow room, and a microwave—my first. I have resisted owning a microwave for all these years. It isn't simply a matter of principle—though there is that—but a matter of practicality. You can't fit a fax machine and a microwave on the same kitchen counter and still have room to cut veggies. Now that I have the space, I find I also have a need—twenty-something relatives due for the family Christmas in a couple of weeks, and there's no way I can keep everything warm in the oven.

While we are off-Cape, we will also patronize the new Home Depot, where Harry wants to buy a table saw. I feel more than a little uncomfortable with this foray into the world of retail giants. As a consultant to independent booksellers, I believe in the value of local ownership. I believe also in owner-occupied stores where you are noticed, indeed welcomed, and where your purchase matters in a direct way to another human being. I've never been inside a Home Depot, and until two weeks ago, my only acquaintance with Wal-Mart was through Billie Lett's novel *Where the Heart Is.* The pregnant protagonist, having left her no-good boyfriend, drives halfway across the country and ends up living in a Wal-Mart. That book softened my attitude a little, though I still think if I were going to hide out somewhere, I'd follow the example of the kids in *From the Mixed-up Files of Mrs. Basil E. Frankweiler.* In that one, two kids—a brother and sister, as I recall—manage to hide out in the Metropolitan Museum of Art in New York. As host institutions go, the Metropolitan has a lot more to see. On the other hand, you can grocery-shop in a Wal-Mart.

This Wal-Mart is busy with people piling stuff into overflowing shopping carts. It is the week before Christmas, I reason. Still, I get the feeling that everyone shops here except me. But here I am, watching Harry heft the studio futon ($59.99; I saw it when I was in my first Wal-Mart ever, two weeks ago, on an errand for the bookstore in Maine) into our cart. We proceed to the appliance aisle, where I select a Magic Chef microwave without those annoying little food icons on the front. It's white with a single timing knob. "Kinda retro," Harry says. "Go get another cart." We proceed to the register with two shopping carts. The cashier rings me up. For less than $200, I have acquired a new appliance, a spare bed for the yellow room, and a baker's rack to hold my plants in the office. All made in Third World countries, I scold myself. Possibly by children in sweatshops.

At Home Depot, I am underwhelmed. It is vast, true, but I find that the closer I look, the less they really carry. Yes, they carry windows and doors and paint and floors and plumbing and electrical supplies and rugs and tools. But within each category, they carry items from only a couple of manufacturers. They also don't have deals like my old friend, the Bargain Box at the Mid-Cape Home Center, or wide-plank wooden floors like those at my favorite hardware store. But the man who helps Harry select a table saw is helpful and knowledgeable. And he turns out to be a musician who knows Harry.

Okay. I got some good stuff cheap at Wal-Mart. And Home Depot wins points for good service and providing at least one

musician with a day job. But I still feel like I should visit the
Virgin Mother when we get home and say a few Hail Marys. *

* IN THE HALLWAY, Tony is holding the canister vacuum
cleaner while Howard vacuums the sawdust off the walls and
ceiling. Howard is standing on the stepladder that John left
behind. I take a photo of them, Howard intent on his job,
Tony so serious in the way he holds the vacuum he appears to
be taking part in a solemn ceremony. They can't speak over
the sound of the vacuum, so their ceremony is wordless. I
offer to run for lunch. Howard declines, planning to leave a
little after noon, but Harry and Tony place their orders and I
run out for Indian food. "It's your chance to try some Indian
food," I say to Howard. I've learned during our days together
that Howard's son-in-law—the one who isn't handy around
the house—is East Indian. Howard's told me he plans a trip
over the holidays to install that wire molding and do a few
more things around his daughter's house. By now, I'm convinced that Howard is not so displeased with his son-in-law's
lack of building talent. Howard's superior skills assure him of
his place in his daughter's heart—and home.

"You can heat up the leftovers in the microwave," Tony says as
we finish our meal. It becomes a refrain for the weekend,
Tony pointing out all the uses I will find for the shiny new
appliance that Harry has unpacked and placed on the corner
counter. After lunch, we get to the business of moving, but
not until I have taken pictures of Harry's beautiful handiwork
from all angles: desk alone on refinished wood floors, sunshine
streaming through windows; desk with desk maker leaning on
it; desk with a Bog Boy hefting each end; and after we lay the

carpet that pulls the wood tones and the blue walls together, desk with Harry seated at it, striking an executive pose.

My new desk is beautiful, cherry-topped with purple-heart accents and copper-pipe legs. And it's huge. I'll be able to open a blueprint on my new desk and still have room to make notes. In the past, all layouts and architectural drawings were spread out either on my bedroom floor, my dining room table, or—often—my bed. Egypt prefers the floor option, but I find it tricky to see through his bulk when he is stretched across a crucial element of a plan.

That night, Tony claims the futon in the yellow room after we test it out as a couch—the three of us sitting side by side, knees up to our chins. We must look idiotic. Egypt confirms this hypothesis by sitting just out of reach, tail-side facing us, on the little blue chenille rug in front of the futon. "Maybe I'll actually get some sleep tonight," Tony says. He's thrilled to be a house-width away from Harry's legendary snoring. Harry, past the stage where he denies that he snores, takes the remark in stride. ✳

✳   BY THE END of the next day, the office is in place. My bedroom is a little lopsided now, the room robbed of exactly half its function. But I find I enjoy sitting in my bed under the new matching windows and staring at the empty space. I'll keep my eye out for a comfy armchair, but for now, I inhale the space where my desk used to be. It will be good for dancing, I think. More room to move, and easier to close the door and use the full-length mirror I hung for practicing. Good for flute practice, too. The acoustics will improve with less furniture in the room.

The first day of my new commute, I make myself a cup of morning tea and stroll down the hallway. I am thrilled—and, to be honest, a little scared. It's so lovely, the blue walls, the deep wood wainscoting, the yellow pine floors, Harry's hand-made furniture. When I sit down at my desk, I feel as though I will have to do great things, think great thoughts, write great words, and not because I feel inspired, but because I feel like I need to live up to my surroundings. I'm in my new, longed-for office, and I find I am entirely intimidated.

The phone rings, and I reach for it. John. "Do you have the wood for the hall?" I have grown unused to these early morning logistics and it takes me a minute to comprehend his question. Oh—he means the birch flooring.

"I haven't picked it up yet, but it has arrived," I tell him.

"I'd like to put the floor in this week, if that's okay with you." We'd planned on the week after Christmas, but he is feeling as though we are cutting it too close for the family party, sched-uled for the day before New Year's Eve. It is the new deadline, this party, and so far it is working to my advantage. Kevin promises I'll have plumbing in the cottage before the party, the tile man says he'll finish the bathroom floor in time, and John says we'll finish the hallway, no problem.

I should have had the family party in October.

"The wood is supposed to sit in the environment for a few days," I remind him.

"But you have some there already." He is talking about the three boxes I found months ago at the Bargain Box.

"Forty-five square feet," I say. The numbers are easy to retrieve. Six more boxes were required for the job. And they weren't cheap. Birch, I learned, is used more rarely for floors than the standard oak, or even fir. It wasn't easy to match the boards I found at the Bargain Box, and when I finally tracked down a distributor, I paid a premium for the beautiful blond wood from Canada—the special-order flooring cost three times as much per box.

"They're in the house?" John asks.

I confirm that the wood from the Bargain Box is now stacked in the hallway. Over the weekend, I had Harry and Tony haul the three boxes up from the basement.

"Good. We'll start with those. If we pick up the other wood today, we can let it adjust for a couple of days. I have to work at the station tomorrow anyway," he says. "I'll be there in about half an hour—as soon as the girls are off." On those mornings when John isn't at the firehouse, he takes the morning duty with Katelin and Nicole. Often I can hear breakfast activity in the background of his calls.

By nine, John is at the door, and I am adequately presentable. I am aware as he enters that I am truly happy to see him, and not just because he is here to make me a beautiful floor for the hallway. I've missed him. "It's good to see you," I say.

"It's good to see you, too," John says. To a stranger, ours might sound like an automatic exchange, but there is a smile between us, a meeting of our eyes, and a two-beat pause after we greet each other. I am pretty sure that John senses, as I do, the warmth behind the words. I think back to the days when I wasn't sure of him, when I wished for John's calm and steady dad instead. I cannot locate in my mind the exact moment when things shifted between us, when John began to enjoy the project, and I began to enjoy—and fully appreciate—John. Perhaps it was the slow, steady process of working together, of talking, deciding together, of laughing together. John and I have had fun, and maybe that is at the root of our unforeseen friendship. We have become collaborators; we have developed a mutual respect for each other, for our differing ideas and ways. We have learned to joke, we have learned to listen, and we have discovered we are perfect partners. What I could imagine, he has made real—and often, more beautiful.

It is over quickly, this moment of mutual recognition, and John gets down to business. I lead him to the boards, still in boxes leaning against the hallway wall. It's cold outside, and he has brought the smell of winter inside with him. You smell this most keenly on children wearing parkas, I have noticed, but on a strong winter day, you can smell it on grown-ups, and even cats. The first time I picked up an incoming Egypt and noticed that blunt scent, I realized it must not be the clothing that creates the winter smell, but some odd inter- action of body warmth with weather cold. Damp wool mit- tens, cold plastic coats, the fragrance of chill and stillness, heightened by a hint of wood fire; a heady combination of temperature and temperature, a bubble of the outdoors that comes indoors to burst.

We talk about how to lay the floor, the direction of the wood. I have this idea that the wood planks should carry us down the hallway, that they should follow the direction of the hall. But John points out I will see more nails that way. He explains that he can hide the nails for a certain number of planks, nailing sideways into the boards, but as he gets closer to the wall, he will have to hammer from above. There is a name for this: face-nailing.

"Can you start on the edges and work toward the middle?" I ask. I am thinking this may give him more elbow room in the narrow hallway.

He considers this, but points out that we would end up with a very visible row of nails right down the center of the hallway. He'd also have to split planks, do a lot of cutting and advance planning, so the skinniest planks wouldn't end up in the middle.

We open the boxes as we consider the issue, and John lays out some boards for me. We do a section of the hallway with the planks running the long way, and a section with the planks running side to side.

"I'm fine with this," he says, pointing to the lengthwise planks, "so long as you're okay with the nails showing."

"The nails don't bother me so much. But I'm not sure I like the way the wood fits together."

"You've got a lot of short boards," John says. And I realize, yes, that is a big part of my problem. I'd imagined long glossy rows of matching boards, leading you from the living room to the back door. But the package we have opened is packed with two- and three-foot sections. We open another box, and another. Same thing. A couple of six-foot boards, everything else much shorter. "That's usually the way this prefinished stuff comes," John confirms.

"Hmmm." I say it out loud. I am stalling. John knows this, and he is patient with me. We have learned that we can solve a problem together as long as I am allowed to examine the alternatives before making a decision. "Let's talk about the trapdoor," I suggest. It's a way to get something done while I am considering the long-versus-wide problem.

The trapdoor will be built on top of the four-by-four section of plywood that covers the plumbing and heating and electrical connections between the house and cottage. We are thinking ahead to issues of home repair—or, more optimistically, home improvement. We might want these pipes and wires later, if I ever build that upstairs room.

"Would it have a hinge?" A stupid question, I realize. A hinge above would look awful and rise up to meet innocent toes. A hinge below would require massive engineering and special materials, not to mention more time than we have to finish the hallway. Before John has to answer me, I retract the question.

"Screws in each corner, was what I was thinking. I can do it with some nice brass screws, so they won't look bad, and I'll sink them." We figure out the size of the opening, and he describes how he will arrange the boards. The trapdoor will be a feature, a bit of parquet in the hallway, at just about the midpoint. I leave the pattern to John. He's made one before, in his own house. "I'll figure it out as I go," he says, and I can tell he is looking forward to it.

"I've got it on the floor. What about this?" I place three boards end to end against each wall, house and cottage, and I add another row of three on each side, also running the long way. Then I take some of the shorter planks and run them side to side, crossing the hallway between the lengthwise boards. The effect is a floor that is framed around the edges, a subtle echo of the parquet we imagine.

"That'll work." John says. The practical issues of visible nails and short boards and wood edges are resolved. He smiles. I smile.

"Let's do it." I say, as if I will hold the boards while he aims the nail gun. ✱

✱ WHILE JOHN WORKED on the hallway floor yesterday, I picked up the remaining boxes of flooring in two trips to Falmouth. John and I actually measured the interior of my car and the boxes from the Bargain Box. We figured I could probably haul all six boxes in one crammed trip, as long as the passenger seat was down flat. The guy at the dock was patient, if disbelieving. I kept telling him we'd measured the car, that it should work. Finally, I realized the boxes were an entirely different shape and size. It turned out the boxes I had at home were two feet shorter than the boxes I was picking up. We persevered, and managed to get three boxes in, cramming them between the foothold on the passenger side and the trunk of the car, which is partially exposed with the back seat folded down. I could still shift, but I lost use of my emergency brake for the ride home.

The wood is in the house now, acclimating to its new environment. I am acclimating too. I am back in my office today, and still feeling uncomfortable. It occurs to me that I welcomed yesterday's wood trips as a chance to get away from this space. Not a good sign. Am I truly inhibited by the beauty of my new surroundings? As the day wears on, I realize it is more than that. We have some serious issues with the layout. For one thing, the phone—located on the computer table Harry made so that my desk can be free of electronics—is too far away. And the new desk light—with a telescoping arm and a milk-glass shade with stained-glass accents—rather than lighting my way, seems to be in the way. I shift the lamp on my desk, move the phone, and crawl around on the floor to work out the cord logistics. Then I sit and stare at the holly tree, loaded with deep red berries. Nice view. But it's still not right. I call Harry.

"Well, the space really is set up more for a right-handed person," he says.

Of course. I am painfully both-handed, so I didn't take this into account, but I realize now that I always reach for the phone with my left hand, and I usually listen with my left ear. The right-sided phone means I am in a tangle of curly cord. No wonder I'm uncomfortable. After we hang up, I relocate the phone to my left, which requires additional phone cord taped to the underside of my desk. While I'm at it, I wrap the light cord around one copper leg. It feels a little better. Maybe I just need to get used to the space. But that night, staring at my bedroom dance floor, I realize the truth of the matter—the desk is facing the wrong way!

Before John arrives on Wednesday, I've reversed the desk. Now my view is out one window and my new, full-view door. I see the mahogany-red railing on the walkway, the treetops in the bog. It is a much larger view, expansive even. In the light snowfall, it is stunning. With the desk oriented toward the holly, I realize, I was replicating the view from my old office from just a slightly different angle. Facing the holly, I was also facing the original house, my old office—the past. Now I am positioned with a view of the present, a view that reminds me what we have done in these last twelve months, a view that only my cottage addition can afford. If I squint, I imagine, I might even catch a glimpse of the future.

As soon as I sit at the desk, I understand all this—my insecurities, my desire to keep an eye on my old space, to cling a little to my crowded office, to have a view of the comfort zone. I feel the power in the simple act of flipping the desk as I remove the taped phone cord. I relocate the little table that holds the printer—an engagement present from my grandfather to my grandmother—so it sits in front of the window that looks out on the holly. When I retrieve what I print, I will be reminded of my roots. Satisfied with my tiny feng shui victory, I return to my desk and turn to my left to send off an e-mail to Harry, just as John knocks twice on the French doors and lets himself in.

the twelve days of christmas

IT IS SNOWING OUTSIDE, and John keeps his table saw covered with a blue tarp. The saw is set up on the deck, conveniently plugged into the outlet that Stan installed to the left of the French doors. The boards require a certain amount of cutting as John works to fit them, like a jigsaw puzzle, into the hallway. I had no idea that laying a prefinished floor would be so complicated. John tells me that the narrowness of the expanse is part of the reason so much cutting is involved. All week, John has been moving between the warmth of the hallway and the bitterness outside. He fits, measures, runs outside if a cut is required, comes in to hammer the wood into place. For this back-and-forth operation, John wears a T-shirt and jeans.

I am outside in a hooded parka, snapping pictures with a gloved index finger. I'm hoping for a good shot of the house and cottage united: green shutters and red-bowed wreaths on the windows, ivy with white lights wrapped around the lamppost, a dusting of snow not quite covering the red roof. I am thinking it will make the perfect December photo for the calendar I plan to give to John and Ed.

The snowfall is lovely. The branches of the spruce are white, but not yet heavy. We are only supposed to get a couple of inches; the birds, busy at the feeder, confirm this forecast. You can pretty much predict any weather by watching the birds.

During a small snow, the birds visit the feeder nonstop. When they expect a big snow, they flock to the feeder before the weather begins. Then they disappear into silence and white, returning only after the storm has passed.

Like my first foray into gardening, my backyard birding habit was encouraged by Barbara. She gave me a thistle feeder many years ago. "It will bring the little finches," she told me. I wasn't sure I'd recognize a little finch if it came. But I bought the seed she told me to get and I hung the feeder by my dining room window. That winter, the color of the birds, their tenacious living in the midst of all the winter dead, heartened me and gave me hope for spring. I realize now that Barbara gave me the feeder because her winter bird-feeding days were over.

Barbara's mother died in the wintertime, only a few months before Barbara made the first trip down the path to my house. Two years later, Barbara mentioned her mother's death to me for the first time, confessed how hard it had been for her to live through the winters ever since. Barbara, I learned, had struggled all her life with depression. Another year or two later, she invited me up the hill to read her medical history. "You just read it," she said to me, as she stationed herself in her mother's rocker. Egypt had come up the hill with me, and he was moving between the two of us, catching a pat wherever he could. The record was grim, and kept in her own hand. She'd been subjected to electroshock treatment, psychotherapy, intermittent hospitalizations, and every brand of psychopharmaceutical you could name. Some of the side effects were worse than the cure, which in any case had never been effected.

After her mother's death, winters in that house became impossible for Barbara to manage. I came to expect her annual hospitalization; she would usually disappear shortly after her birthday on December 31. In the spring she would return, stronger, but never quite as good as new. These last couple of years, her return seemed premature, her departure delayed, her suffering more long-standing. Winter's agony, it seemed, had stretched into spring; fall was an anticipation of the pain to come, and even summer days were longer than she could bear. When she came home this past spring—after the robins, but before the catbirds—she was distressed a lot of the time. She'd call me often in the middle of the day. "Come up, please. I can't get the safe open."

The safe was ancient, big and clunky, and hard to open. Even with the combination written out in Barbara's neat handwriting, I could never get it the first time. She'd fidget and complain, convinced we wouldn't be able to get it open. Three tries usually did it, after I had some practice. Inside were some miscellaneous papers and her unused checks. Her compulsion to touch those papers, I think, was a compulsion to feel that some part of her life was in order. Outside that locked-up safe, there was disorder all around her.

Late last summer, her friend and companion summoned me up the hill. "Barbara's in a very bad way," she said on the phone. "Maybe you can help?"

I found Barbara in her bedroom—once her mother's room—in physical and emotional pain. "I'm dying, Katie," she said. "I am dying." She said it in her incongruously loud voice, a declaration, not a protest.

"We're all dying, Barbara," I said. "It's just a matter of timing."

"Where are my glasses?" I found them for her so she could look up at me. I think she was a little surprised by my response. I wasn't being glib, and she knew it. There is something about Barbara—at her best and at her worst—that invites you to be candid, blunt. Perhaps because she gives you nothing less in turn.

"Barbara," I said. "You have a very strong body. It isn't going to die without a lot of help. You aren't going anywhere right away, Honey."

She didn't say anything, but lay her head back down on the pillow.

"Do you want to die, Barbara?" I asked her. I knew it was Barbara's very nature that was pushing me to this boldness. Why mince words, she would have asked if she were feeling better.

Silence.

I sat down on the bed next to her. The mattress was ancient; it was awful for her back. Not to mention the room itself. Dark, and full of pain. I wondered whether I could get her out of this bedroom, move her into another room where the memory of her mother might not seep through the wallpaper.

"I don't know, Katie," she said.

"Of course you don't."

"I need my pills." I got her a fresh glass of water, and she swallowed her medication. She handed back the glass, then her glasses. "I want to sleep now."

I tucked her in, for even on that August day she was cold, and needing two woolen blankets. I resisted the urge to kiss her on the forehead. I knew Barbara wasn't big on physical affection. Instead, I squeezed her hand and said good-bye. ✶

✶ I THINK OF BARBARA NOW, as I watch the cardinals moving between the spruce and the green feeder, its roof white with snow. I have grown used to the beauty of this sight, red on evergreen, a dusting of white. One morning after a big snow, I counted sixteen cardinals around my feeders. When guests spy a single cardinal through the living-room window, they tend to interrupt themselves mid-sentence— "Oh look! A cardinal!" I always oblige with a look, because the cardinals are always beautiful, and always worth the momentary interruption. Sometimes I tell my bird-spotting guests how many cardinals I have that year, the mating pairs, their babies, who, when they are old enough, are brought to the feeder and instructed by example how it works.

It's fun to watch the teenage cardinals, still reddish-orange and more fluffy than feathered, their sex determined but not entirely obvious at first glance. They stare as one of their parents— usually the male—flies to the feeder and settles down for a snack. The female stands guard, signaling for danger or departure if needed. This is part of the teaching, too: one sentinel; one eater at a time. They exchange places; the female, glamorous, orange-gold with her lipsticked beak, eats some seed. The teenagers, nearby, beg their parents to feed them. They squeak and squawk and flap their wings, baby birds in the nest. But their parents ignore them, keep eating. On the first visit, the parents eventually give in to the kids. The father bird carries some seed to feed the youngsters. The movement of seed, beak-to-beak, is a beautiful and delicate operation, which I love watching in springtime when the male feeds his mate in a ritual of courtship.

This first round of family feeding is designed, I believe, to teach the kids that the feeder is a genuine food source. They will make another trip to the feeder as a family—probably the next day. This time, the parents will repeat the process of feeding themselves, one by one at the feeder, but they will not give in when the young birds make their flapping, noisy demands to be fed. Instead, the adults will urge them, by example, to the feeder. Perhaps the braver of the two will make the flight, and land on the green roof. There, he or she will squawk and flap and beg, as if to say, haven't I been brave enough? After a few moments, one parent will reward the little one with a seed or two, moving from the birdhouse ledge to the roof, back and forth.

After a few visits with their parents, the youngsters will make it to the feeder on their own. Their first efforts are clumsy, and they are a little frightened by the mechanism that closes the feeder up tight if a heavyweight lands on the feeding bar. The siblings urge each other along, one watching, the other flying to the roof, squawking, flapping. When no papa bird arrives to feed the brave baby, she makes her hesitant way to the landing area. Once there, she radiates uncertainty, looking to her watchful sibling for encouragement as she clings to the wooden bar. Sometimes the feeder closes at this point, mistaking her lopsided, flappy weight for that of a larger bird or robber squirrel. Or sometimes a chickadee or finch appears, startling the young cardinal up and off the feeder. But eventually, the bird—or her braver sibling—will settle long enough, calmly enough, to get some of the black-oil sunflower seed; after two or three trips to the feeder, she will be a pro. And her parents are freed from feeding duties. Free to court and breed again, to repeat the process that begins with the bird calls of spring, the flapping of wings, the sunflower seed passed so gently from male to female, beak to beak.

Last summer's babies are well grown now, and all the birds look a little scruffy in their winter coats. Already it is hard to tell which is the older generation. By spring, it will be nearly impossible. My little camera is unequipped to capture the birds on film without disturbing their morning, so I restrict myself to shots of the house. Looking for the right angle for the calendar photo, I shoot up from the driveway and down from the path that leads to Barbara's house. I move to the walkway deck and photograph the bog, which is white and magical, a forest of bare, glistening limbs. I take a shot of my insulators capped in snow and sitting on the bench by the front door. I am burning film now, wanting to develop the roll for the sake of the calendar effort.

I make my way back to the side of the house and I surprise John at the saw. When I snap his picture, he is looking up from his work for a moment, and there is the blur of snowfall between us. You can see his strong bare arms, and you can see a snowflake or two, not yet melted in his short black hair. "A document to your macho nature," I say, as I steal the shot. ✳

✳ HAVING JOHN AROUND the house, without Peter or any of his crew, feels different from having Howard here. Aside from the sound of the nail gun, John works quietly, and he moves lightly. More than once I am startled when he comes to the doorway of the office to ask me a question. Finally I realize that he is in stocking feet, that his heavy boots are stashed by the door. But there's something else. It takes me two whole days to figure it out: he is working without a tool belt. There is no clanking of tools when he moves, no sound to give him away when he approaches the opening to the cottage. In this quiet between us, I feel a strange sort of intimacy. He is unarmored, working in my home. I wonder what it is like to be Margaret, his wife, or to be one of his kids, used to the fact of their dad fixing things at home, working on projects, tool-belted or not, bare-armed or stocking-footed. It isn't a fantasy, exactly, but a desire to understand what it would feel like to have such a capable man around the house.

The cobbler's kids go shoeless, I know, but I suspect that John does not neglect the projects at home. He sent me to his house to see the stone he'd used there, to see if I liked it for my cellar wall. He has been talking about building an addition, and just this week he referenced the prefinished flooring he installed at home. Somehow, between his all-night shifts at the firehouse and his day-long building projects for his many clients, John finds time to work at home, too. He has his father for a role model. Ed keeps his home in perfect repair, never shies from a project. Susan jokes that she "married her handyman." I don't know the whole story, but I do know that Ed's wife died young, and he and Susan met when she needed some work done. Since they have married, they have expanded Susan's summer cottage into a two-story home with a beautiful deck, a hot tub, a tidy little shed out back. Their project list is ongoing, it appears, and the house is well loved by Ed's skillful hands.

I feel a little envious of Margaret and Susan, and I wonder about the assortment of wives to all these men who hammer and saw and climb on roofs, paint shutters, glaze windows, and mix mortar. I wonder if the women appreciate their men, or whether they take it for granted that their husbands can build a deck in a weekend. More than that—do they appreciate that they are married to men who are willing to give up their weekend to build that deck? Or do they think nothing of it; have they simply married men who do what they expect men to do? I wonder what the women do in turn, whether they are locked into gender typecasting in their marriages, and at least for a minute, I wonder if that would be so bad. Maybe I need to look for a man with a contractor's license— or at least a man who knows how to use a Sawzall.

On the other hand, if I had a man like that, I would not have John in my hallway right now. John, in his wooly stocking feet.

I would be quite content to have John and his father work on my house forever. ✳

✳   JOHN FINISHES THE HALLWAY late on Friday. It's dark, and he doesn't have time to clean up. "I'll come back tomorrow morning," he says. I protest. I don't want to intrude on his holiday weekend, but he does not want me to live with wood scraps and sawdust and his equipment littering my new deck on Christmas Day.

Saturday morning, John arrives with his daughters, Katelin and Nicole. They go straight for the fishing game, a little mechanical pool of fish with mouths that open and shut to reveal shiny metal inside. Wind up the pool, watch the fish swim around, and try to catch as many as you can with the little fishing rods with magnets on the ends of their lines. Katelin and Nicole fish for awhile in the living room before we adjourn to the little yellow room. They are drawn to this room with the bright-colored walls, the low futon, and all the children's books. They pick out a story for me to read: *The Twelve Days of Christmas.* We begin by reading the words and looking at the illustrations, before I discover the girls do not know the song. So I teach it to them. Singing is not something I usually do in front of anyone except Egypt, who generally leaves the room when I begin to so much as hum a few notes. I'm not sure what has gotten into me, but here I am singing the one Christmas carol that rivals the national anthem in unsingability. Maybe it is the room, the yellow that is so bold, or maybe it is the company—accepting, and not surprised that I would sing for them.

We read the words and examine Jan Brett's wondrous artwork to learn the gift of each day; then we sing the next verse of the song: "Five golden rings, four calling birds, three French hens, two turtle doves, and a partridge in a pear tree." Nicole, only three, struggles with some of the words, but she's getting the hang of it, and for the first time, I understand the beauty of this song. It isn't meant for grown-ups, I realize, but for little kids. The repetition is a form of learning, even if the gifts, archaic, are a bit beyond a child's grasp.

We are on the eleventh day when John comes back inside. He's packed up his table saw and has finished sweeping the deck, clearing off as much of the frozen sawdust as he can. When he comes to the doorway of the yellow room, we don't hear him approach. He's in stocking feet, and we are singing. ✳

＊ THAT AFTERNOON, I am in the yellow room again, this time with my friend Cindy's kids: Drew and Brooke. Cindy and I have been best friends since high school. We live several states apart, but we maintain a habit of long phone visits that we began as teenagers. Our phone calls shortened for a while, when her kids were really young. I remember Cindy calling once when I wasn't home. "I had this awful thought," she told my machine. "Just when my kids are old enough to leave me alone when we're on the phone, you'll be having babies. I just know it."

Not quite two years ago, Cindy lost her husband, Bob, to pancreatic cancer. It is an old man's disease, but Bob was only forty when he died. The pain began just two months after the huge surprise birthday party Cindy had organized for her husband. Bob was unable to work, barely able to speak. Cindy suspected the worst from the start, even as I urged her to be more optimistic. She dragged him from doctor to doctor, and there was no diagnosis. He was hospitalized, but still no clear diagnosis. One doctor suggested a psychiatric evaluation. Another suggested prayer. Furious, Cindy took matters into her own hands, yanked Bob's records, sent them to a specialist at another hospital. Within hours, they had the beginning of the horrible, unlikely, deadly diagnosis.

Bob and Cindy fought hard; his illness became a full-time job for both of them. They blended conventional and alternative treatments; they sought out cancer research doctors and clinical trials, followed every lead. Bob outlived his prognosis by almost six months, but he died on Memorial Day, 1999.

Cindy is a strong and powerful woman, and she remains powerfully angry that she has lost Bob. They had a beautiful relationship, a partnership of equals who never fell out of love. They were the couple you would mention if someone brought up the impossibility of true love, of long-lasting marriage. They were the role model you hoped you could imitate. And not because they had it easy, either. Their son, Drew, is saddled with the unfortunate combination of a slew of learning disabilities and a high IQ. He lives his life at an elevated level of frustration, and this only fuels an already-fierce sibling rivalry with his younger sister, Brooke. Another couple might have divorced over their mutual focus on an inability to "fix" Drew and the tension that his condition bred in the family, but Cindy and Bob simply shared responsibilities, divided up the duties, and reminded themselves how much they loved each other every day.

My friend resents the fact that she is alone now, and I don't blame her. I could never live her life, a life that starts at quarter of six in the morning, moves through breakfast quarrels to the bus stop, then to work. There, she spends her day—frenetic with customer requests and employee questions, interrupted by phone calls from school, visits to doctors, counselors, tutors. Then the after-school activities begin. Basketball, soccer, cornet lessons, vision therapy, ski club, more doctors, 4-H. Supper is often late, and it is not uncommon for Cindy to feed several members of Bob's family on any given evening. I'm not sure when Cindy cares for the growing menagerie of animals. A few weeks ago, she called me, disappointed that she'd missed out on buying a goat that was advertised in the paper. "I called too late," she said.

"I'd say you called right on time." I am always trying to get her to slow down, to relax for a few minutes, to let go of one or another activity. She laughed at me, admitted a goat would have been some work, but soon enough she was waxing rhapsodic about the type of goat that was offered, and how hard it would be to find another. I have no doubt she'll locate another one, and sooner than she needs it. "I need a nap after just listening to your schedule," I have said more than once. "I don't know how you do it." *

* TODAY IS THE FIRST TIME Cindy and the kids have seen my revised home. Cindy has kept the project a secret from Drew and Brooke, wanting to see their reactions. "Wow," Drew says. "What did you do?" We walk around the house, and I remind Cindy and the kids where the walls and doors and windows used to be. They shake their heads and ask an occasional question.

When Cindy heads out for some last-minute errands, Drew and Brooke and I gravitate to the yellow room, where Brooke shows off her kitten. Snuggle, smuggled in past the Cat-in-Charge, is an easy-going baby, with dark stripes and a loud purr. She doesn't mind being passed from person to person, and she is only vaguely curious about her new surroundings. They tell me she was very good on the trip, that she slept most of the way, that she hardly cried at all.

We squeeze side by side onto the little futon, ready to begin what is becoming our annual tradition: Christmas charades. There is something about the three of us together, the way that two of us work to guess the answer while the actor pantomimes his concept, that warms relations between Drew and Brooke. We laugh a lot, at ourselves and at each other. We act out Christmas concepts: Stockings, Trees, Angels, Reindeer, and Carols—"Silent Night," "Jingle Bells"—before we move on to other categories: Things in the Kitchen, Jungle Animals. You name it. Between turns, we pass the kitty around.

Cindy returns, and we move to the living room to open presents. She has given me a guest book with a picture of a house on the cover. "It's so everyone can write their impressions of your beautiful new home," Cindy tells me, and I love the idea. "We'll begin." And so the first entry in my house book is in Cindy's familiar hand, the handwriting I have known for twenty-seven years. Brooke and Drew are next, mature in their observations, childlike in their handwriting, creative in their spelling. It is a beautiful gift.

That night, they fold themselves back into Cindy's truck, crammed full of suitcases and Christmas presents, to head to Cindy's mother's house for the holiday. I know Cindy will be up all night baking, that her holiday will be anything but restful. "Take it easy," I say to my friend as I give her an extra-long hug good-bye. She squeezes me back, but she does not agree to my demand. *

* FOR CHRISTMAS, I make a complicated Algerian lamb stew from a recipe I clipped out of the Williams-Sonoma catalogue. The recipe was included to help them sell a big expensive pot, and as the pile of chopped vegetables grows, I understand why a giant pot is required. But I make do, cramming everything into a something that is almost big enough. It will work. The array of spices is complex, and so is the flavor when my mother and I sit down to dinner in midafternoon. We eat in the newly arranged living-dining room, at the big

round table that is now by the windows. My mother approves of the new layout, the openness of the room now that many of the bookcases have been taken out. "There were too many books in this room," she declares, as if my English-teacher mother were in no way instrumental in my affinity for reading objects. "It felt heavy." I quell my objections. Can there ever be too many books? I know she is right about the heaviness and the openness. It is easier on the digestion to eat in the open space, with the view of the birds at the feeder. I suspect I will use this room more now, that I will consume fewer meals hunched over the kitchen counter.

We enjoy our meal, and open our presents before two friends of my mother's arrive for dessert. I have made brownies and some odd little goat cheese desserts inspired by a cheese-course recipe in *On Rue Tatin*, a wonderful combination cookbook-memoir by Susan Herrmann Loomis that I devoured in the fall. I blended soft goat cheese with a little raspberry jam and, lacking molds, packed the mixture into rinsed-out scallop shells and put them in the fridge to firm. It wasn't easy getting the treats out of the shells without losing some of the ribbing, but I got better at it as I progressed through the tray. I dribbled warm lavender honey on top of each and served them rib-side up. I think the shell shapes look elegant on the blue glass plate, and I am proud of myself for making them, but my mom's friends are simply polite about the goat cheese creations, each eating exactly one. The brownies, gooey, chewy, and stuffed with chocolate chips, are a hit.

On the second tour of the day, I show off the progress in the cottage bathroom to my mother and her friends: The floor is mostly tiled—pale, pale blue-green and creamy white, arranged in a checkerboard pattern—unfinished because we ran out of my remnant tiles. I have to hunt down some more this week. The toilet arrived only yesterday, and the shower is not yet operational. We have to order a custom-made enclosure because there is nothing standard that will fit in this odd little space. Thanks to the burst pipes in the cottage, the bathroom has turned into a major project. I comfort myself with my bargain floor, as my guests admire the full-price tiles I have chosen for the shower: shiny white, with two rows of small blue-green accent tiles. The clear glass enclosure will show off the design, and the blue matches the bathroom walls perfectly. "I want to come sleep over," my mother announces, "just so I can use this bathroom. When it's all done," she adds. ∗

∗ ON NEW YEAR'S EVE, Bruce and Tina and I gather at the round table for another big meal: pork tenderloin, hopping john, bitter greens. For dessert, two more recipes from the pages of *On Rue Tatin:* a simple marble yogurt cake and a more complex, egg-yolk-laden Breton butter cake. "I guess I am missing France," I say to Tina, and she assures me my new obsession is a worthy substitute for an overseas trip.

My thoughts drift to the start of this year, to the Millennium Party. My friends are scattered this New Year's Eve. Tony and Anna, now married, are in Italy, visiting Anna's parents. I wonder if they will break the news on this trip. Katrina and Ruben are having a romantic dinner alone. Bill and Erika are at Bill's sister's house.

That leaves Harry and Tina, no longer an item. Tina isn't ready for what Harry wants right now. It is a time for her to be light in relationships, and a time when he is looking for solidity, permanence. Neither of my friends seems to have been hurt in this discovery, and I am glad for their brief connection. In her time with Harry, Tina reopened her sweet, sad heart.

Harry, meanwhile, is seeing someone new, and they are celebrating this New Year with her friends. I suspect this one might turn serious—if it hasn't already. I have met his new sweetheart only once, but she and Harry seem in sync. They laugh a lot together, and I take that as an excellent sign.

In lieu of a big New Year's celebration, I plan to gather friends to welcome spring. The family Christmas, postponed by snow, will wait for springtime, too. In my mind, I see a warm day in May; a big crowd on my deck, grab gifts in the center of a family circle, joking all around.

At midnight, our toast is quieter; our gathering is smaller than last year's, but the company is excellent, and the house is warm. The next morning, we breakfast on the Breton butter cake and we finish off the leftover Christmas stew for lunch. We take Bruce to the ferry at Woods Hole. We joke about starting the New Year with a serious intention to eat when Tina and I stop for a bite on the way back. There's no time for dessert before Tina boards the bus, so I send her home to Boston with two kinds of cake. ✴

✴ ON THE FIRST NIGHT of the New Year, Egypt and I patrol our new house, complete, or close to it. We move from house to hallway. With the smooth wooden floors and the vaulted ceilings, this space is gorgeous and a little frightening. Feng shui would dictate that I slow down the energy here; indeed, there is a sense we might be carried right out of the house on an invisible inner wind. "I've ordered a couple of rugs," I tell Egypt, "and I'll hang some pictures." He doesn't seem to mind, as he races down the hall, and at the last minute turns into his skid, landing on the rug in my office. I've noticed he never merely steps into the cottage; king of his expanded castle, he *arrives*.

I unscrew the clear bulbs on each of the five Christmas candles in the cottage windows, and shut down the computer after one last e-mail check. Back down the hallway to the house, seven more lights to unscrew, turn down the heat, flip the switch on the fairy lights climbing up the ivy on the outdoor lamppost. It's time for bed.

The darkness in my bedroom is interrupted by the nearly full moon. The moonlight travels through the skylight in the hallway, shadowed by the white mullions on the two new windows over my bed. The rectangular patterns of silver light play on the center of the pale blue pillowcase next to me. When Egypt claims that very spot, he draws the moonlight into his fur until it disappears.

marriage

I HAVE NOTICED that when an established couple, especially
a married couple, looks back on their courtship, they are able
to identify specific, chronological phases in their relationship.
The beginning: Was it love at first sight, or a long friendship
that one day turned inexplicably romantic? And the middle: It
may have been a little rocky then, the time when some couples
discover that their respective beloveds are not always entirely
lovable. But those couples who push through the so-called
disillusionment period reclaim their love, hold fast, and decide
to stay for the ride. They marry.

Ever since Ed first said to me, "We will marry the houses
together," I have held this image, this metaphor in my head. I
laugh, thinking I am the yenta who spotted the lonely cottage
and brought it to my very eligible home.

As is often the case in human courtship, preparation was
essential. In this case: clearing trees, moving gardens, digging
holes, and generally making a large mess of the place. And
then the cottage came, ably transported by a crew of three
men, escorted by state troopers, followed by friends. It didn't
approach the house that first night, but instead was nestled
beneath the pines in the bottom circle of the driveway. Still, I
imagine that the house knew that it had a new neighbor. They
sensed each other, as fated couples can, before they have even
met. The next day, when the cottage was lifted into place, they

were at last within sight of one another. And through each day of the next two months, they sat side by side. I felt they were eyeing each other.

In my ritual walks from house to cottage, the reverse circle that was the longest distance and the only way to get from house to cottage during that time, I was tracing some invisible line, some pulse of energy, electricity, connection. Then, Vito made the foundation wall, and I thought—first date? And the skeleton of the hallway: certainly progress, a more consistent connection. Next the roof, which connected them fully, irrevocably. Each roof changed a bit in this design; the new roofline was elegant, perfect, and a little unpredictable. I had thought that the roof connection would be the marriage, but as the project progressed, I realized, no—we were not married yet. I joked with Ed, "The houses aren't married, but I think they are dating exclusively." On the weekend that Harry and Tony and I took down the exterior shingles that were then inside the hallway, I felt another turning point, as the houses revealed something of their original tongue-and-groove construction. They were stripped bare, each in the face of the other.

Just a few days before, Ed and Howard had moved the window in the cottage, and that weekend we could slide in and out of the cottage through a narrow slot in the wall where half the window used to be. Soon afterward, more of the wall came down, the header was installed, and the opening to the cottage was complete. "They are engaged now," I told Katrina when she came over for a visit. She suggested I might be taking this metaphor a little too seriously. I laughed with her. But the truth was—and is—that these two small houses are real to me, distinct and with their own personalities.

Sandy, the Jungian psychotherapist who cat-sat in October, saw the marriage metaphor immediately, before I said a thing about it. She went even one step further in her anthropomorphic thinking: "Which is the female, do you think?" Indeed, I had thought about this, and in a moment of gender bias, I cast the cottage as the feminine; "she" let down her walls first. By the time Sandy arrived, the house had yielded its kitchen wall: another major opening, encompassing the first stretch of hallway as part of the kitchen, expanded to meet the cottage. Are they married yet? I wondered. And I realized I was entirely unsure. I thought that perhaps the marriage would come with the moving in, the full integration of house to house. Then, I thought that perhaps the marrying moment would be the completion of the hall floor, the laying of beautiful birch boards, the moment when Egypt and I could walk indoors across a smooth floor to reach our new addition.

And now, I am at a small distance, and the houses are most nearly one. Still, sometimes, when asked where something is, I say, "Oh, that's in the cottage." Or I call it "the other side," even sometimes calling the original the "main house" as if my three original rooms and 750 square feet were a mansion of much larger proportions. It seems to me now that I might have reached that point—the way couples do—where I can identify the progress in hindsight, to point to that first moment, that first movement of love that led to marriage. But I can't. I have the sneaking suspicion that the houses have married secretly. Just as they quietly eyed each other that night before the lift and landing, sending signals through the trees, just as they sat quietly, companionably, side by side, communicating in a language I could not understand, now they are quiet in their married ways. They are as mysterious to me as human married couples, speaking in a code I have never been able to crack. ✳

✳ I HAVE NEVER MARRIED, and this is a fact more puzzling to me at age forty-two than it has ever been. I have hoped for a partner, and I still do. I've been in significant and long-term relationships. I have loved and been loved. But I remain unattached, almost eerily so at this juncture. Sometimes I think I was born into this world lacking the marriage chromosome, and—who knows—perhaps some day, genetic engineers will be able to predict our mating patterns as surely as they predict our propensity for illness and health. I look around me at the predominance of married persons in my age and demographic group, and I don't know what to make of what seems to me to be a random pattern of coupling. I watch couples in public places and I try not to stare, obsessed as I have become in unraveling how they have landed together, wed, happily or not. I have the single, never-married person's curious combination of idealistic and cynical beliefs about all this. How does this wonderful man end up with this critical, impatient woman? Why does such a remarkable woman put up with such a possessive boor of a man? I contemplate all this rather dispassionately while the inner princess still hopes her knight will arrive before she gets *really* old.

In the course of moving the cottage and joining the houses together, I have often wished for a co-conspirator, a partner. The princess imagined conversations over dinner, planning and plotting progress with one very special man. Instead, my league of friends has offered an embarrassment of riches, helping, marveling, supporting me in ways that perhaps no one Ideal Man would ever be able to do. Still, I have wished for him. I have wished that I was not alone, that I was not bearing the emotional and financial burdens by myself. For friends go home to their own troubles at the end of the day, home to their own joys—and often to their own partners, and that leaves me and the cat and the house-in-progress. On our own.

But the woman who observes the many apparently mismatched and unhappy couples in the world knows this project might just as easily have ended a relationship as made one. I am glad for the freedom I have had, the ability to work in the moment, without feeling as though I needed to consult anyone, least of all a husband. While the inner princess imagines romantic tête-à-têtes, another part of me cannot bear the thought that I would lose autonomy, lose the capability to say, after a few moments' consideration and a brief conversation with John or Ed or Stan about some key detail, "Yes. Let's do it that way." Somewhere I hold the knowledge—and the fear—that I could be a woman who would wait until my husband comes home before deciding to relocate a window, install an unplanned electrical outlet—hell, move a cottage twenty-something miles and set it down on my challenging site.

I am not that woman, and perhaps this explains my unmarried state. A better explanation might be that the man I would marry would not require me to have his permission. The man I would marry would have faith in my imagination, support my creative impulses, not attempt in word or deed to rein in the boldness of thought that has carried me this far in life.

But of course the man I would marry would be willing to listen to me on those days when I am indecisive, obsessing about the smallest detail. Walker Percy says in *The Last Gentleman* that we seek someone just to tell us what to do, to guide us gently and firmly through the daily maze. Sometimes the man I would marry would need to do that, too. Never tell me what to do, but please— *tell me what to do!* It is a tall order. My expectations are only as high as the moon.

The moon that I can see tonight, if I lie back on my pillows and look up, through the windows above my bed, into the hallway, and up through the skylight. I told Tina I could see the moon this way, and she said, "Did you ever imagine that?" As a matter of fact, I did. I've lived on this hillside for almost fourteen years now. I understand the relationship of this piece of earth to the sun, the moon, the stars. I think of Barbara, and Barbara's mother, knowing she had similar considerations in mind when she instructed her builder-husband how this house would be positioned, told him to put windows in every room—and lots of them. Clearly, she had an appreciation for light, an understanding of how it moves through rooms. I like to imagine that she approves of the changes I have made, the awareness I have kept of light, my conscious invitation to invite the sun and moon into my home.

The sun and the moon—together, another symbol of marriage, of masculine and feminine—I can't seem to get around this marriage question. Are they married yet? Last week in the pouring rain, the town assessor came to measure and evaluate the worth of my new home. I am hoping he bids low. Next week or the week after, the bank's appraiser will come, evaluating the same, but this time I am looking for a high bid, a bid that will enable me to refinance house and cottage and all related debts into one big fat mortgage payment each month. It's the right thing to do, I've decided, though I am worried about coming up with the cash every month for the next twenty or thirty years.

As I look ahead to the closing, I think in fact it is probably the final opening, the legal sanction of these domestic partners. Yes, as unromantic as it is, I suspect the merging of finances, the passing of papers, the assumption of shared responsibilities and demands—yes—I suspect this may be the way houses marry. Astrology teaches that love is ruled by Venus, but it is the more rigorous Saturn who claims supremacy in the House of Marriage. Saturn structures love as surely as buildings; requires we make certain our foundations are strong, our paperwork in order.

The more I consider it, I am certain the mortgage is the marriage.

Which means I'll have to plan a closing party. A party that exorcises all my money worries, and celebrates love and imagination and friendship and hands that build homes. A housewarming, a wedding reception, a welcome home, and a bon voyage party. A party with music in the hallway and dancing on the deck. Lots of good food prepared in my expansive kitchen with a view. Conversations, laughter swelling up the house. Friends meeting friends. Sunset, then stars.

There will be long good-byes and many good wishes as the moon sets in time for the sun to rise, and at last house and cottage will sleep. We'll wake up late in the morning, when the morning sun hits the skylight. The house will sneak an admiring glance across the hallway at his mate, just before she wakes. And Egypt will walk across my chest, wondering if I ever plan to serve him breakfast. We will rise, cat and Kate, house and cottage, scoop cat food onto a dish, fill the teakettle, stretch, sigh and smile, reveling in the daylight of home.

acknowledgments

THIS BOOK would not be possible without the people in it:
the real men who moved a real cottage, who built for me a real
home; the friends and family members who lent help and support along the way. I thank you all for being present during the
house-moving year, and for allowing me to write about you. In
a few cases, I have changed names or blurred details, confident
you know who you are and how much your help meant to me.

When the little bits and pieces I was writing about the project
threatened to turn into a book, there were many people who
encouraged me to take the plunge. I thank my early readers:
Cristina Lopez, Tina Maravich, Jay Leutze, Gail Harriman,
Katrina Valenzuela, David Kalan, and Jill Baldwin. Another
round of thanks to my listeners, to whom I read aloud,
sometimes on the phone, and sometimes in person: Cindy
Donaldson, Bruce Anderson, Victoria Kane, and Martha
Eastman. One particularly steadfast listener, Anne Williams
Sweeney, sat through several readings of the same material,
and lent me her studio and audio production skills—as if I
didn't already owe her a huge thank-you for the author photo.
Special thanks, also, to three book business colleagues who
have provided the moral support I needed to imagine a book
of my own: Bob Hugo, Dan Cullen, and Marshall Smith.

Every book needs a spiritual advisor, and this book has blos-
somed under the guidance of several special souls. Tom Hallock
not only shared his publishing expertise, but also lent his

unstinting belief in the project—which I borrowed whenever my own faith wavered. Editor Emeritus Bob Wyatt gave me the gift of his enthusiasm, a good dose of insider knowledge, and plenty of laughs. Ginger Curwen, a.k.a. Great Connector, offered encouragement, a generous helping of her professional editorial insight, and an introduction to the best agent ever. Julia Lord took this book—and this writer—under her wing, and flew with us. When we touched down at Commonwealth Editions, I met Webster Bull, who turned out to be my ideal publisher: a rare combination of careful reader, personal cheerleader, and spirited entrepreneur—graced with imagination, humor, and boldness of purpose.

At Commonwealth Editions, *Cottage for Sale* morphed from manuscript to finished book, thriving in the expert and gentle care of Managing Editor Penny Stratton. Thank you, Penny, for pulling it all together into one extraordinary package, and for assembling one extraordinary team: Ann Conneman, Sarah Weaver, Elizabeth Muller, and Jeff Walsh. Another bundle of special thank-yous to Sales Director Katie Bull, Special Sales Manager Jill Christiansen, publicists Kathy Shorr, Emily Miles Terry, and Linda Phelan—and I must not forget my all-time favorite sales rep, Tony Giordano.

When people ask me why I wrote this book, I answer truthfully that writing was a way to extend the enjoyment of my house-moving, home-building adventure. For making home improvement fun, I want to give an extra thank-you to Bob Hayden, Ed and John Oberlander, Harry Hussey, and Tony Savoie. Thank you all for your very special assistance in helping one woman achieve her classified destiny.

postscript

THREE YEARS AFTER house and cottage were married, with his inspections complete, his nine lives lived long and large, Egypt Whouley died of the complications of old age. So much a part of my home, Egypt now resides in my heart. And a few nights ago, he appeared in my dreams, banging on my bedroom window, demanding my attention. Before I could lift the screen to let him in, Egypt walked across the window sill, gave my outstretched hand a solid head-butt, and—wouldn't you know it—headed straight for his food dish.